THE CAMBRIDGE COMPANION TO
BRITISH LITERATURE OF THE FRENCH REVOLUTION
IN THE 1790S

The French Revolution ignited the biggest debate on politics and society in Britain since the Civil War 150 years earlier. The public controversy lasted from the initial, positive reaction to French events in 1789 to the outlawing of the radical societies in 1799. This Cambridge Companion highlights the energy, variety and inventiveness of the literature written in response to events in France and the political reaction at home. It contains thirteen specially commissioned essays by an international team of historians and literary scholars, a chronology of events and publications, and an extensive guide to further reading. Six essays concentrate on the principal writers of the Revolution controversy: Burke, Paine, Godwin and Wollstonecraft. Others deal with popular radical culture, counter-revolutionary culture, the distinctive contribution of women writers, novels of opinion, drama and poetry. This volume will serve as a comprehensive yet accessible reference work for students, advanced researchers and scholars.

PAMELA CLEMIT is Professor of English Studies at Durham University.

THE CAMBRIDGE
COMPANION TO

BRITISH LITERATURE OF THE FRENCH REVOLUTION IN THE 1790s

EDITED BY
PAMELA CLEMIT

CAMBRIDGE
UNIVERSITY PRESS

CAMBRIDGE
UNIVERSITY PRESS

University Printing House, Cambridge CB2 8BS, United Kingdom

Cambridge University Press is part of the University of Cambridge.

It furthers the University's mission by disseminating knowledge in the pursuit of education, learning and research at the highest international levels of excellence.

www.cambridge.org
Information on this title: www.cambridge.org/9780521731621

© Cambridge University Press 2011

First published 2011

A catalogue record for this publication is available from the British Library

Library of Congress Cataloguing in Publication data
The Cambridge companion to British literature of the French Revolution in the 1790s / edited by Pamela Clemit.
p.   cm. – (Cambridge companions to literature)
Includes index.
ISBN 978-0-521-51607-5 (hardback) – ISBN 978-0-521-73162-1 (paperback)
1. English literature – 18th century – History and criticism.   2. Literature and society – Great Britain – History – 18th century.   3. France – History – Revolution, 1789–1799 – Influence.
4. France – History – Revolution, 1789–1799 – Foreign public opinion, British.   5. Great Britain – History – 1789–1820.   I. Clemit, Pamela.   II. Title.   III. Series.
PR448.S64C36   2011
820.9´3584404 – dc22   2010051868

ISBN 978-0-521-51607-5 Hardback
ISBN 978-0-521-73162-1 Paperback

For Marilyn Butler,
who blazed the trail

CONTENTS

List of illustrations   *page* ix
Notes on contributors   xi
Preface   xv
Acknowledgements   xvii
List of abbreviations   xviii
Chronology   xx

1 The political context   1
   H. T. DICKINSON

2 Burke, *Reflections on the Revolution in France*   16
   DAVID BROMWICH

3 Paine, *Rights of Man*   31
   MARK PHILP

4 Burke and Paine: contrasts   47
   DAVID DUFF

5 Wollstonecraft, *Vindications* and *Historical and Moral View of the
   French Revolution*   71
   JANE RENDALL

6 Godwin, *Political Justice*   86
   PAMELA CLEMIT

7 Wollstonecraft and Godwin: dialogues   101
   NANCY E. JOHNSON

CONTENTS

8 Popular radical culture   117
   JON MEE

9 Counter-revolutionary culture   129
   KEVIN GILMARTIN

10 Women's voices   145
   GINA LURIA WALKER

11 Novels of opinion   160
   M. O. GRENBY

12 Revolutionary drama   175
   GILLIAN RUSSELL

13 Politics and poetry   190
   SIMON BAINBRIDGE

   Guide to further reading   206
   Index   218

ILLUSTRATIONS

4.1 *Frontispiece to Reflections on the French Revolution*,
anonymous etching attributed to Frederick George Byron,
published 2 November 1790. © The Trustees of the British
Museum.   *page* 51

4.2 *The Knight of the Wo[e]ful Countenance Going to
Extirpate the National Assembly*, anonymous etching
attributed to Frederick George Byron, published
15 November 1790. © The Trustees of the British
Museum.   52

4.3 *Don Dismallo Running the Literary Gauntlet*, anonymous
etching attributed to Frederick George Byron, published
1 December 1790. © The Trustees of the British Museum.   53

4.4 *Contrasted Opinions of Paine's Pamphlet*, anonymous
etching attributed to Frederick George Byron, published
26 May 1791. Courtesy of The Lewis Walpole Library,
Yale University.   54

4.5 *Tom Pains Effegy or The Rights of a Sed[i]tious Poltroon*,
anonymous etching possibly by John Nixon, published
16 January 1793. © The Board of Trinity College Dublin.   58

4.6 a and b Creamware jug with black printed designs of Paine and
Burke, manufactured in Liverpool *c.* 1795. Photographs
reproduced with the kind permission of The Royal Pavilion
& Museums (Brighton & Hove).   59

4.7 *The Contrast 1792*, etching by Thomas Rowlandson from
a design by Lord George Murray, published December
1792. © The Trustees of the British Museum.   60

4.8 *An entire Change of Performances?*, satirical broadside,
published in London *c.* 1795 and sold by 'Citizen Lee'.
© British Library Board. All Rights Reserved.   61

4.9 Title page to Kit Moris (pseud.), *The Rights of the Devil, or, The Jacobin's Consolation* (Sheffield, 1793). © British Library Board. All Rights Reserved.   64

9.1 William Jones, *One Penny-worth More, or, A Second Letter from Thomas Bull to His Brother John*, London, 1792. From the copy in the Rare Book Collection, the University of North Carolina at Chapel Hill.   136

9.2 Title page to Hannah More, *The Way to Plenty; or, The Second Part of Tom White*, London and Bath, 1796. © British Library Board. 4418.e.70 (2).   141

NOTES ON CONTRIBUTORS

SIMON BAINBRIDGE is Professor of Romantic Studies at Lancaster University. He is the author of the monographs *Napoleon and English Romanticism* (1995) and *British Poetry and the Revolutionary and Napoleonic Wars: Visions of Conflict* (2003), the editor of *Romanticism: A Sourcebook* (2008), and has written many essays and articles on the writing of the Romantic period. He is a past president of the British Society for Romantic Studies.

DAVID BROMWICH is Sterling Professor of English at Yale University. His books include *Hazlitt: The Mind of a Critic* (1983) and *Disowned by Memory: Wordsworth's Poetry of the Nineties* (1998). He has edited a selection of Edmund Burke's writings, *On Empire, Liberty, and Reform* (2000), and is completing an intellectual biography of Burke.

PAMELA CLEMIT is Professor of English Studies at Durham University and held a Leverhulme Major Research Fellowship from 2007 to 2010. She is the author of *The Godwinian Novel* (1993) and has written many essays on William Godwin and his intellectual circle. She has published a dozen or so scholarly and critical editions of Godwin's and Mary Shelley's writings, including an Oxford World's Classics edition of *Caleb Williams* (2009). She is the general editor of *The Letters of William Godwin*, for which she is also editing volumes one and two.

H. T. DICKINSON taught for forty years at the University of Edinburgh and was Richard Lodge Professor of British History there from 1980 to 2006. He is now an Emeritus Professor and an Honorary Professorial Fellow at Edinburgh. He is the author and editor of over twenty books on eighteenth-century British politics and political ideas, including *Liberty and Property: Political Ideology in Eighteenth-Century Britain* (1977); *Britain and the French Revolution, 1789–1815* (1989); and *The Politics of the People in Eighteenth-Century Britain* (1995).

DAVID DUFF is Senior Lecturer in English at the University of Aberdeen. His books include *Romance and Revolution: Shelley and the Politics of a Genre* (1994); *Modern Genre Theory* (2000); and *Romanticism and the Uses of Genre* (2009). He has also co-edited a collection of essays, *Scotland, Ireland, and the Romantic Aesthetic* (2007). He is editor of the forthcoming *Oxford Anthology of Romanticism*.

KEVIN GILMARTIN is Professor of Literature at the California Institute of Technology, and a regular visiting professor in English at the Centre for Eighteenth-Century Studies at the University of York. In addition to articles on the politics of literature and print culture in the Romantic period, he is the author of *Print Politics: The Press and Radical Opposition in Early Nineteenth-Century England* (1996) and *Writing against Revolution: Literary Conservatism in England, 1790–1832* (2007). His current book projects include a study of the politics of William Hazlitt's critical prose and a study of eighteenth- and early nineteenth-century writing on poverty and agricultural change.

M. O. GRENBY is the author of several studies of late eighteenth-century culture, including *The Anti-Jacobin Novel: British Conservatism and the French Revolution* (2001). He has produced new editions of a number of political novels from the period of the French Revolution, and is editing volume three of *The Letters of William Godwin*. He is the co-editor of *The Cambridge Companion to Children's Literature* (2009), author of *The Child Reader 1700–1840* (2011) and is currently Reader in Children's Literature in the School of English Literature, Language and Linguistics at Newcastle University.

NANCY E. JOHNSON is Associate Professor of English at SUNY New Paltz, where she teaches eighteenth-century literature and literary theory. She is the author of *The English Jacobin Novel on Rights, Property and the Law: Critiquing the Contract* (2004) and articles on law and literature in the 1790s. She is currently editing volume VI of the court journals of Frances Burney (forthcoming, 2012) and writing a book on law and literature in the eighteenth century.

JON MEE is Professor of Romanticism Studies at the University of Warwick and held a Philip J. Leverhulme Major Research Fellowship from 2006 to 2009. He has written widely on politics and culture in the Romantic period, including *Dangerous Enthusiasm: William Blake and the Culture of Radicalism in the 1790s* (1992) and *Romanticism, Enthusiasm, and Regulation: Poetics and the Policing of Culture in the Romantic Period* (2003). He has written many essays on popular radicalism and co-edited the eight-volume *Trials for Treason and Sedition 1792–1795* (2007–8) with Professor John Barrell.

MARK PHILP teaches political theory in the Department of Politics and International Relations, University of Oxford, and is a Fellow of Oriel College. His books include *Godwin's Political Justice* (1986); *Paine* (1989); *The French Revolution and British Popular Politics* (ed.) (1991); *Napoleon and the Invasion of Britain* (with Alexandra Franklin) (2003); *Thomas Paine* (2007); and *Political Conduct* (2007). He has edited collections of the writings of Paine and

Godwin and has written widely on radicalism and loyalism in Britain at the end of the eighteenth century. He is the director of the Leverhulme-funded project William Godwin's Diary: Reconstructing a Social and Political Culture (http://godwindiary.politics.ox.ac.uk/).

JANE RENDALL is Honorary Fellow in the History Department and Centre for Eighteenth-Century Studies at the University of York. Her research focuses on eighteenth- and nineteenth-century British and comparative women's and gender history. Recent publications include: *Defining the Victorian Nation: Class, Race, Gender and the British Reform Act of 1867* (with Catherine Hall and Keith McClelland) (2000); *Eighteenth-Century York: Culture, Space and Society* (ed. with Mark Hallett) (2003); and *Soldiers, Citizens and Civilians: Experiences and Perceptions of the Revolutionary and Napoleonic Wars, 1790–1820* (ed. with Alan Forrest and Karen Hagemann) (2008).

GILLIAN RUSSELL is an Australian Research Council Professorial Fellow in the School of Cultural Inquiry at the Australian National University, Canberra. She is the author of *The Theatres of War: Performance, Politics, and Society, 1793–1815* (1995) and *Women, Sociability and Theatre in Georgian London* (2007).

GINA LURIA WALKER is Associate Professor of Women's Studies at The New School, New School University, New York City. She is editing the Chawton House Library Edition of Mary Hays's *Female Biography*. Her publications include *The Feminist Controversy in England 1788–1810* (1974); *Memoirs of the Author of A Vindication of the Rights of Woman* (ed. with Pamela Clemit) (2001); *The Idea of Being Free: A Mary Hays Reader* (ed.) (2006); *Mary Hays (1759–1843): The Growth of A Woman's Mind* (2006); *Rational Passions: Women and Scholarship in Britain, 1702–1870* (ed. with Felicia Gordon) (2008). She and G. M. Ditchfield are guest editors of 'Intellectual Exchanges: Women and Rational Dissent', a special issue of *Enlightenment and Dissent* (2010).

'If it be asked – What is the French Revolution to us?', wrote Thomas Paine in 1791, 'We answer... *It is much*. – Much to us as men: Much to us as Englishmen... the French Revolution concerns us *immediately*.'[1] The French Revolution ignited the biggest debate on politics and society since the Civil War 150 years earlier. The public controversy lasted from the initial positive reaction to French events in 1789 to the outlawing of the radical societies in 1799. It was not just a debate about politics: it also changed the language of politics, and created new forms of political communication. The debate drew in workers, artisans and tradespeople as readers for the first time. Poets, novelists and dramatists sought to influence the course of events. The themes and techniques of the Revolution controversy laid the foundations of British political progress in the early nineteenth century and helped to shape the imaginative concerns of Romanticism.

Study of the political and literary responses to the French Revolution has been facilitated by the recent publication of many previously unavailable primary texts. Pickering and Chatto have published scholarly collections of the works of the principal authors of the 1790s, such as Mary Wollstonecraft, William Godwin, Charlotte Smith and the Anti-Jacobin novelists, together with facsimile reprints of contemporary political pamphlets, papers of the London Corresponding Society and documents relating to the trials for sedition of 1792–4. A wide range of political writing of the 1790s, and beyond has been made available in popular selections, notably Marilyn Butler's *Burke, Paine, Godwin, and the Revolution Controversy* (1984), Paul Keen's *Revolutions in Romantic Literature: An Anthology of Print Culture, 1780–1832* (2004), and Iain Hampsher-Monk's *The Impact of the French Revolution* (2005). In addition, there has been a steady increase in paperback editions of works by individual writers. The most notable authors – Burke, Wollstonecraft, Paine and Godwin – are now part of university courses in eighteenth-century literature and Romanticism, as well as courses in political thought and history.

This Cambridge Companion presents an opportunity for critical reassessment of the British authors, genres and themes of the 1790s written in response to events in France and political reaction at home. The volume falls into two main sections. After an indispensable historical overview, six chapters engage with the best-known works of the four major writers of the Revolution debate. The chapters which follow range more widely, both chronologically and thematically: they deal with popular radical culture and counter-revolutionary culture; the distinctive contribution of women writers; novels of opinion on both sides of the political divide; and drama. The final chapter opens up the connections between the Revolution controversy and Romantic poetry. The chapters do not follow a single pattern. Some of them focus on the arguments of individual texts; others on formal and stylistic innovation. A few generalize from many texts, while others investigate readers' responses – both literary and visual, in the case of Burke and Paine – and the circumstances of production. This variety reflects the nature of the subject, which spans several different disciplines.

The writers covered in this volume do not stand in isolation: their works are dependent for meaning on each other, and display a high degree of intertextuality, allusiveness and cross-reference. Writers not only responded to each other's publications, but were often acquainted personally. Burke and Paine were drawn into friendship before they took opposing views on the French Revolution, while Godwin and Wollstonecraft were briefly married before her early death in 1797. Writers reached out to all sections of society, and women were as intensely engaged in political debate as men. Authors chose different ways to reach their public, defined by the price that readers were willing to pay. Some works were published in book form, intended for a limited audience, but many originated as pamphlets, and were published at prices ranging from three shillings (Burke's *Reflections on the Revolution in France*) to sixpence (the second part of Paine's *Rights of Man*). The French Revolution prompted the first modern, socially inclusive political debate in Britain. This debate set a pattern for the future, and remains influential today.

NOTE

1 Thomas Paine, *Address and Declaration, of the Friends of Universal Peace and Liberty, held at the Thatched House Tavern, St James's Street. August 20th. 1791* ([London], 1791), pp. 2, 3.

ACKNOWLEDGEMENTS

I thank the Leverhulme Trust for the generous award of a three-year Major Research Fellowship, which gave me the time to complete this volume, and Jenny McAuley for her expert assistance in preparing the typescript.

ABBREVIATIONS

Bennett   Betty T. Bennett, ed., *British War Poetry in the Age of Roman-
                     ticism: 1793–1815* (New York and London: Garland, 1976)
Blake, *Poems*   William Blake, *The Complete Poems*, 2nd edn, ed. W. H.
                     Stevenson (London and New York: Longman, 1989)
British Theatre   *The British Theatre*, ed. Elizabeth Inchbald, 25 vols. (London:
                     Longman *et al.*, 1808)
Duffy   Michael Duffy, 'William Pitt and the Origins of the Loyal-
                     ist Association Movement of 1792', *Historical Journal* 39
                     (1996), 943–62
EB Corr.   *The Correspondence of Edmund Burke*, gen. ed. Thomas
                     Copeland, 10 vols. (Cambridge: Cambridge University Press,
                     1958–78)
EB Writings   *The Writings and Speeches of Edmund Burke*, gen. ed. Paul
                     Langford, 9 vols. in progress (Oxford: Clarendon Press,
                     1981–)
Goodwin   Albert Goodwin, *The Friends of Liberty: The English Demo-
                     cratic Movement in the Age of the French Revolution*
                     (London: Hutchinson, 1979)
Jefferson, *Writings* Thomas Jefferson, *Writings*, ed. Merrill D. Peterson (New
                     York: Library of America, 1984)
Kegan Paul   C. Kegan Paul, *William Godwin: His Friends and Contempo-
                     raries*, 2 vols. (London: Henry S. King, 1876)
Macaulay, *Letters* Catharine Macaulay, *Letters on Education: With Observa-
                     tions on Religious and Metaphysical Subjects* (London: C.
                     Dilly, 1790)
MW Letters   *The Collected Letters of Mary Wollstonecraft*, ed. Janet Todd
                     (London: Allen Lane, 2003)
MW Works   *The Works of Mary Wollstonecraft*, ed. Janet Todd and Mar-
                     ilyn Butler, 7 vols. (London: Pickering and Chatto, 1989)
Paine, *LMW*   *The Life and Major Writings of Thomas Paine*, ed. Philip S.
                     Foner, 2 vols. (Secaucus, NJ: Citadel Press, 1948)

Paine, *RM*   Thomas Paine, *Rights of Man, Common Sense and Other Political Writings*, ed. Mark Philp (Oxford: Oxford University Press, 1995)

Palmer   Roy Palmer, *The Sound of History: Songs and Social Comment* (Oxford: Oxford University Press, 1988)

PBS Letters   *The Letters of Percy Bysshe Shelley*, ed. Frederick L. Jones, 2 vols. (Oxford: Clarendon Press, 1964)

Political Writings *Political Writings of the 1790s*, ed. Gregory Claeys, 8 vols. (London: Pickering and Chatto, 1995)

Prelude (1799)   William Wordsworth, *The Prelude* (1799), in *The Prelude: 1799, 1805, 1850*, ed. Jonathan Wordsworth, M. H. Abrams and Stephen Gill (New York and London: W. W. Norton & Co, 1979)

Prelude (1805)   William Wordsworth, *The Prelude* (1805), in *The Prelude: 1799, 1805, 1850*, ed. Jonathan Wordsworth, M. H. Abrams and Stephen Gill (New York and London: W. W. Norton & Co, 1979)

STC Letters   *Collected Letters of Samuel Taylor Coleridge*, ed. Earl Leslie Griggs, 6 vols. (Oxford: Clarendon Press, 1956–71)

STC Poetical Works Samuel Taylor Coleridge, *Poetical Works*, ed. Ernest Hartley Coleridge (London: Oxford University Press, 1969)

Trials   *Trials for Treason and Sedition 1792–1794*, ed. John Barrell and Jon Mee, 8 vols. (London: Pickering and Chatto, 2006–7)

WG Novels   *Collected Novels and Memoirs of William Godwin*, gen. ed. Mark Philp, 8 vols. (London: Pickering and Chatto, 1992)

WG Writings   *Political and Philosophical Writings of William Godwin*, gen. ed. Mark Philp, 7 vols. (London: Pickering and Chatto, 1993)

WH Works   *The Complete Works of William Hazlitt*, ed. P. P. Howe, 21 vols. (London: J. M. Dent, 1930–4)

	France	Britain
1789	Meeting of Estates-General (May); Third Estate votes to adopt title of 'National Assembly' (June); storming of the Bastille (July); Declaration of the Rights of Man and the Citizen (Aug.); Paris mob march to Versailles and force Louis XVI to go to Paris (Oct.); nationalization of church property (Nov.)	London Revolution Society meets to celebrate the 'Glorious' Revolution of 1688, after which Richard Price delivers sermon later published as *A Discourse on the Love of Our Country* (Nov.). Astley, *Paris in an Uproar*; Dent, *The Triumph of Liberty*; Kemble, *Henry V*; St John, *The Island of St Marguerite*
1790	Prohibition of monastic vows and suppression of religious orders (Feb.); abolition of aristocratic titles (June); Civil Constitution of the Clergy (July)	Motion for repeal of Test and Corporation Acts defeated. Barbauld, *An Address to the Opposers of the Repeal of the Corporation and Test Acts*; Blake, *The Marriage of Heaven and Hell* (conc. 1793); Burke, *Reflections on the Revolution in France*; Macaulay, *Observations on the Reflections of the Rt Honourable Edmund Burke, Letters on Education*; Merry, *The Laurel of Liberty*; Opie, *The Dangers of Coquetry*; Williams, *Letters Written in France*; Wollstonecraft, *Vindication of the Rights of Men*

	France	Britain
1791	Louis XVI and his family attempt to flee France but are stopped at Varennes (June); Champ de Mars massacre of republican protesters (July); Louis XVI accepts the new constitution (Sept.)	Birmingham Riots (July). Burke, *An Appeal from the New to the Old Whigs*; Christie, *Letters on the Revolution*; Gifford, *The Baviad*; Mackintosh, *Vindiciae Gallicae*; Merry, *Ode for the 14th of July*; Paine, *Rights of Man*, Part One; Pigott, *Strictures on the New Political Tenets of Edmund Burke*; Sayer, *Lindor and Adelaïde*, Smith, *Celestina*; Thelwall, *Ode to Science*
1792	France declares war on Austria (Apr.); Prussia declares war on France (June); overthrow of the monarchy (Aug.); September Massacres; French defeat Prussians at Valmy (Sept.); France declared a republic (Sept.)	London Corresponding Society founded (Jan.); Society of the Friends of the People founded (Apr.); Royal Proclamation against seditious writings (May); Association for the Preservation of Liberty and Property against Republicans and Levellers founded (Nov.). Bage, *Man As He Is*; Barlow, *The Conspiracy of Kings*; 'John Bull' broadsheets begun; Holcroft, *Anna St Ives*; More, *Village Politics* (conc. 1795); Paine, *Rights of Man*, Part the Second, *Letter Addressed to the Addressers*; Parkinson, *The Budget of the People*; Pigott, *The Jockey Club*; Smith, *Desmond*; Wollstonecraft, *Vindication of the Rights of Woman*

	France	Britain
1793	Louis XVI executed (Jan.); France declares war on Britain, Holland and Spain (Feb.); Committee of Public Safety established (Apr.); purge of the Girondins (May–June); Terror begins (July); Toulon surrenders to Lord Hood (Aug.); execution of the Girondins and Marie Antoinette (Oct.)	Grey's motion for parliamentary reform defeated (May); Muir and Palmer convicted of sedition and sentenced to fourteen and seven years' transportation respectively (Aug.–Sept.); 'British Convention' meets at Edinburgh (Oct.–Nov.). Eaton, *Hog's Wash, or a Salmagundy for Swine* (conc. 1795); Godwin, *An Enquiry concerning Political Justice*; Hanway, *Ellinor; or, The World as It Is*; Hays, *Letters and Essays*; Smith, *The Old Manor House*; Spence, *Pig's Meat, or Lessons for the Swinish Multitude* (conc. 1795); Thelwall, *The Peripatetic*
1794	Slavery abolished in French West Indies (Feb.); Danton executed (Apr.); Festival of the Supreme Being (June); Robespierre overthrown and executed (July)	Skirving and Margarot convicted of sedition and each sentenced to fourteen years' transportation (Jan.); Gerrald convicted of sedition and sentenced to fourteen years' transportation (Mar.); suspension of Habeas Corpus (May) (renewed annually until 1801); Hardy, Thelwall and Horne Tooke tried for treason and acquitted (Oct.–Dec.). Coleridge and Southey, *The Fall of Robespierre*; Godwin, *Caleb Williams*; Holcroft, *Hugh Trevor* (conc. 1797); Parkinson, *Pearls Cast before Swine*; Smith, *The Banished Man*; Wollstonecraft, *Historical and Moral View of . . . the French Revolution*

	France	Britain
1795	Formal separation of church and state (Feb.); peace with Prussia, Holland and Spain (Mar. –June); Vendemiaire uprisings (Oct.); dissolution of the National Convention (Oct.); establishment of the Directory (Nov.)	Food riots (June–July); meeting in St George's Fields to petition for annual parliaments and universal suffrage (June); meeting of London Corresponding Society in Copenhagen Fields (Oct.); attack on King at the opening of Parliament (Oct.); Seditious Meetings Act and Treasonable Practices Act outlaw mass meetings and public lectures (Dec.). Edgeworth, *Letters for Literary Ladies*; Fenwick, *Secresy*; Gifford, *The Maeviad*; Inchbald, *Every One Has His Fault*; Lee, *King Killing*; More, *Cheap Repository Tracts* (conc. 1798); Pigott, *Political Dictionary* (posthumously published); Spence, *The End of Oppression*; Thelwall, *Poems Written in Close Confinement*, *The Natural and Constitutional Right of Britons*; Watson-Taylor, *England Preserved*
1796	Napoleon opens his successful Italian campaign (Apr.)	Bage, *Hermsprong*; Burke, *A Letter to a Noble Lord*; Coleridge, *Poems on Various Subjects*; Hamilton, *Letters of a Hindoo Rajah*; Hays, *Memoirs of Emma Courtney*; Helme, *Farmer of Inglewood Forest*; Inchbald, *Nature and Art*; Lewis, *The Monk*; Southey, *Joan of Arc*; Thelwall, *The Rights of Nature, Sober Reflections*; Walker, *Theodore Cyphon*; Wollstonecraft, *Letters Written during a Short Residence in Sweden, Norway and Denmark*

	France	Britain
1797	*Coup d'état* of 18 Fructidor (Sept.)	Bank of England suspends payments (Feb.); naval mutinies at Spithead and the Nore (Apr., June); defeat of Dutch fleet at Camperdown (Oct.). *Anti-Jacobin, or, Weekly Examiner* (conc. 1798); Colman the Younger, *The Heir at Law*; D'Israeli, *Vaurien*; Franklin, *A Trip to the Nore*; Godwin, *The Enquirer*; Mathias, *The Pursuits of Literature*; Southey, *Poems*; Spence, *The Rights of Infants*
1798	French occupy Rome (Feb.), invade Switzerland (Apr.) and land in Egypt (July)	Irish Rebellion (May–June); Nelson defeats French at battle of the Nile (Aug.); alliance between Britain and Russia against France (Dec.). *Antijacobin Review and Magazine* (conc. 1821); Baillie, *De Monfort*; Godwin, *Memoirs of the Author of a Vindication of the Rights of Woman*; Hays, *Appeal to the Men of Great Britain*; Holcroft; *Knave or Not?*; King, *Waldorf; or, The Dangers of Philosophy*; Kotzebue, *The Stranger*; Polwhele, *The Unsex'd Females*; Smith, *The Young Philosopher*; Wollstonecraft, *The Wrongs of Woman; or, Maria* (posthumously published); Wordsworth and Coleridge, *Lyrical Ballads*
1799	*Coup d'état* of 18 Brumaire: Napoleon overthrows Directory and establishes the Consulate (Nov.)	London Corresponding Society and other radical groups outlawed (July); Combination Acts against formation of unions. Godwin, *St Leon*; More, *Strictures on the Modern System of Female Education*; Robinson, *The Natural Daughter*; Sheridan, *Pizarro*; Walker, *The Vagabond*

	France	Britain
1800	France defeats Austria at Marengo (June) and Hohenlinden (Dec.)	Bowles, *Reflections on the Political and Moral State of Society*; Burges, *The Progress of Pilgrim Good-Intent in Jacobinical Times*; Bisset, *Douglas; or, The Highlander*; Craik, *Adelaide de Narbonne*; Dubois, *St Godwin*; Hamilton, *Memoirs of Modern Philosophers*; Moore, *Mordaunt*
1801	Napoleon re-establishes French Church	Act of Union with Ireland (Jan.); Pitt's government defeated over Catholic Emancipation (Feb.); Addington Prime Minister (Mar.). Bullock, *Dorothea; or, A Ray of the New Light*; Godwin, *Thoughts Occasioned by the Perusal of Dr Parr's Spital Sermon*; Hamilton, *Letters on Education*; Holcroft, *Deaf and Dumb*; Lucas, *The Infernal Quixote*; Beaufort [pseud. for Thelwall], *The Daughter of Adoption*
1802	Treaty of Amiens between France and Britain (Mar.); Napoleon becomes Consul for life (Aug.)	Treaty of Amiens between France and Britain (Mar.). Holcroft, *A Tale of Mystery*
1803	War renewed with England (May)	War renewed with France (May). Hays, *Female Biography*
1804	Napoleon crowns himself Emperor of the French (Dec.)	Pitt returns as Prime Minister (May). Edgeworth, *Popular Tales*
1805	Napoleon defeats combined Austrian and Russian army at Austerlitz (Dec.); Treaty of Pressburg between France and Austria forces Austria out of coalition with Britain (Dec.)	Formation of Third Coalition against France; British Navy under Nelson defeats Franco-Spanish fleet at Trafalgar (Oct.). Opie, *Adeline Mowbray*

	France	Britain
1806	Wars against Prussia and Russia	Death of Pitt (Jan.); ministry of 'All the Talents' under Lord Grenville; death of Fox (Sept.)
1807	French invade Portugal (Nov.); Russia signs Treaty of Tilsit, withdrawing from war with Napoleon (July)	Abolition of slave trade in British dominions (May); Grenville resigns over Catholic Emancipation and is succeeded by Duke of Portland (Mar.)
1808	French invade Spain (Mar.)	British troops land in Portugal, beginning Peninsular War (conc. 1814); Convention of Cintra (Sept.) allows French evacuation of Portugal. Scott, *Marmion*
1809	Napoleon annexes Papal states and captures Vienna (May)	Portland resigns, Perceval Prime Minister (May)
1810	Napoleon annexes Holland (July)	
1811		George III declared permanently insane (Feb.); Prince of Wales made Regent; Luddism (machine-breaking by workers) begins in Midlands (Nov.)
1812	Napoleon invades Russia (June) and occupies Moscow (Sept.), then retreats (Oct.–Nov.)	Perceval murdered; Lord Liverpool Prime Minister (June); America declares war on Britain (June). Byron, *Childe Harold's Pilgrimage* (conc. 1818)
1813		Shelley, *Queen Mab*
1814	Napoleon abdicates and is exiled to Elba; Bourbons restored, with brother of Louis XVI reigning as Louis XVIII (Apr.)	Treaty of Ghent ends American war after British capture and burn Washington DC (Dec.). Austen, *Mansfield Park*; Wordsworth, *The Excursion*

	France	Britain
1815	The 'Hundred Days': Napoleon escapes from Elba and enters Paris (Mar.), but is defeated at Waterloo (June); monarchy restored (July) and Napoleon exiled to St Helena (Oct.)	Economic depression; Corn Law Bill
1816		Spa Fields riot (Dec.). Byron, *Manfred* (conc. 1817); Maturin, *Bertram*
1817		Coercion Acts (Mar.); Pentrich uprising in Derbyshire (June). Coleridge, *Biographia Literaria*; Shelley, *Laon and Cythna*
1818		Congress of Aix-la-Chapelle (Sept.), attended by Castlereagh
1819		Peterloo Massacre: crowd gathered at St Peter's Fields, Manchester, to hear speech on parliamentary reform broken up by cavalry (Aug.); 'Six Acts' limiting right to hold meetings and freedom of the press (Dec.)
1820	Revolts in Spain and Italy against the Bourbons	Death of George III (Jan.) and accession of George IV; 'Cato Street Conspiracy' to assassinate government ministers foiled (Feb.); trial of Queen Caroline (July). Shelley, *Prometheus Unbound*
1821	Greek War of Independence begins (March) Napoleon dies on St Helena (May)	
1823	War between France and Spain	

	France	Britain
1824	Death of Louis XVIII and accession of his brother Charles X	Repeal of Combination Acts (June) leads to rapid development of trade unionism
1825		Financial crisis (Nov.). Hazlitt, *The Spirit of the Age*
1827		Liverpool resigns; Canning Prime Minister (Apr.); Canning dies (Aug.)
1828		Wellington Prime Minister (Jan.); repeal of Test and Corporation Acts (May)
1829		Catholic Emancipation (Apr.)
1830	July Revolution: Charles X abdicates and his cousin Louis-Philippe, Duc d'Orléans, is installed as King of France; a new Constitution provides for elected monarch	Death of George IV (June); accession of William IV; Wellington's ministry falls (Nov.); Earl Grey Prime Minister of Whig administration
1832		Reform Act introduces wide-ranging changes to the British electoral system (Mar.)

I

H. T. DICKINSON

The political context

The French Revolution began with the astonishing events of 1789, but it has to be seen as an intense and profound process that changed and developed dramatically over the following decade and more. Its political and social experiments changed a great many aspects of French life, and these changes also had a major impact on all of France's neighbours, including Great Britain. The Revolution led to a bitter dispute across Europe about the French principles of 'liberty, equality and fraternity', and, because the French revolutionaries sought to export these principles to the rest of Europe, it helped to provoke a war that posed an enormous challenge to France and all its neighbours. The French Revolution and the French Revolutionary war were the most discussed issues in British politics and the British press. The Revolutionary debate of the 1790s in Britain had a profound influence on the political, religious and cultural life of the country, while the French war produced almost unprecedented economic and social strains, and forced Britain to make a huge military, naval and financial effort to counter French ambitions. For a great many Britons the 1790s were a decade of crisis that polarized British society into the friends and enemies of the French Revolutionary cause. To understand the nature of this crisis, we need to appreciate the ideological disputes in Britain about French Revolutionary principles, to explore how these disputes encouraged Britons to support or oppose these principles, and to examine how these disputes strengthened the party of government, and seriously undermined the opposition in Parliament.

The ideological disputes about French principles and the French war

British radicals and reformers had been developing a political programme for constitutional reform, and intellectual justifications for such a programme, for at least two decades before the outbreak of the French Revolution in 1789. They wished, in particular, to promote a reform of the electoral system that would see the House of Commons elected by a much higher proportion of adult males. Since 1780, the more advanced radicals had been advocating universal manhood suffrage, annual general elections, equal-sized constituencies, the secret ballot, the abolition of property qualifications for parliamentary candidates and the payment of MPs. These proposals were justified by historic appeals to the ancient rights of Englishmen, and to the universal rights of man. More moderate proposals were debated in Parliament in 1783 and 1785. Although the movement for parliamentary reform weakened in the later 1780s, these years still witnessed favourable discussions of the new American federal constitution, attempts to repeal the Test and Corporation Acts for the benefit of Protestant dissenters and a widespread popular campaign to abolish the slave trade. The failure to achieve any success in the late 1780s disheartened the radicals and reformers, but they were galvanized into renewed action by the outbreak of the French Revolution in 1789. The events in France received a positive response from many Britons of liberal and advanced views. The veteran radical, Richard Price, a Protestant dissenting minister, offered the first sustained panegyric on the French Revolution when he addressed the Revolution Society in London on 4 November 1789.[1] In this oration, subsequently published in early 1790 as *A Discourse on the Love of our Country*, Price rejoiced that he saw the ardour for liberty catching and spreading, and a general reform of human affairs beginning in France. He undoubtedly hoped that the events in France would revive the reform movement in Britain.

More conservative British observers of the events in France were surprised and somewhat shaken, but they were not at first concerned about their possible consequences for Britain. Edmund Burke was initially undecided on how to respond to the amazing events in France, but, more than any other politician of the day, he made a serious attempt to understand what was happening. When he produced his *Reflections on the Revolution in France*, in November 1790, he was as much concerned with the way Richard Price and others were using the French Revolution to promote and justify radical reform in Britain as he was with the consequences of the Revolution for French politics and society. He devoted much of his famous tract to the threat posed by British radicals, who he feared were being seduced by dangerous French principles into giving fresh impetus to the cause of reform at home. Burke warned his readers that a new political society was being erected in France on the most abstract general principles and the wildest speculative theories. In their appeals to universal and inalienable natural rights, and to abstract concepts of liberty, equality and fraternity, the French were placing far too much reliance on human reason. They were ignoring divine providence, the flawed nature of man and the hard lessons of history. The French revolutionaries were acting under the dangerous delusion that social arrangements and political institutions were simply the artificial products of human reason. This unwarranted confidence in human reason needed to be rejected. Men had to recognize that the social and political order in any country was, in part, the creation of divine providence and, in part, the result of innumerable small changes, slight adjustments and even sheer accidents occurring over hundreds of years. The French revolutionaries were ignorant, self-seeking and mean-spirited men, who were determined to seize power from their social superiors. They had no understanding that firm government was needed to restrain human passions and to prevent the tyranny of the ignorant majority over the talented minority. The consequence of placing too much confidence in human reason, and of elevating human will above religion, justice and experience, would be an inevitable and rapid descent into social anarchy and unrestrained terror.

Burke's *Reflections* was an immediate publishing success, though there were many who believed that his reactions to the French Revolution were exaggerated, unbalanced and unjustified. Many radical critics, including Thomas Paine, Mary Wollstonecraft, Joseph Priestley and James Mackintosh, rushed to counter his arguments and his fears, while other writers came to Burke's defence. Over the next few years several hundred published contributions were made to the profound and bitter discussion on the merits or dangers of the French Revolution. Some of the radical responses to Burke defended the character and principles of Richard Price, attacked Burke for reneging on his former liberal principles, condemned the abuses of the *ancien régime* in France and justified the French efforts to achieve reform. James Mackintosh's *Vindiciae Gallicae* (1791) was probably the best attempt to defend the principles of, and to vindicate the actions taken by, the French Revolutionaries. Other radicals used the opportunity created by the excitement aroused by Burke's *Reflections* to advance their own political agenda without replying directly to Burke's arguments. In the first part of his *Rights of Man* (1791), Thomas Paine deliberately abandoned any appeal to the past or reliance on prescription, insisting instead that each age had the right to establish any political system that would best serve its own ends and purposes. The present age must be free to reject the tyranny of the past, and to inaugurate a new age of more extensive liberty. All men were created equal, and possessed the inalienable natural rights of liberty, property and the pursuit of happiness. To maintain these natural rights in civil society, the authority of those in power must be subjected to the sovereign power of the people. A written constitution must place limits on the executive and the legislature, and must clearly delineate the civil liberties of all subjects.

In the even more influential second part of the *Rights of Man* (1792), Paine demonstrated how a reformed political system could alleviate the distress of the poor by reducing taxes on the many, and imposing a property tax on the rich to finance social welfare reforms, including old age pensions, child allowances and maternity benefits.

In his *Enquiry concerning Political Justice* (1793), William Godwin offered the most sophisticated critique of the existing political and social order, and advanced the most optimistic and utopian radical vision of the future if only men were governed by reason and not their passions. He attacked monarchy and aristocracy as unjustified by reason, and he argued that the unequal distribution of property was the greatest source of all social evils. He urged universal benevolence, advocated the promotion of the public good and believed in a future of unlimited human perfectibility. He wished to see the abolition of all government institutions and the radical extension of individual liberty. In her *Vindication of the Rights of Woman* (1792), Mary Wollstonecraft mounted a spirited case for the rights of women, but she argued primarily to free women from male oppression rather than to grant them an active role in politics. She wanted to free women from the authority of fathers and husbands, to grant them greater rights over their property and their children and to give them greater access to education and the learned professions. She believed that women were potentially the intellectual, moral and legal equals of men, but she did not explicitly demand that they should be granted the right to vote or to sit in Parliament or serve in government. A handful of radicals did broach the subject of women being granted political rights, but only tentatively. Thomas Spence conceded that women should be allowed to vote, but he did not expect them to take an active role in public life because of the delicacy of their sex. Spence's radicalism rested primarily on his Land Plan, which he discussed in most of his publications. He urged the elimination of the private ownership of landed property or natural resources, and wished to see these placed under the control of parochial corporations that would lease them out to the highest bidder. The money so raised would be used to pay for the limited expenses of a reduced national government and for the building of various public works and amenities. The remainder of each parish's income would be shared out equally every three months between every man, woman and child living in the parish. Under his system, Spence believed that excessive wealth and power would no longer be accumulated, and that dire poverty would be eliminated.

Although the needs of the poor, and the question of redistributing wealth, were discussed by only a few British radicals – the vast majority were content to advocate parliamentary reform – their arguments did much to alarm conservative opinion in Britain. They led to repeated accusations that all British radicals were intent on confiscating private property, by force if necessary. Aware of the damage that such charges were doing to the cause of reform, many radical societies published handbills explicitly rejecting any suggestion that they wished to undermine the principle of private property or the right of inheritance. The Sheffield Society for Constitutional Information, for example, insisted that its members sought equal political representation, and were 'not speaking of that visionary equality of property, the practical assertion of which would desolate the world, and re-plunge it into the darkest and wildest barbarism'.[2] Despite such disclaimers, it is clear that the more popular radical societies hoped that, if their demands for full political rights were met, they would see a freer press, a fairer judicial system, cheaper and more honest government, lower taxes, lower prices, more schools and a lower prison population.[3]

The political demands of the British radicals, expressed particularly strongly in 1792–3, alarmed conservative opinion in Britain because they coincided with growing violence and instability in France, and the outbreak of war in Europe. The ultra-radical ideas and practices of the French Jacobins, as they faced the possibility of internal counter-revolution and foreign invasion, seemed to confirm the fears that Burke had expressed in his *Reflections*, and this released a flood of conservative propaganda that deluged Britain with warnings about the danger posed to the political and social order in Britain by French Revolutionaries and their radical admirers in Britain. A host of British propagandists, including John Bowles, William Jones, Robert Nares, Arthur Young, Samuel Horsley and Hannah More, joined Burke in seeking to halt the spread of French principles across Britain. They produced propaganda written in simple language and an impassioned tone so that it might elicit a militant response from the middling and lower orders of British society. They argued that, in their pursuit of unrestrained liberty, the French Jacobins were lurching from crisis to crisis, and were letting loose the mob and rendering all property insecure. The Jacobins were blamed for unleashing the 'Terror' in France, and condemned as armed fanatics, who, having destroyed monarchy and aristocracy, were now conspiring to destroy all laws, all government and all religion. More alarming still, deluded British radicals were threatening to emulate the French Jacobins in their efforts to reform the British constitution. If they were not stopped, they would destroy all order and hierarchy in the British state, and encourage the poor to pillage the rich.

Once Britain was at war with Revolutionary France, from February 1793, arch-conservatives in Britain urged the nation to strain every sinew until ultimate victory was achieved. They saw the war as an ideological struggle of supreme importance, as almost a new war of religion, which had to be won at all costs. The British people must support the war effort in order to preserve a constitution that guaranteed their liberties, their personal security and their property. The war was necessary to save the nation from anarchy, revolution and internal violence. Burke, in his *Letters on a Regicide Peace* (1795–6), insisted that there could be no compromise with the French Jacobins. Others were even more forthright:

> It is for national existence, that we arm. It is for Religion against Atheism; for justice and security against universal depredation; for humanity against barbarous cruelty; for social order; for legal freedom; for all that distinguishes men in civil society, from a band of robbers, or an horde of savages. The British sword is drawn in the cause of God, and of our Country, and in defence of our lives, our families, and our all.[4]

Radical societies and loyalist associations

Several organizations supporting political reform, including the Revolution Society and the Society for Constitutional Information, had been established in Britain well before the French Revolution, but they had declined in the late 1780s. They revived because of the political excitement engendered by the French Revolution, and they were soon joined by more radical and more popular societies dedicated to political reform. The most important of these new societies was the London Corresponding Society (LCS), founded on 25 January 1792 by a small group of artisans led by Thomas Hardy, a shoemaker. They agreed to meet at a tavern each week to discuss political issues, and they began to levy a weekly subscription of one penny. This society drafted a political programme dedicated to the radical reform of the electoral system. Several branches were established across the metropolis, with each one sending a delegate to the general committee, which met each Thursday evening. This general committee elected in turn a smaller executive committee that coordinated the objectives and policies of the society as a whole. The LCS drew up several addresses to the people, urging the cause of parliamentary reform, and began corresponding with reformers in France and across Britain. It is difficult to be precise about the size or social composition of the LCS. It claimed a total membership of 5,000, but attendance at meetings fluctuated considerably, and the active membership was probably around 3,000. When subjected to government repression, the membership declined to about a thousand by the end of 1796, and to a few hundred by 1798. Many members were small craftsmen and artisans, with little formal education, though others were attorneys, booksellers, printers and shopkeepers. There is no evidence that the LCS ever had much appeal for unskilled day-labourers or the very poor.

Similar radical societies sprang up in many old and new towns across Britain, including Norwich, Newcastle, Leeds and Manchester. There were certainly many dozens of these popular radical societies, though we cannot be sure of their exact number. The most active and famous in the English provinces was the Sheffield Society for Constitutional Information, which was set up at the end of 1791. Total membership of this society may have reached 2,500 by June 1792, though the active membership was probably around 600. Many of these were connected to the steel industry. They were organized much like the LCS. The local newspaper, the *Sheffield Register*, supported them; and they distributed political literature in the vicinity of Sheffield, and communicated with other radical societies further afield. The Sheffield radicals secured 4,000 signatures for their petition for parliamentary reform in the spring of 1793, and they attracted more than 5,000 people to an open-air protest meeting on 28 February 1794. In Scotland, there were several branches of the Friends of the People that did much to organize in Edinburgh first a Scottish, and then a British, convention of radical delegates to promote parliamentary reform in 1792–3. The last of these conventions adopted French Revolutionary procedures, forms of address and songs. Despite such efforts, the radicals were never united into a single organization with clearly identified leaders.

The popular radical societies organized debates, public addresses and petitions, including a campaign against the government's repressive legislation in 1795 that resulted in 95 petitions signed by over 130,000 protesters. John Thelwall and Henry Redhead Yorke went on lecture tours to speak to radical groups, and some large open-air public meetings were held, especially in 1795. The radicals were active in producing or supporting several radical newspapers and periodicals, and they also made determined efforts to educate the people about their political rights and the abuses of the government. When war broke out, most popular radicals were opposed to any interference in the internal affairs of France, regarding British involvement as unwise, unnecessary and unjust. There were many crowd disturbances provoked by industrial disputes, the high price of food and the impressment of men into the army, militia and navy, but little effort in Britain (though there was in Ireland) to start a violent revolution on the French model. When the government resorted to arrests and repressive legislation, most British radicals lost heart, or moderated their public activities. Some did emigrate rather than submit, and some began to arm themselves and to contemplate revolution should the French ever invade Britain, but only in Ireland was there a large-scale revolutionary movement committed to an armed rising.

The resulting Irish rebellion of 1798 was crushed with considerable ferocity before a small French army could land and provide effective military
support.

The French Revolution did much to galvanize British radicals into political action in the earlier 1790s, but the French 'Terror' and the French war
did much to undermine their efforts thereafter. Just as the French Revolution revitalized the British reform movement after 1789, so did it stimulate
a powerful conservative reaction against reform. There was a conservative
reaction to the efforts in 1787–90 to repeal the Test and Corporation Acts
(restricting office under the crown and in borough corporations to members of the Church of England) that led to the formation of many Church
and King clubs designed to defend the existing order in church and state.
Members of such clubs attacked Protestant dissenters and political radicals
celebrating Bastille Day in Birmingham in July 1791, and attacked the property and printing press of the radicals in Manchester in December 1792.
Growing violence in France, and the outbreak of war in Europe, helped to
produce some 386 loyal addresses to the King in support of the existing
constitution in Britain by September 1792. In the winter of 1792–3 effigies
of Thomas Paine were publicly and ceremonially burned in hundreds of
towns and villages across the country. Although officially sponsored, large
numbers of ordinary Britons were very willing of their own accord to join
in these demonstrations of loyalty to the status quo and hostility to radical
change.

On 23 November 1792 a public announcement appeared in the *Star*,
a pro-government newspaper, urging the founding of an Association for
the Preservation of Liberty and Property against Republicans and Levellers
(APLP). The advertisement was placed by John Reeves, who later claimed
to be acting independently, although it has recently been proved that the
government did know of his plans in advance, and did subsequently amend
his proposal to serve its own political ends.[5] After consulting with the government, the APLP declared that it would not only endeavour to halt the
distribution of radical publications, but would disseminate its own cheap
publications in order to persuade the poor not to be seduced by radical aims,
and to recognize the benefits they enjoyed under the existing political and
social order. The first APLP was set up at the Crown and Anchor tavern
in London in November 1792, and within a few months many more similar loyalist associations had been established across the country, until they
formed the largest popular political movement in the country. There were
soon hundreds of these loyalist associations, perhaps even as many as 2,000.
Active membership was largely confined to local men of property, and to
Anglican clergymen and magistrates, though they did gain the support of

more humble men. They were able to submit dozens of loyal addresses to the crown, many signed by hundreds of local people, and some by several thousand. It seems likely that the loyalists in Britain came to outnumber the radicals.

The loyalist associations produced and disseminated their own political tracts, and they also distributed hundreds of tracts written by such conservative propagandists as John Bowles, William Jones, William Paley and Hannah More. Some associations resorted to overt violence against the radicals, especially in Lancashire, and many warned innkeepers and publicans that they risked losing their licences if they allowed radical groups to hold meetings on their premises. This often had the desired effect. Men of property were also encouraged not to rent land or offer employment to, or make purchases from, those who could be regarded as seditious radicals. In many areas, the loyalists acted as the eyes and ears of the government, and reported any suspicious political behaviour to the Home Office or to local magistrates. Loyalist associations were encouraged to assist the war effort by offering bounties to men who would enlist in the army or navy, and by providing extra blankets, gloves and stockings for the British troops serving and suffering in Flanders in the winter of 1793–4. As the war expanded and the threat of invasion grew, the loyalist associations became a source of recruits for a voluntary and part-time armed force that could resist any armed invasion from France, and that might also be used to intimidate British radicals. In March 1794 the government decided to raise just such a force, the Volunteers, that soon attracted substantial sums of money, and many tens of thousands of recruits. Men of property, who had demonstrated their loyalty to the existing constitution, commanded the Volunteer corps, and they recruited into the ranks only those poor men that they believed they could trust. The parades, military exercises, celebrations, and patriotic speeches and addresses of the Volunteers demonstrated the loyalty of the propertied classes, intimidated their radical opponents and promoted a patriotic reaction among the people at large. The Volunteers 'rendered disloyalty unfashionable, sedition dangerous and insurrection almost impossible'.[6]

The APLP and other loyalist associations did much to weaken the influence and disrupt the activities of the radicals by 1796, and many of the latter lost focus, commitment and direction. As the radicals weakened, so did the organization of the loyalists, but this did not prevent repeated demonstrations of political loyalty and popular patriotism in the later 1790s. In 1795–6, and in 1800, hundreds of loyal addresses were sent to the King after attacks on his person. There were similar massive demonstrations after every victory in the war against France, and after the ending of the alarming naval mutinies of 1797. The clergy and ministers of all the various Christian churches in Britain delivered thousands of sermons, and printed hundreds of them, in opposition to French principles, in defence of the British constitution and in support of the war effort. Many leading conservative evangelicals, most notably Hannah More, contributed essays to the enormously successful *Cheap Repository Tracts* that began to pour from the press from 1798, and which were distributed as free or cheap publications to the poor. More militant loyalists produced such long-lasting periodicals as *The Anti-Jacobin* and *The Anti-Jacobin Review and Magazine*. There seems little doubt that, by the late 1790s, the loyalist movement had done much to condemn French principles and to weaken the appeal of the radicals at home, as well as offering considerable support to the government's war effort against the French Revolutionaries abroad.

Government repression and opposition weakness

William Pitt and his ministerial colleagues were originally prepared to be mere spectators of the astonishing events in France; and they saw no reason to interfere in the internal affairs of France, even when Austria and Prussia chose to do so in 1792. It was the French success in hurling back the forces that had attacked them, their issuing of the Edict of Fraternity in November 1792, offering military support to any people wishing to overthrow their rulers, and the French invasion of the Austrian Netherlands (modern Belgium) that brought Britain into the war. Once involved in the war, the members and committed supporters of the British government were divided on how best to conduct operations, with Henry Dundas and others preferring to wage a war at sea and in the colonies; with William Grenville and others believing that a land war in Europe was essential; and with yet others convinced that the ultimate aim must be to overthrow the French Revolution and restore the Bourbon monarchy. When British forces achieved very little on the continent and French forces became increasingly successful, and when several British efforts to make peace were rejected by the triumphant French, the British government became increasingly concerned that the French might launch a successful invasion, and that the invaders might find a welcome from British radicals. The British government was not content to rely on the virtues of the British constitution, or the arguments of their loyalist supporters, to counter the appeal of the radicals. It was determined to use its own resources to defeat the radical movement at home. While Prime Minister Pitt was genuinely concerned that the French might find many supporters in Britain who might support their cause, he was also ready to exploit the situation in order to increase his own support within

Parliament and the nation, and to reduce support for his parliamentary opponents.

The government's first step to exploit its executive, legislative and judicial powers in order to destroy the radical threat at home was to issue a royal proclamation against seditious writings on 21 May 1792, urging the public to inform magistrates of the appearance and circulation of politically dangerous publications. By November the situation at home and abroad was even more alarming, and the King was advised to issue a second royal proclamation urging the prosecution of the authors and distributors of seditious publications. On 19 November 1792, Justice William Ashurst distributed his *Charge to the Grand Jury of Middlesex*, which urged active support for the King's most recent royal proclamation. Once at war with France, the government embarked on a campaign of repression that has sometimes been termed 'Pitt's Reign of Terror'. Although Pitt's repressive policies in Britain produced far fewer deaths than the Jacobin Terror in France, it inflicted unwarranted suffering on many honest and moderate reformers who only sought limited political reforms by constitutional means. It needs also to be borne in mind that there were many thousands of people killed, wounded and arrested and a vast amount of physical damage to property inflicted in crushing the Irish rebellion of 1798.

Once the British government had convinced itself that the radicals posed a serious threat to the political and social order, the Home Office was instructed to investigate their activities, and to scrutinize their writings. In 1793 an Alien Office was set up as a sub-department with instructions to monitor all foreign visitors to Britain, particularly the French. A small secret service section was also set up. Information was collected from hundreds of justices of the peace, post office and customs officials, and private individuals across the whole country, and from diplomats serving abroad. Some of the information collected was clearly alarmist and exaggerated; and some reports were motivated by spite, by a desire for revenge and by hopes of financial reward or career advancement. The Home Office was not always gullible, but it did employ some spies who were not above fabricating evidence and agents provocateurs who deliberately misled foolish men into uttering seditious words, or engaging in subversive activity, before betraying them. It did, however, also employ some agents who successfully penetrated the LCS and other radical societies, and provided the government with detailed and reliable reports on their political activities.

When the Jacobin Terror took hold in France, and Britain's military efforts on the continent proved ineffective, the government resorted to sterner action against radicals at home. The most notorious examples of judicial prosecution were the trials for sedition in Scotland in 1793–4 and the treason trials in England in 1794. Handpicked juries and partial judges in Edinburgh secured the conviction of Thomas Muir and several other leading radicals in Scotland, and their transportation to Australia. In England, however, several leading radicals, including Thomas Hardy of the LCS and the veteran radical John Horne Tooke, were acquitted of the charge of treason, in part due to the brilliant defence mounted by Thomas Erskine, an opposition Whig MP and the leading defence lawyer of the day. These popular acquittals persuaded the government to abandon its attempts to secure convictions for high treason against other English radicals, though it did secure the conviction and execution of one Scottish radical planning to attack Edinburgh Castle in 1794 and one Irish conspirator plotting treasonable actions with the French in early 1798. The government was much more successful in convicting several prominent English radicals, such as Thomas Spence and Daniel Isaac Eaton, of publishing seditious works. A few radicals were also imprisoned for a time during the periods when habeas corpus was suspended. The total number of convictions secured by the government in the 1790s did not exceed 200, but this number included some leading radicals; and such treatment undoubtedly persuaded some radicals to emigrate, and intimidated others into silence. The government may not have entirely abandoned due judicial procedures in its efforts to crush the radicals, but it certainly bent and abused these procedures in a ruthless effort to silence its radical critics.

As well as prosecuting radicals in the law courts, the government secured support in Parliament for new legislation that would strengthen its hand in combating the efforts of the radicals. To persuade Parliament to support its legislative proposals, the government produced a mass of written material, and a host of witnesses and informers, before secret committees of the whole House of Commons in 1794 and 1799. Parliament agreed by large majorities to suspend habeas corpus between May 1794 and July 1795, and between April 1798 and March 1801, thus allowing the government to imprison its opponents without convicting them in a court of law. Only a few radicals were in fact imprisoned without trial. The two notorious Gagging Acts of 1795 were also more significant as indicators of government alarm and as threats to hold over the radicals, than as effective means to bring radicals before the courts. The Treasonable Practices Act (1795) extended the law of treason in an alarming fashion, to include efforts to force the King to change his ministers or to overawe Parliament, but no radical appears to have been prosecuted under this act. The Seditious Meetings Act (1795) gave wide powers to magistrates to license or forbid public meetings, but only one radical appears to have been prosecuted under this act.

Other repressive legislation was also less effective or less often implemented than was once thought, but this does not mean that it played no part in intimidating the radicals or inhibiting their actions. In 1797 an act made it a capital offence to encourage mutiny in the armed forces. There was only one prosecution under this act, and even in this case the death sentence was not invoked. In 1798 the Press Act required the registration of all printing presses, and urged the prosecution of all publications that excited hatred of the King, government, or constitution. It was little used. In 1799, the LCS and other radical societies were banned by law. Few were active at this time. In 1799, and again in 1800, Parliament passed legislation making illegal all combinations of workers, because they were held to be in restraint of trade. It failed to destroy all trade unions, or to make it impossible for workers to combine in industrial action. Despite the limited prosecutions that resulted from the government's repressive legislation in the 1790s, the mere threat of invoking this legislation did much to silence the most active radical organizers and propagandists and to persuade many ordinary radicals to abandon their support for political reform. The civil liberties of the people at large were infringed and many brave men suffered unjustly for holding radical views that they sought to pursue by constitutional means.

Pitt's government was able to secure large majorities for its repressive legislation not only because many of the propertied elite feared French principles and were alarmed at the possibility of a French invasion, but also because the more liberal men in both Houses of Parliament failed to mount an effective defence of the nation's civil liberties. When the French Revolution broke out in 1789, the Whig opposition in Parliament was already in disarray because of their gross mismanagement of the Regency crisis, which made them appear factious, and even disloyal, in seeking to give the Prince of Wales full powers because of the ill health of the King. When George III recovered, Pitt's position was strengthened, and that of Charles James Fox and his Whig allies was severely weakened. In 1789 Fox welcomed the French Revolution with great enthusiasm, and hoped it would help him reduce the influence of the crown, and regain both his credibility in Parliament and his popularity in the country. Instead, he so misjudged the nature of the French Revolution that he eventually lost the support of most of his own party. From the outset, Fox failed to understand the nature and significance of the French Revolution; and he never learned from his initial mistakes, but continued to hold views that became increasingly unpopular with his own party and with his natural supporters in the country. His views on the Revolution were dominated by English assumptions and expectations, rather than being based on French circumstances, or the true aims of the revolutionaries. He ignored the profound differences between British and French experiences in the eighteenth century, instead emphasizing the superficial similarities between them. He wrongly concluded that the French were imitating what the British had achieved by the Glorious Revolution of 1688–9 when they erected a limited or parliamentary monarchy. He optimistically hoped that the French would speedily and easily resolve their constitutional difficulties. Although he occasionally voiced concerns about the motives and violence of the French revolutionaries, he too often saw only the best in them, and blamed their faults on their doleful experiences under the *ancien régime*, or their need to resist outside interference in the affairs of France. He was not persuaded by the counter-arguments put forward in the *Reflections* by his long-time friend and political ally, Edmund Burke. When, on 6 May 1791, Fox again praised the French Revolution in the House of Commons, Burke declared their friendship at an end, and he soon began to support Pitt's government.

Fox regretted this breach, but it did not lead him to alter his position, or even to exercise greater control over his more reform-minded Whig colleagues. Fox himself continued to criticize the influence of the crown, and he helped to secure the passage of the Libel Act of 1792, which allowed the jury, not the judge, to decide if the offending words were in fact seditious libel or not. On the other hand, he was never committed to even moderate parliamentary reform, and he claimed never to have read Paine's *Rights of Man*. He did not prevent close allies and younger disciples, however, from going further than he was prepared to go in advocating reform. He stood by while Richard Sheridan, Charles Grey and others established the Society of the Friends of the People, which set out the faults in the existing electoral system, corresponded with more radical societies and implied that it would give a lead in Parliament to the cause of reform. Grey even introduced into the House of Commons a motion for moderate parliamentary reform in 1793.

Fox's failure to restrain his Whig colleagues, and his outspoken attacks on the government's war effort, led to growing concern among the more fearful, and more conservative, members of his opposition party. Throughout 1793 a number of Fox's party split from him, though they did not immediately rally behind Pitt. The Duke of Portland, the nominal leader of the Whig opposition, refused to support Fox's position on the war against France. In June–July 1794, Portland and about half the parliamentary opposition negotiated a grand coalition with Pitt and secured several leading posts in the reconstructed administration that was determined to counter the radical threat at home and to wage a vigorous war against Revolutionary France. Fox's attitude to the war, more than his early enthusiasm for the French Revolution, split his party asunder and rendered the opposition increasingly ineffective. Fox and his remaining allies, reduced to about fifty or sixty MPs in the House of Commons, bravely and honourably protested against the new administration's repressive policies, but to no avail. Fox and his small band were outraged by the trials for sedition in Scotland, but he could not save the convicted radicals from being transported. His ally, Thomas Erskine, did much to prevent the English radical leaders being convicted of treason in 1794, but that was the last effective action by the Foxite rump. Only a few dozen Opposition MPs voted against the two Gagging Acts of 1795, and in that year the Society of the Friends of the People suspended its activities. In 1797 the small Foxite party seceded from Parliament and failed to attend any debate for some months. The opposition in Parliament had been effectively destroyed by its apparent sympathy for French principles, and even more by its hostility to the war against Revolutionary France.

In the late 1790s, Pitt's administration was unable to bring the war to a successful conclusion. It was facing major financial problems and social unrest, and it struggled to contain an explosive rebellion in Ireland. And yet, Pitt's majority in Parliament was greater than ever, the loyalists were firmly in the ascendant and the support for radical reform had almost totally collapsed.

NOTES

1 The Revolution Society had been set up some decades before to commemorate and celebrate the Glorious Revolution of 1688–9. There is a good account of it by Rémy Duthille in the online version of the *Oxford Dictionary of National Biography*.
2 William Cobbett, ed., *The Parliamentary History of England*, 36 vols. (London: T. C. Hansard, 1806–20), vol. XXXI, col. 738.
3 See *Address from the London Corresponding Society to the inhabitants of Great Britain, on the subject of Parliamentary reform* (dated 6 August 1792) (London, 1792), p. 6.
4 Thomas Hardy, *Fidelity to the British Constitution, the Duty and Interest of the People* (Edinburgh: David Willison, 1794), pp. 33–4.
5 Michael Duffy, 'William Pitt and the Origins of the Loyalist Association Movemant of 1792', *Historical Journal* 39 (1996), 943–62; 950.
6 J. R. Western, 'The Volunteer Movement as an Anti-Revolutionary Force, 1793–1802', *English Historical Review* 71 (1956), 613.

2

DAVID BROMWICH

Burke, *Reflections on the Revolution in France*

A necessary step towards understanding the place of Edmund Burke's *Reflections on the Revolution in France* in the broader debate on the Revolution is to recognize that Burke was not an orthodox apologist for monarchy. He was, as Richard Pares called him, a high and dry anti-monarchist.[1] Having written and spoken steadily in defence of aristocratic society, Burke had long opposed democracy in the sense of the word that implies popular sovereignty, or active participation by the people in government. He wished to keep the King in the British constitution, not, as his earlier writings make clear, for sentimental reasons but rather as an offset against the possibility of ministerial aggrandizement. France he considered as less prepared than England for modern liberty; it was a place, to him, unimaginable without a king and queen. These views are consistent in Burke's thought from 1770 through 1791. Yet there are tensions and contradictions in his thinking, too, which emerge under the pressure of events in 1788–90; and these have a place in an honest rendering of the subtlety, the richness and the peculiar understanding of political prudence that come together in the *Reflections*, his first full-length reaction to the Revolution in France.

Few persons who knew Burke's public character had expected him to declare himself so entirely opposed to the Revolution. But few had followed closely the impact on Burke of two events: the Gordon Riots of 1780 and the Regency Crisis. The riots were the action of the mob that marched on Parliament on 2 June 1780 to protest the repeal of Catholic disabilities. Disappointed of its demands, it swarmed the streets of London, and largely destroyed or damaged Newgate and Fleet prisons, the Bank of England and the houses of several public officials. The scale of the violence – which lasted almost an entire week – seemed to call into question the social order of Britain. The Regency Crisis issued from the onset of the madness of George III, in November 1788, and took the form of a protracted contest between rival claims to emergency authority by William Pitt and the Prince Regent. These events forced Burke to imagine a contingency that could deprive the state of authority, or deprive the country of a monarch. In both episodes, Burke had taken a position consistent with his belief in the principles of civil liberty and the system of constitutional checks; but, though he favoured a regency to cover the madness of George III, and argued behind the scenes for clemency in the punishment of the Gordon rioters, his letters and recorded actions, during both crises, testify to the tremendous disturbance that shook his mind. *Reflections* gives the first unmistakable evidence that the doubts and fears of those emergencies of the 1780s had come to stay.

One may describe Burke in the 1770s and 1780s as the theorist and to some extent the strategist of the Rockingham party: a group not less aristocratic than the other Whig connections, but less corrupt, and more adequate to the work of parliamentary opposition. From his work as ambassador for Lord Rockingham (in treating with the outlawed radical politician John Wilkes among others) and from the fame of his own published writings and speeches, Burke had substantial and mostly friendly contact with the body of religious dissenters who formed, besides, a major section of the Bristol constituency which he served from 1775 to 1780. He was tolerant of republicans and spoke admiringly, for example, of the radical Joseph Priestley in the autumn of 1782, after a visit during which Burke and his son Richard had been shown Priestley's library and laboratory; Priestley was 'the most happy of men, and most to be envied' (*EB Corr.*, vol. v, p. 54). As late as August 1788, Burke could write to his disciple French Laurence: 'I am just going to dine with the D. of Portland in company with the great American Paine, whom I take with me' (p. 412).

Circumstances like these greatly complicate the picture of Burke as an apologist for 'a dull, sluggish race' with 'a sullen resistance to innovation'– a self-portrait he achieved by arbitrary emphases and shadings in the *Reflections* (*EB Writings*, vol. VIII, pp. 106, 137). There is a break in his career, but it comes after the *Reflections*: a divided work itself, intended more to split the Whig party, or to reunify it on terms agreeable to Burke, than to halt the momentum of reform in England. As the central sentences of the book declare: 'A disposition to preserve, and an ability to improve, taken together, would be my standard of a statesman. Every thing else is vulgar in the conception, perilous in the execution' (p. 206). Roughly the first half of the *Reflections* addresses the vulgarity of the French conception, and the second half deals with the perilousness of the execution. Within British politics, Burke's stance is harder to assess; but on the last page of the book he sketches once again the combined disposition to preserve and ability to improve which he believes his own career to have exemplified.

Yet it can hardly be doubted that, as a work of political thought, Burke's *Reflections* is a *causerie* against the Revolution, founded on a catastrophic theory of democracy. A question for the reader of the *Reflections* thus becomes to what extent one can agree with its analysis of the Revolution without assenting to its whole-length argument against democracy. Thomas Paine in the first part of his *Rights of Man* (1791) argued that to accept democracy was to reject Burke. Mary Wollstonecraft in her *Vindication of the Rights of Men* (1790) had implied the same judgement; but in later works like *An Historical and Moral View of the French Revolution* (1794), she came closer to Burke's reservations, while still supposing that the general movement of Europe towards democracy was an enlightened progress and deserved to succeed.[2]

How could Burke believe that he somehow supported the interests of the people while utterly deprecating the cause of mass-suffrage democracy? The difficulty of giving a clear answer, in Burke's own terms, derives from a certain ambiguity in his definition of 'the people'. He assigned various senses to the phrase, often under the exigent pressure of events like the Wilkes crisis of the late 1760s, or the county petition movement of 1779–80. Yet his uses exhibit sufficient coherence to be treated as a guide to his strictures on popular government in the *Reflections*. The truth is that Burke's suspicion, which sometimes crosses into disgust, at what the French have made of their first year of experiment, is all the severer from his initial hopes regarding a form of government that he thought Britain itself should strengthen. The French have given representative government a repulsive turn which will weaken its prospects elsewhere. (And yet it is to be noted and pondered that the example of America is never mentioned in the *Reflections*.)

The following passages from his earlier writings suggest the broad lines of development of Burke's thinking about the people in relation to government. From *Thoughts on the Cause of the Present Discontents* (1770):

> I am not one of those who think that the people are never in the wrong. They have been so, frequently and outrageously, both in other countries and in this. But I do say, that in all disputes between them and their rulers, the presumption is at least upon a par in favour of the people. Experience may perhaps justify me in going further. Where popular discontents have been very prevalent; it may well be affirmed and supported, that there has been generally something found amiss in the constitution, or in the conduct of Government. The people have no interest in disorder. When they do wrong, it is their error, and not their crime. *(EB Writings*, vol. II, p. 255)

Thus, the people are not automatically assumed to have the mind of a mob; indeed it is persons of a different class, 'turbulent, discontented men of quality' or 'the political men of letters', who create the psychology of the mob (*Reflections*, in *EB Writings*, vol. VIII, pp. 97, 160). The Revolution, therefore, though ostensibly a popular movement, is taken by Burke to be one of those 'situations where those who appear the most stirring in the scene may possibly not be the real movers' (p. 59).

Of the role of an assembly, Burke supposed that if properly energetic and properly informed, it should act as a restraint on the rashness of the people even as it brings forward their cause. In *Thoughts on the Cause of the Present Discontents*, he asserts that 'The virtue, spirit, and essence of a House of Commons consists in its being the express image of the feelings of the nation' (*EB Writings*, vol. II, p. 292). He goes on to say that, though meant to serve as a sort of control, a true Commons will be a control acting for the benefit of the people. In the middle of the American war, at his most radical, and fiercely jealous on behalf of civil liberties, Burke in *A Letter to the Sheriffs of Bristol* (1777) writes in a higher strain, with what can seem a democratic motive: 'If any ask me what a free Government is? I answer, that, for any practical purpose, it is what the people think so; and that they, and not I, are the natural, lawful, and competent judges of this matter' (*EB Writings*, vol. III, p. 317). Finally, from a letter to the Chairman of the Buckinghamshire meeting (Burke's own back yard where the County Movement was simmering high) on 12 April 1780: 'The people may be deceived in their choice of an object. But I can scarcely conceive any choice they can make to be so very mischievous as the existence of any human force capable of resisting it' (*EB Corr.*, vol. IV, p. 227). The last passage is less positive than it sounds; Burke was at this time concerned to make a tactical stand against anti-popular forces *without* promoting the democratic cause of the moment: reform of parliamentary representation. His version of popular rights accordingly has the limited form of a defence of the people against those who would override their urgent protests.

Still, the note that Burke strikes, in all these remarks on the people of the 1770s and early 1780s, is notably warmer in point of sympathy than anything one can find in the *Reflections*. The intervening decade had seen not only the flashes of near emergency in 1780 and 1788–9, mentioned above, but also the rise of an insurgent agitational movement, exemplified by leaders such as John Cartwright, John Sawbridge and, increasingly, Burke's disciple Charles Fox. This was a kind of popular politics into which Burke could only equivocally enter. The 'betrayal' of the 1784 election when the people turned the Fox–North coalition out of office, and the slow progress of Burke's own cause, the prosecution of Warren Hastings and the East India Company, were disappointments he took to heart. India reform was a high-republican cause centred on an issue of accountability, and hence suitable to representative government, but it did not find favour with petitioners for annual parliaments and manhood suffrage. A symptom of the restless politics of these years may be noticed in the way that Fox, who had been his close friend, and Sheridan, a wary ally of Burke's, were alike attracted to the democratic mood even as their enthusiasm for the reform of India was cooling. Burke's split with Fox is usually dated from May 1791 when, in a dramatic public display, repelling the scornful assaults of Fox's young associates in a debate on the constitution of Quebec, he declared that their friendship was at an end. In fact, the depth of the separation had become clear by 5 February 1790, in Burke's 'Speech on the Army Estimates', where he announced that France 'was to be considered as expunged out of the system of Europe'.[3] Yet it is misleading to think of Burke's hostility to the French Revolution as mainly a matter of British politics and the vicissitudes of parties. From training in political thought as well as by disposition, Burke was distrustful of such distinctions as those promulgated by the republican theorist Jean-Jacques Rousseau between private inclination and public will, and between natural and civil freedom. Rousseau (whose writings Burke knew better than he pretended) had supposed an original antagonism between private and public as between natural and civil matters; and in the *Social Contract*, above all, he favoured the second term of these comparisons: public will, and civil freedom. No such divisions mark the political thought of Burke, and none theoretically could: for him, politics is at once a natural and an artful extension of society; it is not a transcendent expressive activity that redeems the oppressions of social life. Rousseau's contempt for the artifice of society and his conviction that only a purifying republican state can transform it, are, indeed, the antithesis of Burke. The lost unity of the person is atoned for, in the doctrine of Rousseau, by a discovered unity of society; and this leads on to an irresistible valuation of the rightness of unanimity. 'Whoever refuses to obey the general will shall be constrained to do so by the entire body: which means nothing other than that he shall be forced to be free.'[4] Burke's revulsion from this idea and from the coercive (potentially confiscatory) principle at its basis, may be felt as the particular motive of many sentences of the *Reflections*. For example: 'Their liberty is not liberal' (*EB Writings*, vol. VIII, p. 131).

The democratic principle of Rousseau – single-minded, participatory and looking to sublimate the person in the transparent composition of persons that forms the public – had an early counterweight in the French Revolution from the mixed constitutional theory of Montesquieu. Radical reformers, such as the renowned jurist of the Constituent Assembly Adrien Duport, had strongly favoured 'balance' in the new French constitution, whereas the orators Saint-Just and Robespierre appealed to simplicity and popular energy. This split has been plausibly linked with a theoretical division between followers of Montesquieu, the theorist of a mixed constitutional government, and the disciples of the republicanism of Rousseau, which always aimed at unanimity.[5] But the theoretical dispute came to be known chiefly under practical pressure regarding the proper representation of the Third Estate – the merchants, shopkeepers, artisans and men of the professions whose understanding of their own merits gave a persuasive immediacy to the clamour for reform. The Third Estate spoke without regard to precedent or prescription; one can hear its voice plainly in the words of its most inspired propagandist, the Abbé Sieyès – a member of the clergy as vicar-general of Chartres, but in spirit and by identification, a revolutionary bourgeois.

Sieyès's pamphlet *What is the Third Estate?*, written at the end of 1788 and published at the start of 1789, begins with a distinct echo of the *Social Contract*: 'What then is the Third Estate? All; but an "all" that is fettered and oppressed. What would it be without the privileged order? It would be all; but free and flourishing. Nothing will go well without the Third Estate; everything would go considerably better without the two others.'[6] Here one sees, in bold outline, the self-image of the new class and the motive of the revolution it hopes to lead. Simplification, uniformity and (implicitly and at a distance, perhaps) confiscation – all these mark the attitude under the design. Sieyès identifies the Third Estate as a unique agent of modernization, and this is understood to be a good thing: the privileged order and its outwork, the clergy, are mere remnants of feudalism, and to that extent decorative; but they are also deeply corrupt. They produce nothing; they yield no profit for the social whole. The great new class, by contrast, is owed a substantial representation, in accordance with its actual utility to the nation. Finally, the Third Estate, as Sieyès conceives of it, is the universal class – an epithet that would be invented sixty years later by Marx to describe the proletariat; but in Sieyès's words on the bourgeoisie the idea is already in view. It is this class that naturally represents the will of all the people. When the Third Estate acts, it necessarily acts as the nation. Therefore nothing ought to restrain it.

The claim that the will of any class or sect of persons ought to stand above restraint – whether restraint by custom or by positive law – is utterly antithetical to Burke. Yet 'a nation', writes Sieyès,

> is always in a state of nature and, amidst so many dangers, it can never have too many possible methods of expressing its will. Let us not be afraid of repeating it: a nation is independent of any procedures; and no matter how it exercises its will, the mere fact of its doing so puts an end to positive law, because it is the source and the supreme master of positive law.[7]

Completeness of command, without check, is here permitted to a certain estate or class within the political order, since that class is felt to be uniquely representative. This was a revolutionary idea; it is also potentially a totalitarian idea. For if nothing can limit the will, nothing can limit the power of a class that by definition represents all of society.

Yet Sieyès and the revolutionary orators of the National Assembly were doing no more than confirm Rousseau's principle that 'the Sovereign [will], by the mere fact that it is, is always everything it ought to be';[8] their only innovation was to guide the general will down to a specific ground. What was lost sight of, in this operation, was the practical wisdom of Montesquieu, who had warned that 'every man invested with power is apt to abuse it, and to carry his authority as far as it will go. Is it not strange, though true, to say that virtue itself has need of limits?'[9]

The triumph of the Rousseau party in the French Revolution obeyed a logic of serial demand followed by disappointment and renewed demand: from the failure to reach an agreement by the King and the Assembly of Notables in 1787; to the edicts of May 1788, which suppressed the power of the parlements; to the declaration of independence from the King by the Parlement of Paris, and its decision that the Estates-General should be convoked for the first time since 1614. Yet, up to this point, as Burke would say in the *Reflections* – and it is a qualification of his argument that has often been overlooked – the change in France was salutary. But now a second sequence of actions followed, tending towards a democracy at once popular and simple. January 1789 saw the doubling of the representation of the Third Estate; on 14 July, the Paris crowd stormed the Bastille to show themselves a stronger force than the soldiery; and on the great day of self-sacrifice, 4 August, the aristocracy renounced seigneurial privileges. To an informed observer like Burke, it was plain the initial struggle for authority between the King and the nobility had been displaced by a more consequential battle that had no precedent. Arrayed on one side were the members of the Third Estate, who wanted to command centralized power of a radically new kind; against them and (it appeared) suddenly nerveless and confused were all the relics of the old order of society and the state. The King had tried at first to ally himself with the Third Estate but, by July, the Third Estate and its instrument, the National Assembly, seemed to stand with the crowd in the streets of Paris: not only the members of debating societies and clubs but all that tide of persons heated by the political changes in such a crisis – in short, a floating constituency without continuous and reasoned views but possessing a continuous and available energy, on which the editors and orators of the moment could easily draw. France in two years had moved from benign despotism to a semblance of representative government, only at last to arrive at democratic tyranny. Or so it appeared to Burke.

Many would have identified, as the high watermark of idealism in the Revolution, the passage on 26 August 1789 of the final article of the Declaration of the Rights of Man and the Citizen. Yet on looking into this document, too, one may suppose Burke was 'alarmed into reflection' (*Reflections*, in *EB Writings*, vol. VIII, p. 132). Though the Declaration was modelled in part on the American Declaration of Independence and the Bill of Rights, two points in the new document stood out ominously. Article III specifies that 'The nation is essentially the source of all sovereignty; nor can any individual or any body of men, be entitled to any authority which is not expressly derived from it.' And Article VI identifies the standard of right and wrong, as embodied by laws, with the dictate of the general will: 'The law is an expression of the will of the community.' Burke warns against precisely this equation of collective will and moral right when he observes in the *Reflections* that it is of 'infinite importance' that the people 'should not be suffered to imagine that their will, any more than that of kings, is the standard of right and wrong' (*EB Writings*, vol. VIII, p. 144). The people may, indeed, be a more incorrigible tyrant than a monarch, because they cannot be made the subject of punishment by any human hand.

These animadversions of Burke's were not so quick to come or so inevitable as is sometimes supposed. His first reaction to news of the tumults in France was not horror or disdain, but wonder. Thus, he wrote to Lord Charlemont (a trusted friend and a Whig, but also the man who in 1779 had commanded the Irish Volunteers in a show of force to press for imperial reforms in Ireland):

> As to us here, our thoughts of every thing at home are suspended, by our astonishment at the wonderful Spectacle which is exhibited in a Neighbouring and rival Country – what Spectators, and what actors! England gazing with astonishment at a French Struggle for Liberty and not knowing whether to blame or to applaud... The spirit it is impossible not to admire; but the old Parisian ferocity has broken out in a shocking manner. It is true, that this may be no more than a sudden explosion: If so no indication can be taken from it. But if it should be character rather than accident, then that people are not fit for Liberty.　　　　　　　　　　　　　　　　　(*EB Corr.*, vol. VI, p. 10)

This is the first of many pictures one finds in Burke's writings – and in the *Reflections* above all – that align the judgement of political action with the stance of a theatrical spectator as witness of the central action of a drama. In the same way, Burke will compare Marie Antoinette to a 'Roman Matron' who carries 'the sharp antidote against disgrace concealed in that bosom', and will add his hope (for the sake of dramatic symmetry), that, if she should die, it will be by her own hand (*Reflections*, in *EB Writings*, vol. VIII, p. 126).

The theatrical advice to the Queen – that she will die a better death by suicide than by execution – is a scandalous thought to revolve in our minds, unless we grant Burke's premise that moral judgement in politics is implicated in aesthetic feeling. (The idea of poetic justice, of course, implies this.) And he entertains a second and parallel thought about the fate of the King: 'If I were to punish a wicked king, I should regard the dignity in avenging the crime' (*Reflections*, in *EB Writings*, vol. VIII, p. 134). In other words, though the revolutionists may be wrong in holding Louis XVI as hostage to their new frame of government, their action might become less wrong – and, because of the dignity added by the ceremony, it would give less aesthetic offence – if they tried the king at a solemn tribunal for crimes against the people of France. Burke's use of such a dramatic criterion in the judgement of politics is most marked in his account of the violent menace of the Queen in her bedchamber and the forcible removal of the Queen and King from Versailles, to be escorted by the mob to Paris. 'No theatric audience in Athens', he remarks, 'would bear what has been borne, in the midst of the real tragedy of this triumphal day' (p. 132).

Burke's tendency is always to appeal from universal principles and rights – in which he believes – to their specific adaptation to the spirit of a people. 'The old Parisian ferocity has broken out in a shocking manner' is a more determined negative judgement than it may at first have seemed. The efficacy of laws is decided most of all by the habits of a people; only the habitual practice of self-restraint can suit a people for the difficult work of maintaining liberty. And that habit may be slow to come to the French, Burke intimates, because individuality is a novel experience to most of them, and because moderation was never among their national characteristics. Anyway, it is the habits and customs of a people that dispose them to one political arrangement or another. We cannot fairly say that all humanity desires to be free and that therefore a restrained liberty will be embraced by any people to whom it is once offered.

In appealing from principle to the adaptations of manners, Burke pressed against an idea of cosmopolitan toleration that leads, in the opposite direction, from manners to principle. The latter movement is plain in the writings of Goldsmith, Sterne and Montesquieu, but cosmopolitan reason takes a step beyond tolerance: it supposes that when once a new and correct principle of justice has been discovered, it ought to be put into practice, since any less assured response amounts to a culpable indifference. The moral discovery in view for those contemporaries whom Burke would have counted as political allies in the 1770s and 1780s, was the new principle tested by the American Revolution: that there are certain inalienable rights belonging to all men, chief among them the rights to live unmolested, to exercise freedom of conscience and action and to own property. It was a restatement of these rights by Dr Richard Price – a renowned dissenting minister, moral philosopher and writer on national finance – that gave the immediate incitement to Burke for the writing of the *Reflections*. In his *Discourse on the Love of our Country*, Price held that a parochial and patriotic love of our country ought to be superseded by the love of mankind; for in the present age, men of all nations were united to overthrow arbitrary governments, and to establish for the first time the rule of enlightenment and universal benevolence. A favourite scriptural text of Price, as of many radical dissenters, was the phrase 'on earth as it is in heaven'.

Perhaps the most simply resistant element of Burke's reply is his assurance concerning the 'sullen' and 'sluggish' mores, the wisdom without reflection that he asserts as timeless traits of the British national character. 'We know that *we* have made no discoveries; and we think that no discoveries are to be made, in morality' (*Reflections*, in *EB Writings*, vol. VIII, p. 137). *We*, in the *Reflections*, generally signifies England speaking to France, the spectators addressing the actors of the experiment in liberty. This style of address Burke thinks entirely suitable, since England was the model for French liberty; and Burke is qualified to deliver the message because his stand against the American war (which was taken to signal his advocacy of the rights of Americans) had given him the stature to instruct Europe about what liberty properly is and is not. And yet, as the *Reflections* soon demonstrates, the defence of liberty for Burke means a defence of familiar ways of doing things – ways that, because they are familiar, can be altered with genuine acceptance only voluntarily. What he offers in the *Reflections* therefore is a defence of gradual rather than violent change. *All* sudden change implies to Burke a kind of violence. It is always psychologically wrenching, and a jolt to the mind and feelings brings other shocks in its train.

The artifice of the epistolary form in which the book is cast – the address to 'a Gentleman in Paris' – allows him to greet the French as a nation already free if only they knew it, and to treat Price's criticism of the British monarchy as an act of ingratitude towards English liberty. And one *ought* to be grateful, says Burke, even when a belief like that of the English in their liberty is partly fictive, since acceptance of 'pleasing illusions' (*EB Writings*, vol. VIII, p. 128) disposes the reformer to act with care and restraint. Such a disposition is always good in itself.

To urge the good of belief in illusions or ideals that earn trust merely by their age – as if that made them truths of a kind – takes Burke to the threshold of his defence of prejudice. For the first readers of the *Reflections*, this argument was the most startling of his paradoxes. Burke defends prejudice because the undoubted confidence with which certain beliefs are held is a sign of a trust which, he believes, may perform a social good in other ways.

Without such confidence, a society has no solid ground of feelings and ideas to build on when it alters its structure in keeping with the demands of utility and justice. So, he writes, 'instead of casting away all our old prejudices, we cherish them to a very considerable degree'; and this reserve of common understanding serves to offset the importuning of individuals or sects. 'We are afraid to put men to live and trade each on his own private stock of reason, because we suspect that the stock in each man is small' (*EB Writings*, vol. VIII, p. 138). A psychological argument underlies this. Character becomes definite, it comes to know its strength, only against a background of choices it can call its own; and in the case of 'the people', this is a larger background than a single person can claim. Also, as Burke has the wit and tenacity to recognize, what holds in the contrast between the individual and the people holds equally in the contrast between the present and the past. By the workings of prejudice (our reliance on an unquestioned stock of practised responses), our action comes to be informed at the instant of crisis: 'Prejudice is of ready application in the emergency; it previously engages the mind in a steady course of wisdom and virtue, and does not leave the man hesitating in the moment of decision, sceptical, puzzled, and unresolved. Prejudice renders a man's virtue his habit; and not a series of unconnected acts' (p. 138). Here the revolutionists are condemned for having discarded those moral helps from common feeling that are available in any society.

A quite different source of Burke's suspicion is his sense of the enormous complexity of politics as a vocation. The nature of government, he believes, is intricate, since the judgements required of a statesman affect so vast and heterogeneous an array of objects. A knowledge of history, of human character in politics and of the probability of success when the powers of men and women are placed in new combinations – all this forms the texture of the training in experience of an honest and intelligent representative or a member of a responsible ministry. But this is not a strength that lies within the grasp of most people. They may judge accurately when things go wrong but are not therefore capable of seeing how to set them right. Burke does profess his belief that certain rights are common to all men: the right to act freely so long as we do not trespass against others; the right to the fruits of our labour; the right to worship in a way of our choosing. Yet he adds a qualification that takes back much of that acknowledgement:

These metaphysic rights entering into common life, like rays of light which pierce into a dense medium, are, by the law of nature, refracted from their straight line. Indeed in the gross and complicated mass of human passions and concerns, the primitive rights of men undergo such a variety of refractions and reflections, that it becomes absurd to talk of them as if they continued in the simplicity of their original direction. The nature of man is intricate; the objects of society are of the greatest possible complexity; and therefore no simple disposition or direction of power can be suitable either to man's nature, or to the quality of his affairs.   (*Reflections*, in *EB Writings*, vol. VIII, p. 112)

This anti-reductionist (and deeply anti-popular) insistence on the complexity of society and the corresponding difficulty of governing well, lends weight to Burke's warning against 'pulling down an edifice which has answered in any tolerable degree for ages the common purposes of society' (p. 111). It is wrong to assume, as the revolutionists do, that one can change many things at once and change them for the better. To do so will always require violence; and the effects of violence corrupt the ends one initially held in view.

Besides this sceptical intuition about the rule of familiar habits and the natural intractability of human society to sudden change, Burke offers one other presumption against the idea of revolution – namely, that there is something unnatural in the attempt to re-invent society from the ground up. To the extent that one does pursue such a radical experiment, decency and prudence require that one conceal it. For resistance here is natural; people are too much the creatures of custom for the mood of transformation to sink deep roots: 'The very idea of the fabrication of a new government, is enough to fill us with disgust and horror' (*Reflections*, in *EB Writings*, vol. VIII, p. 81). People love, with a simple attachment, the things that they already know; and Burke defends this attachment with a ferocious protectiveness. He may seem to prove too much. For on his reasoning, how could the enlightened countries of Europe have made the progress that is now their glory, from the ages of superstition and cruelty? Burke's answer is that they did it slowly, always emphasizing a connection to the past that gave every departure a place in a longer continuity. He leaves out of this account the religious wars of the sixteenth and seventeenth centuries; but then, as Burke frames it, the Reformation itself was a revolutionary movement.

If Burke attacks democracy as posing the threat of a new tyranny, if he defends a liberty that he believes compatible with an aristocratic society, it must be added that this liberty, in its reformed state, has no place for a spirit of haughty domination. Rather, it is infused with the manners of deference and a generous self-sacrifice which Christian Europe inherits from the morale of chivalry. That 'mixed system of opinion and sentiment' (*Reflections*, in *EB Writings*, vol. VIII, p. 127) propounded a view of right and wrong that was reasonless. We love and admire certain things, such as gentleness, charity, fealty, just because these are things we were taught to love and admire:

> It was this, which, without confounding ranks, had produced a noble equality, and handed it down through all the gradations of social life. It was this opinion which mitigated kings into companions, and raised private men to be fellows with kings. Without force, or opposition, it subdued the fierceness of pride and power; it obliged sovereigns to submit to the soft collar of social esteem, compelled stern authority to submit to elegance, and gave a domination vanquisher of laws, to be subdued by manners. (p. 127)

Note that the chivalric morale, as Burke presents it, bears the germ of democratic equality without need of the coercive sanction of laws. The spirit of 'noble equality' was understood by all, without words; no contract was necessary in the mutual recognition of persons of differing status; it required no great charter to subdue a monarch by the remissive force of manners themselves.

Kings, then, were levelled with private men without the scuffle and officiousness of political bargaining. Under the surface Burke here is describing one of the great mutations of history: Rome (the 'domination' that is spoken of) was 'vanquished' by the Christian religion with its central virtue of charity. A revolution took place whose ultimate effect was to chasten and civilize. Burke suspects that no such softening is likely to come from democracy, ever.

His understanding of the weakness of the 'edifice' being built up by the new democracy of France enabled Burke to prophesy the rise of a military leader like Napoleon: 'In the weakness of one kind of authority, and in the fluctuation of all, the officers of an army will remain for some time mutinous and full of faction, until some popular general, who understands the art of conciliating the soldiery, and who possesses the true spirit of command, shall draw the eyes of all men upon himself' (*Reflections*, in *EB Writings*, vol. VIII, p. 266). But that is an incidental prediction. What Burke tells of unmistakably is the coming of democracy itself, in a state so constituted that, by the force of the majority or the dictate of the general will, the virtues and vices of the people submit to no check. He makes his challenge to democracy a matter of moral concern beyond its political disadvantages, and denounces the majority as an always insufficient source of dignity and self-respect. The reason is that the majority, by definition, does not believe in its own responsibility: the people's 'own approbation of their own acts', says Burke, 'has to them the appearance of a public judgement in their favour. A perfect democracy is, therefore, the most shameless thing in the world. As it is the most shameless, it is also the most fearless' (p. 144). This should not be taken to retract the credit that Burke as early as 1770 had given to the people as a counterweight against monarchical aggrandizement and the sinister piety of a cabal. Properly employed, the people have a negative function, yet they are meant to act only as an irrefutable check. As he would write in the *Appeal from the New to the Old Whigs*, in a clarification of the sentences quoted above: 'The people are the natural control on authority; but to exercise and to control together is contradictory and impossible.'[10]

In the *Appeal* again – a third-person defence of his politics that is a vital supplement to the *Reflections*, sober, logical and answerable where the *Reflections* is impassioned, intuitive and domineering – Burke would offer a defence of constitutional liberty: a political ideal he took so much for granted in the *Reflections* itself that many readers have failed to notice its presence. In that sequel, he called to witness the eighteenth-century political writer with whom he seems to have felt the strongest kinship. 'Place,' Burke asks the reader of the *Appeal*,

> before your eyes, such a man as Montesquieu. Think of a genius not born in every country, or every time; a man gifted by nature with a penetrating aquiline eye; with a judgement prepared with the most extensive erudition; with an herculean robustness of mind, and nerves not to be broken with labour; a man who could spend twenty years in one pursuit. Think of a man . . . capable of placing in review, after having brought together, from the east, the west, the north, and the south . . . all the schemes of government which had ever prevailed amongst mankind, weighing, measuring, collating, and comparing them all, joining fact with theory, and calling into council, upon all this infinite assemblage of things, all the speculations which have fatigued the understandings of profound reasoners in all times! Let us then consider, that all these were but so many preparatory steps to qualify a man, and such a man, tinctured with no national prejudice, with no domestic affection, to admire, and to hold out to the admiration of mankind the constitution of England![11]

This apostrophe, recalling the French philosopher who paid the grandest of tributes to the spirit of English laws, may be taken as a solemn counterpoint to the joke on an early page of the *Reflections*, where Burke had doubted whether ideas any more than liquors could be 'meliorated by crossing the sea' (*EB Writings*, vol. VIII, p. 55). The underlying sense is a warning against a political enthusiasm that might make even so moral-minded a cause as the spread of human rights a pretext for usurpation and conquest.

NOTES

1 Richard Pares, *King George III and the Politicians* (Oxford: Oxford University Press, 1953); the larger context for the description is the Whig campaign against

George III in 1780–2 to bring the American war to an end: 'The abatement of this emergency was beginning to reveal the members of this grand alliance in their true colours: some, like Burke and Rockingham's clique, as high and dry anti-monarchists; others, like Fox, popular anti-monarchists; others, like the Grenvilles, conservatives; others again, like Pitt, reformers who believed that they could take service under the monarchy in order to reform the better' (p. 129).

2 See Steven Blakemore, *Crisis in Representation: Thomas Paine, Mary Wollstonecraft, Helen Maria Williams, and the Rewriting of the French Revolution* (Cranbury, NJ: Associated University Presses, 1997).

3 'Substance of the Speech of the Right Honourable Edmund Burke, in the Debate on the Army Estimates, in the House of Commons' (London: J. Debrett, 1790), p. 5.

4 Jean-Jacques Rousseau, *The Social Contract and other Later Political Writings*, ed. Victor Gourevitch (Cambridge: Cambridge University Press, 1997), p. 53.

5 On the Rousseau and Montesquieu lines of influence in the Revolution, see Norman Hampson, *Prelude to Terror: the Constituent Assembly and the Failure of Consensus 1789–91* (New York: Blackwell, 1988) and Carol Blum, *Rousseau and the Republic of Virtue: The Language of Politics in the French Revolution* (Ithaca, NY: Cornell University Press, 1986).

6 Abbé Sieyès, *What Is the Third Estate?*, trans. M. Blondel, in Keith Michael Baker, ed., *The Old Regime and the French Revolution* (Chicago: University of Chicago Press, 1987), p. 156.

7 *Ibid.*, p. 173.

8 Rousseau, *The Social Contract*, p. 52.

9 Baron de Montesquieu, *The Spirit of the Laws*, trans. Thomas Nugent (New York: Hafner, 1949), vol. I, XI.4, p. 150.

10 *An Appeal from the New to the Old Whigs*, 3rd edn (London: J. Dodsley, 1791), p. 98.

11 *Ibid.*, pp. 139–40.

3

MARK PHILP

Paine, *Rights of Man*

The first part of Thomas Paine's *Rights of Man* burst on to the political scene in March 1791. It was an immediate sensation, being far and away the most popular of the replies to Edmund Burke's *Reflections on the Revolution in France* (1790). It was followed almost exactly twelve months later by a second part, which was soon bound with the first and sold in cheap editions throughout the country. Alarmed at the success of the book, and especially concerned that it was being made available to people of the vulgar sort who could not correct for themselves as they read, the government issued a Royal Proclamation against seditious writing, and the Attorney General prepared a case to try Paine for seditious libel. The trial, originally set for July 1792, was deferred until November, by which time Paine had been elected to the French National Convention and had taken up residence in France. In his absence he was found guilty and outlawed; he never returned to his native country.

On the face of it, Paine's *Rights of Man* replies to Burke's *Reflections*. It differs from the host of other pamphlets published in response to Burke by its success in reaching and communicating to a wide audience (with Paine actively promoting its cheap circulation through the auspices of the Society for Constitutional Information) and by the radicalism of its principles. Scholars have appropriately raised questions as to how far the 'Debate on France', or the 'revolution controversy', as it has more latterly come to be known, really is an exchange of ideas or a discussion of principles, rather than being a process of assertion and counter-assertion of principles that do not systematically engage with those of the other side. This chapter argues that it was only as events developed between 1789 and 1791 that it became clear to Burke and to Paine how inescapably at odds they were. While the first part of *Rights of Man* does, in many respects, attempt a reply to Burke's *Reflections*, the second part is something quite other – offering a sketch of political principles and their implications that dramatically radicalizes the controversy. Commentators have pointed to the difficulty in locating Paine's thought within domestic political traditions, even as they acknowledge his success in communicating with a wide audience;[1] this chapter argues that the distinctive character of Paine's arguments derives from the formative influence of American and French experiences and debates on his thinking in the critical years of 1787 through to 1795.

Rights of Man (1791)

The first part of *Rights of Man* is clearly an attempt to respond to Burke. The two men had a cordial relationship before 1790 with Paine staying with Burke at Beaconsfield in 1788. Burke's early references to Paine are favourable and Paine subsequently sent on to Burke letters from Thomas Jefferson with details of events in France. Only as the French Revolution broke did it become clear to each how contrasting their views were.[2] Following Burke's 'Speech on the Army Estimates' in February 1790, and the announcement that he proposed to write against the Revolution, Paine determined to answer the pamphlet when it appeared. This does not mean that what Paine wrote was entirely prompted by Burke: Lafayette's correspondence with Washington shows that Paine was working on material for a history of the French Revolution from about 1789 and some sections of the first part of *Rights of Man* probably came from this draft.[3] These likely included the account of the March to Versailles (6 October 1789), which played a major dramatic part in Burke's *Reflections*, and the fall of the Bastille (14 July 1789). On both occasions, however, Paine was out of the country and he relied on the relatively detailed accounts sent by Jefferson and on first-hand accounts from friends, such as Lafayette.[4] This partly accounts for the way that these episodes in the pamphlet stand out somewhat in style. But if the history is largely borrowed, what about the political theory?

In Paris, Paine was closely linked to Jefferson's circles, in which principles of political reform were being discussed and where he developed the understanding of government that informs *Rights of Man* (advancing his earlier thinking during the American Revolution). He particularly attacks Burke's claim that one generation can bind subsequent generations – a position Jefferson also accepted in the summer of 1789 (Jefferson, *Writings*, pp. 959–64). This theme is central to the first part of *Rights of Man* and is coupled with an understanding of the social compact that creates the constitution, which in turn constitutes and constrains the government. Underlying this structure of authorization and accountability is Paine's conception of rights, which receive a far more developed discussion in *Rights of Man* than in any of his previous publications. Indeed, it is on the question of rights that Paine is often claimed to have been influenced by Burke – in the sense that

'He [Burke] was the *flint* to Mr Paine's *steel*; by the collision of one against the other, the *divine fire* of the Rights of Man was struck out for the benefit of all mankind...'[5] Yet, although Burke attacked the idea of natural rights in his *Reflections* (*EB Writings*, vol. VIII, pp. 109–11), it was not Burke who made these questions a matter of urgency for Paine. Some elements of Paine's position are evident in *Common Sense* (1776) and *Dissertations on Government, etc* (1786), but there are also clear signs that his thinking changes in the late 1780s – that is, well before the controversy.[6]

The most important development is Paine's differentiation between perfect and imperfect rights. This first appears in the first part of *Rights of Man* (1791) but an earlier sketch can be found in a letter to Jefferson, probably written in 1788 (Paine, *RM*, pp. 81–2). In that letter, as in *Rights of Man*, natural rights are distinguished into those where we have a full (or perfect) power to execute them (as in the right to think for ourselves), and those where we need a civil power to uphold the right (as in the right to property). Although the point is developed more fully in *Rights of Man*, this earlier letter demonstrates that rather than responding to Burke's attack on rights by developing a new set of distinctions, Paine had already worked these out. Moreover, he did so following a discussion involving Jefferson, and probably others, of James Wilson's pamphlet on the Federal constitution, which talked about the resignation of a certain proportion of natural liberty to government.[7] The omission of a bill of rights from the proposals for the American Federal Constitution was something that Paine, Jefferson and Condorcet all regretted, and it is the debates and discussions around the Federal Constitution from 1787 to 1789 that encouraged the enumeration of these rights and the demand that they be expressly articulated as the starting point for any political system and constitutional design.[8]

It was, then, the debates on the American Constitution that first prompted these developments in Paine's thinking, but these debates were being conducted in France with leading French thinkers at the same time as the crisis in government finance led to the calling of the Assembly of Notables and, following their failure, to the establishment of the Estates-General. Many associated with Jefferson and Paine, such as Condorcet, were attracted to American constitutional thinking because it rejected the English example of mixed government with the institution of a nobility and advocated the sovereignty of the people. The salience of American constitutional issues for many French thinkers is evident in the discussion of Wilson's pamphlet and in the translation and editing by Jefferson's friends of John Stevens's *Examen du gouvernement d'Angleterre comparé aux constitutions des états unis* (1788), a powerful attack on the English model and its defenders.[9]

Debates on the US, British and French constitutions thus became inter-twined in Paine's Paris circles in the years 1787–9, and his thinking on the central issue of the nature of rights and the relationship between the people, the constitution and the government should be recognized less as a response to Burke than as a sign of his involvement in French discussions of the American constitution and its superiority to Britain's mixed government. *Rights of Man* attacked hereditary privilege as a relevant principle in government and, as in the French deliberations, the attack was primarily directed, not against the King, but against the nobility and its claim to be a separate order from that of the nation as a whole.

There are other elements in *Rights of Man* where the attribution of influ-ence and intention is a complex task. For example, in the first part of *Rights of Man* (1791) Paine gives us an account of events in France and of the French Constitution that treats the actions of the French crowd as instances of regrettable but understandable retaliatory violence. He also defends the property-based franchise of the Constitution. We might read these as exam-ples of Paine distancing himself from the more radical elements of the Revo-lution and their sense of revolutionary justice, in keeping with his links to a section of the leadership of the French Revolution that was wary of popular initiative and popular justice, much as they had hopes for a transformation of the political system in the direction of a representative system. But it is also likely that he was trying to demonstrate to the British public the rea-sonableness of the French innovations, which led him, especially in the light of Burke's highly coloured reaction, to play down more populist elements of the Revolution.

There are two further areas where Paine is curiously reticent. In his dis-cussion of the monarchy he accepts that it is to be a central part of the new order within France, and his withering accounts of hereditary imposition are directed against the aristocracy rather than against the King, in marked contrast to *Common Sense*. Again, he may have been concerned to defend the new institutions of France, to which the monarchy remained central, but he also clearly had some sympathy for the French King, which sprang from the gratitude that many Americans felt for his support during the American Revolution.[10] Was this sheer pragmatism – attacking monarchy in *Common Sense* to break people's attachment to George III as the traditional source of appeal, but tolerating the French King because there was no republicanism in France prior to 1791? In fact, Paine had serious doubts about how far the countries of Europe were open to the kind of government that graced the New World. In *Common Sense* there was a real sense that liberty had flown from Europe because its societies were too systematically corrupt to bear reformation. He became more optimistic about the possibilities for reform in Europe following the opening events of the French Revolution, but this does not mean he was immediately convinced that it was possible to undertake the kind of root and branch reform required by the imposition of a wholly representative political system. It seems that, until the spring of 1791, he thought that the reforms of 1789–90 were as close as the French could get to a fundamental reform of their system. His view of Britain was similar. In the first part of *Rights of Man* he defends the limited reforms of the opening of the French Revolution as steps that can be taken in the least despotic of the monarchical states of mainland Europe, but there is no evidence that he wants to push those states further in the direction of wholly representative government. In *Common Sense* he saw America as exceptional and as having had a unique historical opportunity to begin the world again that set it apart from European monarchies, and his view of the prospects for Europe changes only gradually.

A second 'silence' concerns the franchise. For all Paine's reputation as a democrat, the first part of *Rights of Man* did not advocate universal suffrage, and he defended the limited suffrage of the National Assembly and the distinction between active and passive citizens without apparent embarrassment.[11] It was clear to him that France's arrangements offered something that was dramatically superior to the arbitrary and corrupt system of voting in England, but there is no evidence that he was holding back from expressing his real preferences. Neither part of *Rights of Man* advocates universal manhood suffrage. Only in what has been called the 'third part of *Rights of Man*' – his *Letter Addressed to the Addressers* (1792) – does Paine's position become unequivocal: because every twenty-one-year-old pays taxes out of the product of his labour, 'so has every one the same equal right to vote, and no one part of a nation, nor any individual, has a right to dispute the right of another' (Paine, *RM*, p. 377). The same principle was given still fuller expression in his 'Dissertation on First Principles of Government': 'The right of voting for representatives is the primary right by which other rights are protected. To take away this right is to reduce a man to slavery, for slavery consists in being subject to the will of another, and he that has not a vote in the election of representatives, is in this case' (Paine, *RM*, p. 398). This is a story of changing convictions: Paine had no interest in emphasizing deficiencies in the arrangements in France in 1790 but the contrast that mattered most to him at that point was that between the level and generous suffrage of the French system and the arbitrary and narrow suffrage of the unreformed House of Commons.

The first part of *Rights of Man* is an accomplished performance that focuses in detail on Burke's prolix and elusive argument. There is an insistent reference to what Burke actually said, although that means that the scoring of debating points is often more prominent than detailed engagement with Burke's central themes of the fragility of government and the importance of tradition and order. Moreover, while Paine does tackle a number of Burke's central claims, especially concerning the rights of generations and the nature of the compact, the text itself is episodic and it strikes many modern readers as a mere medley of topics and issues that do not themselves add up to a coherent and consistent argument. This is one result of Paine's attempts to take Burke seriously, to challenge the substance of his claims about the actual events of the Revolution and to counter the deep anti-populism of Burke's essay. In the 'Conclusion' to part one, however, Paine steps back from the details of Burke's pamphlet and begins to speak in a voice that suggests a deeper radicalism:

> it is evident that the opinion of the world is changed with respect to systems of Government... What were formerly called Revolutions, were little more than a change of persons, or an alteration of local circumstances. They rose and fell like things of course... But what we now see in the world, from the Revolutions of America and France, are a renovation of the natural order of things, a system of principles as universal as truth and the existence of man, and combining moral with political happiness and national prosperity.
>
> (Paine, *RM*, pp. 193–4)

Governments are divided into those by election and representation and those by hereditary succession and the two modes are founded, respectively, on 'Reason and Ignorance'. Only the former has legitimacy. He explicitly attacks the doctrine of mixed government and, finally, turns on monarchy:

> The romantic and barbarous distinction of men into Kings and subjects, though it may suit the condition of courtiers, cannot that of citizens; and is exploded by the principle upon which Governments are now founded. Every citizen is a member of the Sovereignty, and, as such, can acknowledge no personal subjection; and his obedience can be only to the laws.   (pp. 193–4)

Paine's 'Conclusion' points to a position that is in several respects significantly more radical than the rest of the text, suggesting that in the course of engaging with Burke and associating with French and subsequently British reformers he had come to see a future for Europe that he had not previously anticipated.

Rights of Man, Part the Second (1792)

In the Preface to the second part of *Rights of Man*, Paine explained that it had been his intention to cast the first part at greater length but had realized that it would become too bulky. He also wanted to gauge public reaction to his style of writing and argument and he wished to see how Burke would reply. Since Burke made no reply, beyond a few comments in his *Appeal from the New to the Old Whigs* (1791), Paine no longer felt constrained to direct his remarks to him and he set out his own principles more directly than he could under the constraints of a reply. It is clear from the conclusion to the first part, that Paine had developed a more radical agenda than is fully canvassed in that text – and that agenda developed further under the pressure of the events of 1791–2 and in the writing of part two. He was further radicalized by the widespread success of the pamphlet and by his stay in France in the early summer of 1791, when the King made his ill-judged flight to Varennes. In the immediate aftermath, Paine, in association with Brissot, Du Châtelet, Lanthenas, Bonneville and Condorcet (members of the influential political club and publishing house, the 'Cercle Social'), formed a republican society calling for the end of the monarchy, and he hurriedly produced a republican manifesto that was translated and posted on the walls of Paris calling for a fully republican and representative system. He did not remain in Paris long enough to see the republican movement suppressed on 17 July 1791 at the massacre of the Champ de Mars (by his old friend Lafayette) but returned to England where he set about writing the second part of *Rights of Man*, which was published in March 1792.

During Paine's republican moment in Paris in June 1791 he engaged with the Abbé Sieyès over the contending strengths of republican and monarchical government and that exchange is reflected in the second part of *Rights of Man* (Paine, RM, pp. 222, 225–6). Indeed, on one reading, the second part of *Rights of Man* can be seen as radicalized by Paine's association with Condorcet and others in the Girondin camp, and consequently as breathing the spirit of Girondin revolutionary enthusiasm.[12] But, while Paine had longstanding links to this group, it is more likely that he was in the vanguard of republicanism and was looked on by his French friends in July 1791 as representing this more extreme position. Moreover, what is most striking about the second part of *Rights of Man* is that it responded to the increasingly complex and messy reality of the French Revolutionary struggle, and to Paine's success in communicating to a very wide English audience, by switching its focus away from France towards America, and by providing a theorized narrative of the American Revolution as an example for English imitation and popular aspiration. This is not to deny French influences, perhaps especially with regard to the practical proposals that fill the last chapter that were probably informed by Paine's acquaintance with members of the Comité de Mendicité in France, but it strongly suggests that Paine now saw the American case as one that could be widely and immediately implemented in the *ancien régime* states of Europe.[13] At the same time, it remains the case that Paine's principal target was Britain and 'the ear of John Bull', and to understand what he was arguing requires that we grasp what he was trying to do with *that* audience in particular. This seems to have been to break its attachment to mixed government and to encourage a movement to express the sovereignty of the people.[14]

For Paine, every government has a sovereign power and in America it is the people. Their sovereignty 'is exercised in electing and deputing a certain number of persons to represent and act for the whole, and who, if they do not act right, may be displaced by the same power that placed them there, and others elected and deputed in their stead, and the wrong measures of former representatives corrected and brought right by this means' (*Dissertations on Government* (1786), in Paine, *LMW*, vol. II, p. 369). 'The sovereignty in a republic is exercised to keep right and wrong in their proper and distinct places, and never suffer the one to usurp the place of the other. A republic, properly understood, is a sovereignty of justice, in contradistinction to a sovereignty of will' (p. 375), a position that sits uncomfortably with more populist interpretations of the sovereignty of the people's will, and leads Paine into direct conflict with the Jacobins. Paine's claim in 'To Messieurs Condorcet, Nicolas de Bonneville and Lanthenas' (1791) to be 'the citizen of a land that recognizes no majesty but that of the people; no government except that of its own representatives, and no sovereignty except that of the laws' (p. 1315) precisely captures his position. He presents the republican system of election and representation as the only one able to protect the fundamental interests of the citizen (p. 1317).

The second part of *Rights of Man* starts with the claim that America had introduced a revolution in the principles and practices of government. In 1791 Paine defended the French reforms that produced a moderate constitutional monarchy; in 1792 he concedes that this is no longer relevant. Instead, the American Revolution becomes the fulcrum on which the political world can be made to turn, eradicating not simply aristocratic privilege but both monarchical and hereditary government, and replacing them with representative democracies. 'Government founded on a *moral theory, on a system of universal peace, on the indefeasible hereditary Rights of Man*, is now revolving from west to east.... It interests not particular individuals, but nations, in its progress, and promises a new aera to the human race' (Paine, *RM*, p. 213). The contrast in *Common Sense* between the New and the Old Worlds, with the principles of the new being of little relevance to the corrupt old orders, has been transformed by seeing the American example as the instigator of progressive revolutionary change to wholly representative government throughout the Old World.

In setting out the political principles of this new order, Paine begins with the distinction between society and government and with the striking suggestion that government is no further necessary than to supply the few cases to which society and civilization are not conveniently competent. Indeed, it is possible for society to manage affairs for some time without disorder in the absence of government, as was demonstrated in America in the two years following the outbreak of the American war. This is in sharp contrast to the picture of *Common Sense*, where government is necessitated by our wickedness, with little sense that this wickedness is of limited extent. In contrast, *Rights of Man* offers a progressive prospect: 'The more perfect civilization is, the less occasion has it for government ... how often is the natural propensity to society disturbed or destroyed by the operations of government! ... *government is nothing more than a national association acting on the principles of society*'. 'Government on the old system, is an assumption of power, for the aggrandisement of itself; on the new, a delegation of power, for the common benefit of society.' Although we might call it a new system of government, it is in fact the oldest 'being founded on the original inherent Rights of Man' (Paine, *RM*, pp. 216, 218, 223).

Paine returns to the contrast between governments founded on reason and ignorance drawn in the 'Conclusion' to part one: all hereditary government is in its nature tyrannical, it treats a people as hereditary property, 'as if they were flocks and herds' (Paine, *RM*, p. 224). In contrast, representative government is a new departure; but it is not to be confused with democratic government, which he understands as direct popular government appropriate only to the small city states of the ancient world (p. 229). The principle of representation was unknown in ancient democracies with the result that these institutions could not adapt as those states grew. Modern states engraft representation on to democracy, ensuring its suitability to any size of state, as America demonstrates (p. 232). In the *Federalist Papers* Madison referred to states with representative government as 'republics'. Paine denies that republics are a type of government. Indeed, 'what is called a *republic* is not any *particular form* of government. It is wholly characteristical of the purport, matter, or object for which the government ought to be instituted' and government that does not make this the end of its activity is neither republican nor good. Many governments claim the title, but 'the government of America, which is wholly on the system of representation, is the only real republic ... that now exists. Its government has no other object than the public business of the nation, and therefore it is properly a republic ... ' It is naturally opposed to monarchy, which essentially signifies 'arbitrary power in an individual person; in the exercise of which, *himself*, and not the *res-publica*, is the object' (pp. 231, 230). Only representative democracy produces republican rule, and only that form of rule has any legitimacy. Hence the sustained critique of monarchy at the end of chapter 3 of part two.

Paine's connections with reform circles in France are important to understanding him, even if much Paine scholarship almost entirely ignores them, but the evidence for seeing Paine as dependent on the intellectual innovations of his French friends is not strong.[15] His attraction for his French friends was in large part his American experience, and they reinforced in him a sense of the importance of that experience and its significance for reform in Europe. His increasing confidence in the potential for change in Europe was influenced by his reading of French events, but it was also affected by his experiences in England where the reform movement was spreading. Moreover, the evidence suggests that it was in the early months of 1791, when he was in England writing the conclusion to the first part of *Rights of Man*, that he settled on the contrast between government by reason, election and representation, as against that by ignorance and hereditary succession, with America epitomizing the former.

Part two also develops further Paine's 1791 argument about constitutions, which Stevens's pamphlet and Sieyès's *What is the Third Estate?* (1789) may have influenced: a constitution should not be understood as the act of a government, but as the act of a people constituting a government. The constitution is the frame of a government established by the sovereign act of the people. In this respect the formation of constitutions in America was the result of a free people, joining together to create a set of institutions by which they would be governed – 'the case and circumstances of America present themselves as in the beginning of a world' (Paine, *RM*, p. 238). Paine offers a narrative of the government of Pennsylvania, also pointing to the convention to be elected every seven years for the express purpose of revising the constitutions (pp. 238–40). He then turns to the formation of the federal government. The federal constitution is not defended as the ideal form of government, indeed, he looks forward to further experimentation: 'The best form of government that could now be devised, consistent with the condition of the present moment, may be far short of that excellence which a few years may afford. There is a morning of reason rising upon man on the subject of government, that has not appeared before' (pp. 240–4). But the central message for his British readers was that those in power had no right to reform the government; only an extra-parliamentary convention would have the sovereign authority to alter the country's constitution. That message set popular reformers an agenda that enjoined them to pursue a popular conventionism; that in turn led to a head-on clash with the government and the Treason Trials of 1794.

In the final and longest chapter of the book, Paine develops further the distinction between civil and court government. It is court governments that are responsible for wars and the intervention in other states that disturb commerce, which is the greatest engine of universal civilization, and that lead to the imposition of crippling burdens of taxation on monarchical countries. In the absence of court government, societies would have only the civil governments that America has and could manage their affairs with infinitely less expense and with the consent and will of the nation. They would engage freely in commerce, following where their interests lay; and they would be relieved of the burden of taxation that presently presses so hard, particularly on the poorest members of society.

He then turns to a detailed analysis of taxation in England, pointing to rises from £500,000 per annum in 1566 to 17 million pounds in 1791, and he lays the blame on the Hanoverian succession and the court wars fought in the eighteenth century. Of that 17 million some 9 million services the National Debt, the rest goes on current expenditure. Paine estimates that, by the spread of peace and the development of agreements with France and America, Britain could reduce its military expenditure and its spending on government to approximately $1^1/_2$ million per annum – roughly the sum the government spent under the extravagant Charles II. This leaves approximately 6 million from current revenues to be disposed of. Since there are difficulties in reducing the tax on many items, because of the way that taxes and trade bind themselves together, he proposes a range of measures that will effectively return taxation to those least able to pay (Paine, *RM*, p. 291). He proposes to abolish the poor rates and to set a national system of poor relief at double the amount of the present poor rates, which would effectively remit the indirect taxes paid by those in poverty. This remission is to be directed to the poor and their children – since the cost of raising children presses hardest upon them – and to those who can no longer work at full capacity or at all. The scheme includes child benefit and pensions for the aged, funding for the education of the poor, the provision of hostels and employment for the young, casual poor in London in search of work, maternity benefit and a grant for newly married couples, and a grant for those who work away from home and need help with funeral expenses. There would also be increased assistance to disbanded soldiers and their officers in the army and navy. Moreover, certain direct taxes should be removed and replaced with a progressive income tax on property, tied to incentives to eradicate primogeniture. In essence he sketches a welfare state that provides support to those in need and taxes the rich. Poverty is explained as a result of high levels of taxation, the costs of having children and the vagaries of disability and old age, and Paine wants the state, rather than wasting its exorbitant revenues in the dynastic wars of courts, to turn them to productive effect. Moreover, he clearly sees this as a matter of right – the poor pay taxation on goods throughout their lives and this ensures that it becomes an investment for their old age.[16]

If the first part of *Rights of Man* sat uncomfortably with British traditions of mixed government and the rights of free-born Englishmen, its second part is still more distant from local traditions: moving the focal point from France to America and promoting popular conventionism among British reformers.[17] Paine's recognition in the early 1790s that European states might follow the American example was powerfully influenced by his experience of the opening stages of the French Revolution and by his discussions with French and English reformers between 1788 and 1792. While he had long nursed an antipathy to kings and aristocrats, the positive American view of Louis XVI, coupled with a sense of American exceptionalism, led him to defend a moderate and limited interpretation of the events of 1789 in the first part of *Rights of Man*. But in the first six months of 1791, from the completion of part one through to the publication of his *Republican Manifesto*, he came to believe that Europe was ripe for a fundamental revolution in its principles and the replacement of hereditary with representative government. The conclusion to the first part of *Rights of Man* intimates the potential for dramatic change, but it is only by the spring of 1791 that Paine thought it possible and necessary to sweep away the whole 'pantomimical contrivance' of kings and aristocracy and the fictions of mixed government, and to replace them with a pure system of representative government. Finally, during the summer of 1792 he became convinced that universal manhood suffrage was a sine qua non for that system (Paine, *RM*, p. 192).

Paine's success in reaching a popular audience in Britain coincided with his own intellectual position becoming simultaneously more extreme – attacking the Burkean reading of the 1688 settlement, setting out the principles of a representative republic founded on natural rights and calling for a popular extra-parliamentary convention to create a constitution for the country in his *Letter Addressed to the Addressers* – thereby setting reformers on a collision course with the government.[18] Loyalist reaction quickly associated Paine's republicanism with king-killing and sanguinary extremism – and the Association for the Preservation of Liberty and Property against Republicans and Levellers, neatly tied the new societies and their principles to the extremist legacy of the English Civil War. From this point, what had started as something like a 'debate' had become an ideological war of considerable intensity. Paine's work was driven underground and was increasingly circulated only clandestinely until the 1820s.[19]

Later thoughts

On this account, the doctrine of Paine's 1795 *Dissertations on Government* is not the same as that of *Common Sense*, written nearly twenty years before, even if they are not radically discontinuous. *Rights of Man* records and contributes to five major developments in Paine's position. The first is his acceptance of commerce and its role as a force for peace in the world, which followed the success of the American Revolution and his association with many leading spokesmen for commercial interests in America. *Common Sense* sees a threat of corruption from commerce (Paine, *RM*, p. 42), but from his *Letter to the Abbé Raynal* (1786) it is increasingly welcomed as an essentially pacific system that could unite the world. That change led him to heap on hereditary institutions all the negative effects of inequality and corruption and to claim that their elimination would enable representative institutions and commercial society to flourish in all states. And, in so far as *Dissertations on the First Principles of Government* (1795) and *Agrarian Justice* (1796) attack wealth and property they do so by challenging aristocratic monopoly rather than commerce and manufacture.

The second change is Paine's growing emphasis on rights as setting the legitimate limits of government action, which emerges in the late 1780s in response to discussions of the federal constitution in France. A third development over the next few years is his conversion to the view that European monarchies could be replaced by representative forms of government. This is intimated at the end of the first part of *Rights of Man*, but it becomes fully explicit only in the summer of 1791, thereafter driving his appeal to popular conventionism in the second part of *Rights of Man* and his *Letter Addressed . . .* The fourth innovation arises from reflections on the nature of citizenship that come to fruition in relation to universal suffrage only in *Letter Addressed . . .* in late summer 1792. This genuine shift in Paine's thinking is influenced both by his French friends and by the demands for universal suffrage and annual parliaments that animated the popular reform movement in England in the 1790s.

A final transition, not fully captured within this period, is that the economic liberalism and the conception of minimal government advanced in *Rights of Man* give way in the concluding proposals for redistributive taxation and welfare rights. These probably owe much both to debates in France and England about the support for the indigent. However, by 1797, in *Agrarian Justice*, Paine moves from his ad hoc suggestion that such redistribution was a way of managing the excess revenues of the state once war was ended, to a principled set of claims for the material and social rights of men arising from the original common ownership of the world. That development responds in part to the work of British radicals, such as Thomas Spence, and to the proto-socialist ambitions of French revolutionaries like Babeuf, but it also stems from pressing still further the natural rights model that Paine first articulated in the late 1780s.[20]

In none of these changes is there much sense that it is by engaging with Burke that Paine is prompted to develop his principles more fully. Burke provides a foil, but the influence of American and French debates is evident in Paine's response in part one, and is worked out still more directly and substantively in part two as Paine leaves behind Burke's text and articulates his own political philosophy. This suggests that Paine barely engages with Burke, but that would be misleading. It is difficult wholly to dismiss the cordiality that existed between the two men in the years before 1790, when it was not clear to either how radically they might come to disagree. Linked by an affection for America, they saw more uniting them than dividing them, but with the outbreak of the Revolution in France their responses begin to drive them apart – so that the *Reflections* is a crystallization and expression of Burke's growing unease with British and continental politics, just as *Rights of Man* crystallizes and expresses a set of hopes and aspirations for the European world that Paine had hitherto associated exclusively with America.

In this sense, the French Revolution provoked a real controversy; it changed the previous terms of debate, producing often dramatic intellectual and theoretical innovations, not least for its principal protagonists. Having retired to private life and concerns with his single-span bridge after 1783, Paine's subsequent experience in France and then in England led him to reflect on and to articulate more fully what he believed to be central to his American experience. In doing so, his thinking changed in significant ways, resulting in a series of iconic texts that more than justify his standing as a founding father of modern representative democracy and as the first international revolutionary.

NOTES

1 J. G. A. Pocock, *Virtue, Commerce and History: Essays on Political Thought and History, Chiefly in the Eighteenth Century* (Cambridge: Cambridge University Press, 1985), p. 276.
2 See Burke's letter to Sir Gilbert Elliot, 3 September 1788, in *The Correspondence of Edmund Burke*, gen. ed. Thomas Copeland, 10 vols. (Cambridge: Cambridge University Press, 1958–69), vol. V, p. 415. Burke's hostility to Paine emerges relatively late – see his letter to William Cusack Smith, 22 July 1791, *ibid.*, vol. VI, pp. 303–4.

3 Lafayette to Washington, Paris, 12 January 1790, *The Letters of Lafayette to Washington 1777–1799*, ed. Louis Gottschalk (Philadelphia: American Philosophical Society, 1976), p. 346.

4 Compare the characterization of the Count de Broglio in Thomas Jefferson, *Writings*, ed. Merrill D. Peterson (New York: Library of America, 1984), p. 88 and in Thomas Paine, *Rights of Man, Common Sense and Other Political Writings*, ed. Mark Philp (Oxford: Oxford University Press, 1995), p. 103. See also J. T. Boulton, 'An Unpublished Letter from Paine to Burke', *Durham University Journal* 43:2 (1951), 49–55.

5 *Manchester Herald*, 28 April 1792, cited in Goodwin, p. 99.

6 See his *Candid and Critical Remarks on a Letter signed Ludlow* (1777) in Philip S. Foner, ed., *The Life and Major Writings of Thomas Paine*, 2 vols. (Secaucus, NJ: Citadel Press, 1948), vol. II, pp. 274 and 273, in which he takes, for the first time, a firm stance on the superiority of natural rights to man-made law.

7 *The Substance of a Speech delivered by James Wilson, Esq. Explanatory of the general principles of the proposed Faederal Constitution* (Philadelphia: Thomas Bradford, 1787), p. 8.

8 See Jefferson to Madison, Paris, 15 March 1789, in Jefferson, *Writings*, pp. 942–6.

9 Joyce Appleby, 'America as a Model for the Radical French Reformers of 1789', *William and Mary Quarterly* 3rd ser. 28:2 (1971), 267–86.

10 The main passage attacking monarchy is in Paine, *Rights of Man*, ed. Philp, p. 175 – see also p. 177 on Hanoverians and p. 180 on the Regency Crisis. Favourable comments appear at p. 97. Essentially Paine is not against Louis but against despotic principles of government – but see pp. 194–5 on monarchical sovereignty.

11 For earlier (1778) comments on the franchise, accepting less than universal suffrage, see *A Serious Address to the People of Pennsylvania on the Present Situation of their Affairs*, in Foner, *Life and Major Writings*, vol. II, p. 287.

12 Gary Kates, 'From Liberalism to Radicalism: Tom Paine's Rights of Man', *Journal of the History of Ideas* 50:4 (1989), 569–87; Richard Whatmore, '"A gigantic manliness": Thomas Paine's Republicanism in the 1790s', in S. Collini, R. Whatmore and B. Young, eds., *Economy, Polity and Society: British Intellectual History, 1750–1950* (Cambridge: Cambridge University Press, 2000), pp. 135–57.

13 Gareth Stedman-Jones, *An End to Poverty* (London: Profile Books, 2004), pp. 16–26.

14 See Paine's letter to John Hall, London, 25 November 1791, in Foner, *Life and Major Writings*, vol. II, p. 1322.

15 Exceptions include A. O. Aldridge's *Man of Reason: The Life of Thomas Paine* (London: Cresset Press, 1960); W. Doyle's 'Tom Paine and the Girondins', in *Officers, Nobles and Revolutionaries* (London: Hambledon, 1995), and Kates and Whatmore, cited above.

16 On the English background see J. Innes, 'The State and the Poor: Eighteenth-century England in European Perspective', in J. Brewer and E. Hellmuth, eds., *Rethinking Leviathan: The Eighteenth-Century State in Britain and Germany* (Oxford: Oxford University Press, 1999), pp. 225–80.

17 See T. M. Parsinnen, 'Association, Convention and Anti-Parliament in British Radical Politics, 1771–1848,' *English Historical Review* 88 (July 1973), 504–33.

18 For an assessment of Paine's prose style, see David Duff's essay in this volume; this chapter focuses on the central principles and commitments in his work, although the medium and the message are undoubtedly related.

19 Formally only the second part of *Rights of Man* was prohibited; but Paine's anti-Christian *Age of Reason* was also suppressed.

20 Gregory Claeys, *Thomas Paine: Social and Political Thought* (London: Unwin Hyman, 1989).

4

DAVID DUFF

Burke and Paine: contrasts

The confrontation between Burke and Paine in the 1790s has been called 'probably the greatest joust in the lists of political philosophy that Great Britain ever witnessed'.[1] This comment by a modern political historian echoes Burke's metaphor of chivalric combat, memorably applied in his *Reflections on the Revolution in France* (1790) to prospective defenders of the French royal family but then used in an ironic sense by his antagonists to characterize Burke's own crusade against the forces of revolution in Britain. Those forces took many shapes, especially in Burke's increasingly paranoiac imagination, but his most dangerous and influential adversary was undoubtedly Paine, and the quarrel between them was seen by contemporary observers, as it is today, as a paradigm of the whole Revolution controversy. Not only did Burke and Paine stake out the two fundamental alternatives in any revolutionary situation – to support radical change or to oppose it – but they did so in terms that transformed the nature of political discourse, altering its language and forms. Within months of the publication of Paine's reply to the *Reflections*, the two parts of *Rights of Man* (1791, 1792), pamphlets were appearing with titles like *Paine and Burke Contrasted, or An Address to the Inhabitants of Great Britain* (1792), wording indicative both of the self-consciousness of the Revolution debate (it was, in part, a polemic on polemic itself) and of the extent to which the war of ideas had become personalized. Reading Burke and Paine, and choosing between them, was a defining experience of the 1790s, and the Burke–Paine binary helped to shape the dualistic mindset of literary Romanticism as it did the broader political culture of post-1789 Britain.

That the names of Burke and Paine became inseparably connected in the public imagination was a source of torment to the former. Responding in an open letter to William Elliot, dated 26 May 1795, to the frequently made charge that he had 'provoked' Paine's pamphlet and thus unwittingly fuelled the radical cause, Burke reminded his accusers that Citizen Paine (who, they will have it, hunts with me in couples, and who only moves as I drag him along), has a sufficient activity in his own native benevolence to dispose and enable him to take the lead for himself. He is ready to blaspheme his God, to insult his king, and to libel the constitution of his country, without any provocation from me. (*EB Writings*, vol. IX, p. 31)

Burke's contempt for his involuntary hunting partner was tempered only by his recognition of Paine's formidable fire power. Paine was, for Burke, the epitome of destructive revolutionary energy, a reformist zealot capable of abolishing in six or seven days 'all, which the boasted wisdom of our ancestors has laboured to bring to perfection for six or seven centuries' (*Fourth Letter on a Regicide Peace*, in *EB Writings*, vol. IX, p. 82). 'Painism', he warned Earl Fitzwilliam, a Whig colleague, in 1791, 'will infuse into the people a disposition to all sorts of mischief... I ought to do all I can against that Man' (*EB Corr.*, vol. VI, p. 313). Elsewhere, he remarks of another influential reply to the *Reflections*, James Mackintosh's *Vindiciae Gallicae* (1791), that, though its ideas were 'better dressed or rather more disguised', 'it is Paine at bottom, – and... indeed all the writers against me are, either Paine with some difference in the way of stating, or even myself' (*EB Corr.*, vol. VI, p. 312). Burke attributes this singular observation to his beloved son Richard (he claims not to have read Mackintosh himself) but it accurately conveys his own near-obsession with Paine, and his sense that between them, he and Paine had spelled out the only real political options available.

Paine, for his part, believed Burke wrote the *Reflections* to spite him, and a note of personal betrayal can be felt throughout *Rights of Man*. Paine had met Burke in 1787 and later claimed to have been 'in some intimacy' with him over the following two years. In light of Burke's previous support for American independence, Paine regarded him as a natural ally and wrote to him from Paris on 17 January 1790 with an enthusiastic account of the French Revolution, which he described as 'a Forerunner to other Revolutions in Europe' and a new form of politics whose 'Contagion' was certain to spread (*EB Corr.*, vol. VI, p. 71). Far from welcoming this news, however, Burke was appalled by it and took it as confirmation of the claim he had already voiced in Parliament and was to make pivotal to the *Reflections*, that France was actively exporting revolutionary principles – Paine himself being a notable trafficker. Paine refers to his January letter several times in *Rights of Man*, expressing surprise and dismay that Burke had spurned their friendship, broken with his liberal principles and declared himself an enemy to the French Revolution (Paine, *RM*, pp. 86, 143). The charge that Burke was guilty of 'incivility' as well as inconsistency and that he had 'abused' both a friend and the French nation sets the tone of *Rights of Man* and of subsequent exchanges, contributing to a perception of the Burke–Paine conflict as a private quarrel as much as a public debate.

The two authors' ability to disturb and provoke one another is matched by their power over other readers. Again, there is a curious symmetry here, notwithstanding the diametrically opposed political messages. Both the *Reflections* and *Rights of Man* had what can only be described as a messianic effect on their readers: the perusal of each was tantamount for many to a conversion experience. Sir Gilbert Elliot wrote to Burke a few days after the publication of the *Reflections* declaring 'Your book contains the fundamental Elements of *all* Political knowledge... I could feel as if it came like the *word* like a *Revelation*, to save us when our own best wisdom or virtue could not suffice' (*EB Corr.*, vol. VI, p. 156). For Burke's parliamentary colleague William Windham, the *Reflections* was 'a work that may seem capable of overturning the National Assembly, and turning the stream of opinion throughout Europe'.[2] The novelist Fanny Burney described it as 'the noblest, deepest, most animated, and exalted work that I think I have ever read'.[3] Even those, like Samuel Parr, who went on to attack Burke's position, acknowledged its 'magic force',[4] a potency confirmed as much by the numerous refutations of the *Reflections* (there were over seventy printed replies, the majority hostile) as by the many public and private endorsements, which included tributes from several European heads of state.

Rights of Man inspired similar raptures and anathemas. As with Burke, many of the eighty or so pamphlets written in reply were hostile but the estimated quarter of a million copies of *Rights of Man* sold by 1793 (with possibly twice that number by the end of the decade) reveal the scale of the positive response. The playwright and novelist Thomas Holcroft caught the mood of public excitement when he declared in a letter to William Godwin, 'Hey for the New Jerusalem! The millennium! And peace and eternal beatitude unto the soul of Thomas Paine' (Kegan Paul, vol. I, p. 69). Joel Barlow, radical poet and pamphleteer, predicted that no work 'that will be written for ages to come, will surely find a reader who will not have read the *Rights of Man*'.[5] A London tailor, roused to political consciousness like hundreds of thousands of other working people by a reading of *Rights of Man*, announced in a London tavern that 'Tom Paine was a Second Jesus Christ' and 'the only Man to save this Country and the Whole World'.[6] The French National Assembly, too, recognized Paine's contribution, bestowing on him honorary French citizenship and electing him deputy for Calais. Legend has it that when Napoleon Buonaparte came to power, he slept with a copy of *Rights of Man* under his pillow.

The celebrity of the two pamphlets and the diversity of responses they attracted are captured by contemporary cartoons. In the *Reflections* Burke likens the misfortunes of Marie Antoinette, forcibly removed by a revolutionary crowd from the royal palace at Versailles to Paris, to those of a damsel in distress in medieval romance:

> It is now sixteen or seventeen years since I saw the queen of France, then the dauphiness, at Versailles; and surely never lighted on this orb, which she hardly seemed to touch, a more delightful vision... Little did I dream when she added titles of veneration to those of enthusiastic, distant, respectful love, that she should ever be obliged to carry the sharp antidote against disgrace concealed in that bosom; little did I dream that I should have lived to see such disasters fallen upon her in a nation of gallant men, in a nation of men of honour and of cavaliers. I thought ten thousand swords must have leaped from their scabbards to avenge even a look that threatened her with insult. – But the age of chivalry is gone. – That of sophisters, oeconomists, and calculators, has succeeded; and the glory of Europe is extinguished for ever.
>
> (*EB Writings*, vol. VIII, pp. 126–7)

Burke's invocation of the 'age of chivalry' to characterize the *ancien régime* and its endangered Queen is a brilliant piece of rhetorical manipulation, cleverly converting literary nostalgia for the old romances of chivalry into political support for the counter-revolutionary cause. Burke intensifies the metaphor by placing himself in the position of the courtly lover, contemplating in horror her threatened physical violation by the revolutionary mob (her 'antidote against disgrace' was an ampoule of poison).

Yet in its hyperbolic rhetoric, anachronistic imagery and unabashed sentimentalism the passage was ripe for parody. A series of caricatures attributed to Frederick George Byron portrayed Burke as a Don Quixote figure, a modern-day fantasist labouring under the delusion that he was a chivalric knight defending the honour of a virtuous woman – and of civilization itself. The first of the series, *Frontispiece to Reflections on the French Revolution* (published 2 November 1790), shows Burke as an infatuated lover kneeling before a vision of Marie Antoinette suspended on a cloud; Cupid inflames his feelings by holding a firebrand to his head (fig. 4.1). Another, *Don Dismallo, After an Absence of Sixteen Years, Embracing His Beautiful Vision* (18 November 1790), reworks this scene in explicitly Quixotic terms, with Burke in full medieval armour and Marie Antoinette as his Dulcinea – and a dowdy Mrs Burke looking on tearfully from the side. Other cartoons in the series use the Don Quixote/Don Dismallo motif to satirize Burke's struggles with his political opponents, real and imagined. The most famous of these is *The Knight of the Wo[e]ful Countenance Going to Extirpate the National*

Figure 4.1 *Frontispiece to Reflections on the French Revolution*, anonymous etching attributed to Frederick George Byron, published 2 November 1790.

Assembly (15 November 1790), a masterpiece of visual mockery which shows Burke, again in full armour, emerging from his publisher mounted on an ass, ready to do battle against the French revolutionaries with his lance (a gigantic ink pen) and his 'Shield of Aristocracy and Despotism' (fig. 4.2).

For present purposes, the most revealing of the series is *Don Dismallo Running the Literary Gauntlet* (1 December 1790), in which Burke confronts his enemies at home (fig. 4.3). Dressed here not as a knight but as a clown, he is shown stripped to the waist and wearing a fool's cap, running ignominiously down a line of men and women who each take turns to flog him. Six of his persecutors are named – Helen Maria Williams, Richard

Figure 4.2 *The Knight of the Wo[e]ful Countenance Going to Extirpate the National Assembly*, anonymous etching attributed to Frederick George Byron, published 15 November 1790.

Price, Anna Barbauld, Richard Brinsley Sheridan, John Horne Tooke and Catherine Macaulay – and represent prominent opponents of Burke who had answered or were expected to answer the *Reflections* (or, in Price's case, who had helped to provoke it in the first place). The other figures are Justice, with her sword and scales, and Liberty, her staff tipped with a *bonnet rouge* (symbolizing the French Revolution), arm-in-arm with an old, ragged man carrying a banner depicting scenes from the storming of the Bastille (he is recognizable as one of the liberated inmates). The speech

Figure 4.3 *Don Dismallo Running the Literary Gauntlet*, anonymous etching attributed to Frederick George Byron, published 1 December 1790.

Figure 4.4 *Contrasted Opinions of Paine's Pamphlet*, anonymous etching attributed to Frederick George Byron, published 26 May 1791.

bubbles articulate various reasons for punishing Burke, a common thread being that he was a turncoat, an erstwhile liberal who had become, in Barbauld's damning phrase, an 'Assassin of Liberty'.

A later cartoon by the same artist depicts differing reactions to *Rights of Man*. Unlike the caricature of Burke, *Contrasted Opinions of Paine's Pamphlet* (26 May 1791) portrays the reading process and shows eight prominent individuals holding a copy of *Rights of Man* and variously responding to it (fig. 4.4). Their reactions are conveyed both by their histrionic gestures (the design is partly modelled on illustrated acting manuals which taught actors how to externalize emotion) and by speech captions which contain quotations from Paine together with approving or disapproving comments. The first respondent (top left) is Burke himself, who shakes his fist and denounces Paine's 'infernal book', quoting a passage in *Rights of Man* where Paine attacks him for 'the disorderly cast of his genius' and his political showmanship. King George III (top row, third from left) gives a similarly angry reaction, saying Paine's book 'is all abuse, all abuse' and 'Flights of madness! Flights of madness!' (the compulsive repetition is an ironic reminder of George III's own chronic mania). Queen Caroline (bottom left) brands it 'a compound of falshoods', singling out a passage in which Paine impugns her German lineage. William Pitt (bottom row, second from right), also shaking his fist, calls Paine a 'damn'd, murderous Republican' and quotes the 'folly of titles' passage where aristocratic titles are compared to 'baby-cloaths' and 'gewgaws' (toys), and to 'circles drawn by the Magician's wand, to contract the sphere of man's felicity' (Paine, *RM*, p. 132). Baron Hawkesbury (top right), a political ally of both Pitt and the King, is shown savouring a passage in which Paine challenges Burke's interpretation of the 1688 parliamentary settlement (the so-called Glorious Revolution) as constitutionally binding 'to the end of time' (p. 93); he misquotes the passage, however, omitting Paine's scornful comments so as to make it read like an endorsement rather than a dismissal of the idea, and concludes with the remark 'o rare Paddy Burke!'.

The three remaining respondents are unambiguously pro-Paine. Charles James Fox (next to Burke) contrasts Paine's 'common sense' with the 'prose run mad' of Burke's *Reflections*, illustrating his point with the passage in *Rights of Man* where Paine rejects Burke's theory of hereditary power and affirms the right of every age and generation 'to act for itself, *in all cases*' (Paine, *RM*, pp. 91–2). Helen Maria Williams (bottom row, second from left)[7] chooses the memorable 'He pities the plumage, but forgets the dying bird' section in which Paine attacks Burke for being the dupe of his own imagination, so dazzled by his fanciful pictures of distressed royalty as to be blind to the true nature of what was happening in France (p. 102). The final reader, Richard Brinsley Sheridan (bottom right), takes as his chosen text a famous statement by the French revolutionary aristocrat the Marquis de La Fayette, quoted in *Rights of Man* as an encapsulation of Paine's rationalist creed of political self-determination: 'For a nation to love liberty, it is sufficient that she knows it; and to be free, it is sufficient that she wills it' (p. 96).

No two images from the 1790s better capture the politics of reading and the centrality of the reading experience at this unique moment of political literacy. *Running the Literary Gauntlet* provides a perfect emblem of the perils of political authorship: of a pamphlet war in which politicians and theorists – many of them personally known to one another – battled for the hearts and minds of the British people through the medium of print. *Contrasted Opinions* provides an equally resonant image of political readership, suggesting both the scale of the mobilization – the unprecedented spectacle of a whole country, from the King and Queen downwards, simultaneously reading the same political pamphlet – and just how divided the 'reading nation' had become. In the wake of the *Reflections* and *Rights of Man*, reading was no longer a passive, private process but an act of public engagement in which every citizen was required to participate, and for which each could be held publicly accountable. The stakes in this great national scene of reading were nothing less than the political future of the country.

Not all readers, however, accepted the simple choice between Burke and Paine. Burke had insisted in his *Appeal from the New to the Old Whigs* (1791) that those who were not for him were against him, and that any countenancing of 'the pretended *rights of man*' was an implicit invitation to revolution.[8] Many disputed this. Replying jointly to the *Appeal* and to *Rights of Man*, Sir Brooke Boothby makes clear in his *Observations* (1792) that 'I am not a *Burkite* – I am not a *Painite*', and that 'The object of the present work is to warn my countrymen from running into either, of what I conceive to be, two very dangerous extremes'.[9] Middle ways of various kinds were proposed. By 1793, with hundreds of pamphlets published, the spectrum of political opinion had broadened sufficiently for an enterprising publisher to produce an anthology entitled *A Comparative Display of the Different Opinions of the Most Distinguished British Writers on the Subject of the French Revolution*, in which extracts from Burke and Paine are juxtaposed with statements from more moderate commentators including Boothby, Catherine Macaulay, Capel Lofft, George Rous and James Mackintosh, whose *Vindiciae Gallicae* supplies the topic headings under which the passages are grouped. That the pamphlet war was being anthologized even as it happened is further evidence of the self-consciousness spoken of earlier: already by 1793, the French Revolution debate was a sufficiently definable phenomenon, with a familiar enough canon of authors, for it to become the subject of what is in effect an academic textbook, precursor of today's anthologies of the Revolution controversy. Compared with other 1790s publications, the anthology is surprisingly impartial – opposed viewpoints are presented without comment – but it captures the polemical essence of the decade in that its organizing principle is *contrast*: the 'comparative display' of conflicting opinions. Like the spectators at a jousting tournament, the public clearly enjoyed the cut-and-thrust, and had internalized the adversarial, contrastive method of modern political debate.

Much was made, too, of the paradox that by attacking the French Revolution Burke had inspired others to defend it, and thus promoted the very radicalism he abhorred. As John Thelwall gleefully put it, 'It was not *Tom Paine* but *Edmund Burke* that made me so zealous a reformer, and convinced me of the necessity of annual parliaments and universal suffrage'; the *Reflections* 'has made more democrats, among the thinking part of mankind, than all the works ever written in answer to it'.[10] Ironic toasts to Burke were a common feature of meetings of the London Corresponding Society and other radical organizations. Yet Paine's writings had a similar paradoxical effect. The spread of popular loyalism from 1792 was as rapid and far-reaching as the rise of the radical movement, and much of it was specifically directed against Paine, as the huge amount of anti-Painite propaganda demonstrates. Indeed, the anti-Paine and anti-Burke camps frequently mimicked one another's methods. One of the more chilling practices of the loyalist associations was to parade through the streets with an effigy of Paine which would then be ritually burned on a bonfire; in the winter of 1792–3, there were over 400 such burnings in towns and villages across the country.[11] An anonymous cartoon (possibly by John Nixon) entitled *Tom Pains Effegy or The Rights of a Sed[i]tious Poltroon* (16 January 1793) depicts an imaginary version of one of these ceremonies, with Burke directing the proceedings, Pitt stoking the fire, and the kilted figure of the Home Secretary, the Scottish lawyer Henry Dundas, performing a celebratory Highland dance (fig. 4.5). The bonfire consists of multiple copies of *Rights of Man* and *Common Sense*, a reminder of the massive print-runs of Paine's pamphlets – and of their incendiary quality.

There are no records of the burning of Burke effigies, but radical groups often made mocking use of Burkean iconography in their public demonstrations. According to a contemporary newspaper report, when five or six thousand workers marched through Sheffield to celebrate the victory of the French army at Valmy in November 1792, they carried a caricature painting of Burke dressed as Britannia riding on a swine, with Dundas as an ass and 'the pole of Liberty lying broken on the ground, inscribed "Truth is

Figure 4.5 *Tom Pains Effegy or The Rights of a Sed[i]tious Poltroon*, anonymous etching possibly by John Nixon, published 16 January 1793.

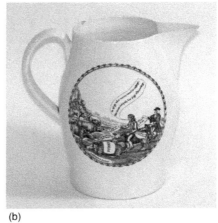

(a)   (b)

Figure 4.6 a & b Creamware jug with black printed designs of Paine and Burke,
manufactured in Liverpool *c.* 1795.

Libel"'.[12] The elaborateness of the iconography is matched by the theatricality of the march itself, an example of the close interconnection in this
period between text, image and street spectacle.

Another radical icon from the early 1790s, now in Brighton Museum, is
a creamware jug manufactured in Liverpool, on one side of which is a full-
length portrait of Paine holding a copy of *Rights of Man*, and on the other
a caricature of Burke addressing a herd of pigs with the words 'Ye pigs who
never went to college, / You must not pass for pigs of knowledge' (figs. 4.6a
and 4.6b).[13] The device of contrast – a staple technique of the caricaturist –
was used extensively as a propaganda tool, not only in satirical cartoons
such as Thomas Rowlandson's *The Contrast 1792*, a much-reproduced and
imitated loyalist print which juxtaposes a beatific image of 'British Liberty'
with a horrifying caricature of 'French Liberty' (fig. 4.7), but also on other
political artefacts, especially two-sided objects like coins, handkerchiefs and
mugs, all of which play their part in the propaganda war of the 1790s. The
Liverpool jug is a particularly interesting example in that here the Burke–
Paine binary is given tangible, visible form.

The pig motif on the jug and painting is an allusion to the notorious passage in the *Reflections* where Burke condemns the expansion of education to
the lower classes as a symptom of cultural decline, describing 'Learning' as
being 'trodden down under the hoofs of a swinish multitude' (*EB Writings*,
vol. VIII, p. 130). The ill-chosen metaphor was a gift to Burke's opponents,
betraying his contempt for the poor and his desperation to prevent them
acquiring the knowledge to better their condition. In a counter-move typical of 1790s polemic, radicals cheekily adopt the swinish persona, using

Figure 4.7 *The Contrast 1792*, etching by Thomas Rowlandson from a design by
Lord George Murray, published December 1792.

it to promote the very knowledge Burke would deny them, and to turn on
their head the snobbish values Burke defends. James Parkinson's *Pearls Cast
before Swine* (1793), Thomas Spence's *Pig's Meat, or Lessons for the Swinish
Multitude* (1793–5), Daniel Isaac Eaton's *Hog's Wash, or A Salmagundy for
Swine* (1793–5) and the anonymous *Rights of Swine: An Address to the Poor*
(1794), are just a few of the many tracts and journals which use the porcine
motif to convey democratic, sometimes openly revolutionary, sentiments.
Most inventive of all is a mock playbill of 1795 sold by the radical London
publisher 'Citizen Lee'. Entitled 'An entire Change of Performances?', the
playbill announces an exciting new street spectacle which will replace the
usual magic show of the arch-illusionist Pittachio (William Pitt) and feature
'The Swinish Multitude', otherwise known as 'the Mobility' (i.e. the mob,
a pun on 'the nobility'), 'STORMING A TOWER' and metamorphosing a
'PALACE INTO A PIG-STYE' and a 'TREASURY CHEST INTO A HOG
TROUGH'. The rebellious herd will then 'DEMOLISH A BASTILLE' and
plant 'THE TREE OF LIBERTY' on its ruins. The performance will conclude
with 'a most diverting display' of 'PIGS IN PATTENS', a clog dance (or trot-
ter dance) to celebrate the new political order (fig. 4.8). The exuberant irony
of this imaginary re-enactment of the French Revolution says much about
the artistic ingenuity and political audacity of the radical sub-culture even at

An entire Change of Performances?

THE Public having been for a long Series of Years entertained at a Prodigious Expence, with the unrivall'd Deceptions of PITTACHIO, and his Fellow Profeffors in the Black Arts, they are now inform'd that Fiction muft give way to Truth, and Reality fupply the Place of Delufion!——In cofequence of which,

The Swinish Multitude

will difplay a Variety of Wonderful Performances, exhibiting ftriking Proofs of their Wifdom, Strength, and Activity, having (to Accommodate the Tafte of the Mobility of this Country), received a courfe of Leffons in the Firft Schools of Paris.——In the Firft place they will agreeably furprize the Spectators with the various Manoevres of

STORMING A TOWER,

which will be done without the Aid of Military Tactics, and unretarded by the regular Operations of a Siege, yet performed with a Dignity, and compofure fuch as never before was witnefsed in a HERD OF SWINE.

N.B. This performance will be Peculiarly interefling to ACQUITTED FELONS.

Secondly, they will with the utmoft Eafe, and Facility (to prove the exquifite refinement of their Tafte) metamorphofe a

PALACE INTO A PIG-STYE,
And then Transform a
TREASURY CHEST INTO A HOG TROUGH.

After which the Audience will be amufed with a Scene reprefenting the infide of a Minifter of State's WORKSHOP, wherein will be exhibited a Brilliant Variety of *Coxcombs,* and Coronets; Stars and Garters; Places and Penfions. The firft of thefe *Baubles* the PIGS will actually hand from the Shelf, and turn it to the

CAP OF LIBERTY

To the marvellous Satisfaction of all prefent——With the *Garters,* they will in a moft ludicrous manner perform the Office of JACK KETCH on certain wicked, and notorious Malefactors, who it is already decreed fhall be

REWARDED *according to their* WORKS.

Thirdly, This inimitable Troop of Performers will moft Effectually

DEMOLISH A BASTILLE

And plant on the ruined Bulwark of Defpotifm

THE TREE OF LIBERTY.

Fourthly, they will proceed to regulate and Purify

A Houfe of Ill-Fame, or, a Den of Thieves

(not a Hundred Miles from St. Stephen's————) containing ample Materials, which after mature deliberation and a fair *Trial* (though not a Nine Day's One), will be found *incorruptible* and fit for decorating and ornamenting

The LAMP IRONS in PARLIMENT STREET.

The whole to conclude with a moft diverting Difplay of

PIGS IN PATTENS.

Vivant la People Soveraigne.

A Variety of other Performances are preparing, and will be announced to the Public in due Time.

At the BRITISH TREE of LIBERTY, No. 45, Hay-Market; may be had a variety of Patriotic Publications, including the following. Liberty Songs.-Precious Morfels; on the blefled Times we live in.—Letter from John Bull to the Pope.—Harlequin Stadtholder.—The Tribute of civic Gratitude an Addrefs to Triumphant Patriotifm.—Nebuchadnezzars Decree for a Faft, Pittachios Exhibition 2 Parts. Muftapha's Adoration of the Sultan Pittander 2 Parts.—Muftapha Vifion's. Dundaffio's Eating Match.—Exhibition of the Swinifh Multitude. Letter to a King. Letter to a People. Duke of York's New March. The Genius of Liberty. Proclamation of Liberty, Equality and Fraternity. Rights of Swine. The Return of Liberty. The Tree of Liberty, &c. &c.

Figure 4.8 *An entire Change of Performances?*, satirical broadside, published in London *c.* 1795 and sold by 'Citizen Lee'.

the height of Pitt's so-called 'reign of Terror', when counter-revolutionary policies had turned Britain into a virtual police state. In the ironic recycling of Burke's 'swinish multitude', we see too the anarchic power of political symbolism: the capacity of a single image or phrase to detach itself from its original context, reverse its connotations and take on a political life of its own.

The after-life of Burke's 'age of chivalry' passage is another example, except that in this case the symbolism served both positive and negative purposes. Many of the hostile replies to the *Reflections* single out this passage as the epitome of Burke's overblown style and falsifying rhetoric. In some cases the critique is made directly, through a critical analysis of Burke's tendentious language. Literary criticism plays a key role in 1790s polemic, another factor that contributes to the strange self-consciousness of the French Revolution debate. In other instances the critique is made by means of satire, with many respondents following the lead of the political cartoonists in depicting Burke as a Don Quixote figure, wallowing in his emotions and unable to distinguish fact from fiction. Ironically, Burke himself may have implanted this idea by comparing the erratic behaviour of the French revolutionaries to that of 'the metaphysic Knight of the Sorrowful Countenance' (*EB Writings*, vol. VIII, p. 58). But Burke's 'Quixot age of chivalry nonsense', as Paine called it (Paine, *RM*, p. 100), was taken seriously by many, and the imaginative association he created between medieval chivalry and modern conservatism had a lasting political effect. By giving a political colouring to the chivalric revival, fashionable since the 1760s not only in the sphere of literature but also in architecture, painting, interior design and other art forms, Burke established an inseparable link between aesthetics and politics. Henceforth, chivalric imagery, with its intrinsic idealization of the ancient institutions of monarchy and aristocracy, could serve as an ideological resource to galvanize patriotic sentiment during the Revolutionary and Napoleonic wars. Writers like Walter Scott make this political agenda explicit, framing their neo-chivalric romances with references to the contemporary world. Scott wrote *Marmion* (1808) whilst he trained with the Light Horse Volunteers, a home guard unit formed to defend Britain against possible French invasion, and the poem's introductory epistles contain stirring elegies for Nelson and Pitt. A measure of how powerful an ideological weapon chivalry had become is suggested by the attempts of some radicals and liberals – notably among second-generation Romantic writers – to reclaim it for progressive causes: the kind of counter-move found in Byron's *Childe Harold's Pilgrimage* (1812–18), Leigh Hunt and William Hazlitt's *Round Table* essays (1815–17) and Percy Bysshe Shelley's *Laon and Cythna, or The Revolution of the Golden City* (1817), an imaginary reworking of the French Revolution in which a radicalized chivalric code plays a prominent part.

Burke's demonic imagery – his characterization of the French revolutionaries as evil magicians, Furies, hell-hounds and other monsters – left a similar imprint on the public imagination, generating a counter-revolutionary
iconography which proved indispensable to loyalist publications like the
Anti-Jacobin and the *Anti-Jacobin Review and Magazine*. Reflecting and
reinforcing the apocalypticism which was part of the spirit of the age in
the 1790s, it also helped to inspire famous cartoons such as James Gillray's
New Morality (1798), which features the pro-French Duke of Bedford as a
giant Leviathan arising from the sea, and *The Apotheosis of Hoche* (1797), a
full-scale vision of a Jacobin heaven and hell. Even this symbolism, though,
was susceptible to reversal. In some radical texts and cartoons, Burke himself becomes the 'literary Lucifer', a fallen angel marshalling the forces of
darkness to counter the spread of political enlightenment and justice. Joel
Barlow's poem *The Conspiracy of Kings* (1792), for instance, is an outspoken attack on Burke's apostasy in which, appropriately, his own apocalyptic
imagery is turned against him, Burke being pictured with his fellow conspira-
tors in the self-made 'hell that springs / From those prolific monsters, Courts
and Kings'.[14] Other radical texts use the opposite tactic, re-appropriating
Burke's demonic imagery in the same way that the swine metaphor gets
reclaimed for radical purposes. The best example is Blake's apocalyptic allegory *The Marriage of Heaven and Hell* (1790–3), where 'The Voice of the
Devil' is a mouthpiece for Blake himself, a visionary traveller confronting
the social and political injustices of his time. A less familiar text built around
the same device is *The Rights of the Devil, or, The Jacobin's Consolation*
(1793) by the Sheffield radical 'Kit Moris' (fig. 4.9). Here, as in Blake, a
Miltonic devil figure becomes a spokesman for radical sentiments, and a trip
to Hell an ironic allegory of the modern political landscape.

Burke's myth-making capability is grounded ultimately in his gift for
figurative language, and the 'magic force' of his writing owes as much to its
metaphoric virtuosity as to its arresting arguments. Other stylistic features
also play a part, as revealed by the following passage from his late tract *A
Letter to a Noble Lord* (1796), which shows his rhetorical method in its
most unrestrained form:

> The French revolutionists complained of every thing; they refused to reform
> any thing; and they left nothing, no, nothing at all *unchanged*. The conse-
> quences are *before* us, – not in remote history; not in future prognostication:
> they are about us; they are upon us. They shake the publick security; they
> menace private enjoyment. They dwarf the growth of the young; they break
> the quiet of the old. If we travel, they stop our way. They infest us in town;
> they pursue us to the country. Our business is interrupted; our repose is trou-
> bled; our pleasures are saddened; our very studies are poisoned and perverted,

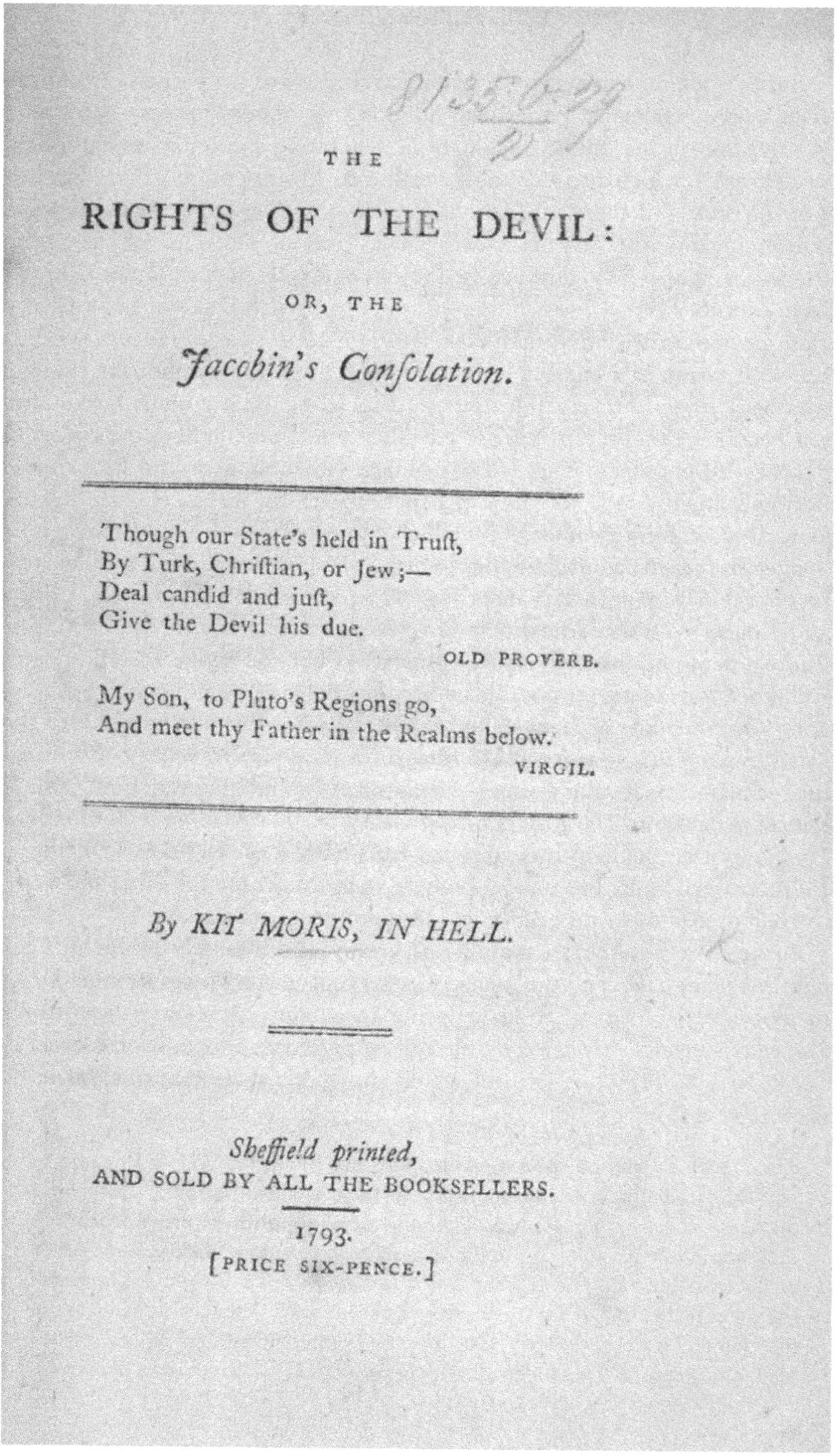

THE

RIGHTS OF THE DEVIL:

OR, THE

Jacobin's Confolation.

Though our State's held in Truft,
By Turk, Chriftian, or Jew;—
Deal candid and juft,
Give the Devil his due.

OLD PROVERB.

My Son, to Pluto's Regions go,
And meet thy Father in the Realms below.

VIRGIL.

By KIT MORIS, IN HELL.

Sheffield printed,
AND SOLD BY ALL THE BOOKSELLERS.

1793.

[PRICE SIX-PENCE.]

Figure 4.9 Title page to Kit Moris (pseud.), *The Rights of the Devil, or, The Jacobin's Consolation* (Sheffield, 1793).

and knowledge is rendered worse than ignorance, by the enormous evils of this dreadful innovation. The revolution harpies of France, sprung from night and hell, or from that chaotick anarchy, which generates equivocally 'all monstrous, all prodigious things,' cuckoo-like, adulterously lay their eggs, and brood over, and hatch them in the nest of every neighbouring State. These obscene harpies, who deck themselves, in I know not what divine attributes, but who in reality are foul and ravenous birds of prey (both mothers and daughters) flutter over our heads, and souse down upon our tables, and leave nothing unrent, unrifled, unravaged, or unpolluted with the slime of their filthy offal.

(*EB Writings*, vol. IX, p. 156)

In part, the passage works through an accumulation of metaphors, or rather the elaboration of a single metaphor, that of the revolutionaries as harpies (the half-bird of prey, half-woman of Greek mythology), an image whose full horror becomes apparent as Burke adds one disgusting detail after another, developing ever more disturbing analogies. By any ordinary standards, the metaphor is hopelessly overdone, but excess here is the essence of Burke's method, the 'overpowering' effect he had theorized forty years earlier in his account of the 'sublime' in his *Philosophical Inquiry into the Origin of our Ideas of the Sublime and Beautiful* (1757). The result in this case is to convert imaginative awe into political fear. The cumulative power of the imagery is reinforced by Burke's syntax, notably the – again, excessive – grammatical parallelism, both in the short staccato sentences of the first half of the paragraph, where anaphoric repetitions ('they shake'; 'they menace'; 'they dwarf'; 'they break'; 'they infest'; 'they pursue') enact the insidious ubiquity of the revolutionary threat, and in the reiterated negative prefixes of the closing sentence ('leave nothing unrent, unrifled, unravaged, or unpolluted'), which take his vision of desecration to an overwhelming rhetorical climax. The carefully placed allusion to *Paradise Lost* (II. 625), supplemented in Burke's footnotes by a long reference to Virgil's *Aeneid*, lends canonical authority to the vision, making the French Revolution a realization of the great poets' darkest imaginings.

On the face of it, Paine's rhetorical tactics could not be more different. Where Burke cultivates excess, Paine practises concision and economy. Instead of the mysterious powers of the sublime, Paine harnesses the resources of common sense, a topic on which he had written his own philosophical inquiry: his American revolutionary tract *Common Sense* (1776). To admirers like Thomas Jefferson, the plainness of Paine's style was the secret of his success as a political communicator. 'No writer', Jefferson declared, 'has exceeded Paine in ease and familiarity of style, in perspicuity of expression, happiness of elucidation, and in simple and unassuming language.'[15] These are exactly the qualities Paine strove for, and used as his trademark. He told readers of a Pennsylvania newspaper in 1778: 'As it is my design to make those that can scarcely read understand, I shall therefore avoid every literary ornament and put it in language as plain as the alphabet.'[16] His 1790s writings contain many similar comments where he defends his plain style and states his preference for fact over fiction, reason over imagination, the literal over the metaphorical. He makes the absence of literary artifice the basis of his appeal to the ordinary reader, and the guarantee of his political honesty. It is on these grounds, in *Rights of Man*, that he mounts his critique of Burke's *Reflections*, whose specious arguments and deceptive rhetoric he exposes in page after page of withering literary criticism and satire. Against Burke's 'tragic paintings' (Paine, *RM*, p. 100) he sets his own prosaic descriptions of the French Revolution, relegating the *Reflections* from the category of history to that of 'dramatic performance' (p. 110) and interpreting its imaginative fecundity not as a strength but a weakness – a failure to grasp the genuinely astonishing quality of what was happening in the real world.

Paine's stylistic self-descriptions should not, however, be taken at face value. As modern criticism has realized, his writing is far more artful than it purports to be, and the plain-speaking manner is as much a rhetorical pose as Burke's self-conscious literariness and prophetic urgency. One source of Paine's power as a writer is undoubtedly, as Jefferson recognized, his perspicuity: the 'happiness of elucidation' manifest both in his brilliant explanations of the philosophy of rights and in the blunt, deflationary logic of his polemical passages. Often, he turns the spotlight on political language itself, pointing out the absurdity of a term like 'counter-revolution': 'There does not exist in the compass of language, an arrangement of words to express so much as the means of effecting a counter revolution. The means must be an obliteration of knowledge; and it has never yet been discovered, how to make man *unknow* his knowledge, or *unthink* his thoughts' (Paine, *RM*, p. 169). This is common sense in its most trenchant, uncompromising form. The 'rights of man' are not only self-evident truths, they are truths that, once exposed, can never be concealed. 'Counter-revolution' is thus a contradiction in terms, as meaningless a concept as an untrue truth. Despite the show of reasoning, however, Paine's argument here rests essentially on a series of puns, and the time-honoured logical method of *reductio ad absurdum* is accompanied by a rhetorical sleight-of-hand in his use of emotive words like 'obliteration' and in the ironic overstatement of phrases like 'it has never yet been discovered' (as if such 'discoveries' have ever been sought). Applied to cherished institutions like monarchy and aristocracy, Paine's reductive method of argument and quietly insolent manner become politically explosive, as in his outrageous pun on the word 'nobility' ('or rather No-ability'), an imaginary etymology he says holds good for the aristocracy 'in all countries' (Paine, *RM*, p. 158).

Notwithstanding the obvious humour, such remarks appalled many readers, and Paine's plain-speaking manner was widely condemned as degrading and dangerous. 'He writes in defiance of grammar,' complained Brooke Boothby, 'as if syntax were an aristocratic invention; and with a disregard of decency worthy of his politics.'[17] At his trial *in absentia* for seditious libel in December 1792 the jury was asked to consider not only the content but also 'the phrase, act, and manner of this author. He dealt in short sentences, and in scoffing and contemptuous expressions.'[18] Recent studies have underlined the rhetorical artifice of Paine's 'vulgar' style – as manipulative in its way as Burkean magniloquence – and the shrewdness of his understanding of the politics of language. Such studies emphasize, too, that Paine is by no means as sparing of metaphor as his linguistic policy statements imply; indeed, page by page, his work is as dense in metaphor as Burke's. Most of the passages featured in the *Contrasted Opinions* pamphlet – incidentally, a brilliant anthology of Paine quotations – owe their effectiveness to some striking metaphor, whether it be Burke's 'genius without a constitution', his immurement within the 'Bastille of a word' or his tendency to 'pity the plumage, but forget the dying bird' (Paine, *RM*, pp. 102, 127, 132). Even when Paine is at his most seemingly anti-metaphorical, in challenging the imaginative distortions of Burke, he inserts his own metaphors. Having condemned Burke's 'theatrical exaggerations' and 'tragic paintings' of the French royal family, he proceeds to explain the workings of regal power in metaphors from *popular* theatre, referring to pantomimes, magic lantern displays, 'the puppet-show of state and aristocracy' (pp. 100, 110, 115).

The fact that Paine often explicitly calls attention to his metaphors is part of his rhetoric of transparency. Where Burke switches straight from literal into figurative language, Paine is liable to prepare his reader with remarks like 'if I may permit myself the use of an extravagant metaphor' (Paine, *RM*, p. 95). The effect, however, is ultimately the same, even if Paine pre-empts the accusation he lays on Burke, of distorting truth with figurative language (*his*, Paine's, 'extravagant metaphors' are 'suited to the extravagance of the case' (p. 95)). The same applies to Paine's literary allusions. Though not as frequent as Burke's, these are indispensable to his writing, invoking the popular literary heritage he shares with his target readership – ordinary working people – and implying that his radical ideas are a natural extension of the folk wisdom which that literature contains. Whether the reference is to the mythical folk hero Robin Hood or to Bunyan's popular allegory *The Pilgrim's Progress*, the point of the allusion is to legitimize revolutionary thought and action: the fall of the Bastille and the overthrow of despotism are not outlandish events beyond the understanding of Englishmen but a 'compounded image... as figuratively united as Bunyan's Doubting Castle and Giant Despair' (p. 102). Nor is his spectrum of literary reference as restrictively demotic as some critics imply: Paine cites Milton and Shakespeare as well as Bunyan, a reminder that these authors too belong to popular culture, and his critique of Burke's Marie Antoinette passage is achieved by means of another literary allusion, to Cervantes. The pattern of literary citation in his work, like the use of metaphor and other rhetorical devices, is not the chance gesture of a naïve writer but the calculated strategy of one in complete control of his means of expression.

A final comment can be made about form. The *Reflections* and *Rights of Man* are commonly referred to as 'pamphlets', a word that then covered any polemical work printed in a certain format. Both, however, are book-length productions, each running to almost 360 pages. Burke's is notionally written in the form of a letter, which, as Capel Lofft observed, 'admits of digression, resumption, studied negligence, artificial confusion, turns of thought and expression, flights of imagination, addresses to the passions, perhaps with more freedom and effect than any other mode of composition'.[19] These stylistic features give Burke a rhetorical flexibility which permits a full expression of his complex theme. The transitions of tone and register, and the turns and counter-turns in the argument, are integral to Burke's account of the startling transformations of the French Revolution. Purposeful, too, is Burke's mixing of genres. Burke's 'revolutionary book against the Revolution', as the German writer Novalis called it,[20] is a generically hybrid text which combines a huge range of expressive modes including biblical prophecy, Milton epic, Scriblerian satire, chivalric romance, elegy, georgic, aphorism and tragedy. Burke's skilful deployment of epistolary form ensures, however, that the shifts of tone, register and idiom are not experienced as abrupt discontinuities. Burke's is an 'organic' text, mirroring its organic theory of the state, which 'smooth-mixes' genres by subsuming its constituent forms in one continuous literary performance, an effect enhanced by the lack of chapter divisions.[21]

Rights of Man is also a generically hybrid text but its formal ingredients and manner of combining them are radically different. The text's literary affiliations are mostly to 'low' genres – popular allegories, parodies, chapbooks, melodrama, street spectacle – and he offsets these with references to, and extracts from, non-literary genres: political manifestos, economic reports, government papers. Paine's prose is punctuated by numbered propositions, statistical tables and arithmetic calculations, and the pamphlet is subdivided into titled chapters. The effect is the opposite of Burke's. Paine 'rough-mixes' genres, juxtaposing rather than synthesizing them, and refusing the impression of organic unity for which Burke strives. The reader of *Rights of Man* is induced into an analytic, anti-organic, sceptical frame of mind, as Paine lays bare his sources, breaks up his text and buttresses his argument with facts and figures in documentary or tabular form. Ultimately, this formal technique, too, is rhetorical in the sense that it is a deliberate part of Paine's persuasive strategy, but it is a compositional method opposite to Burke's seamless, breathless magniloquence.

To read Burke and Paine together, then, as his contemporaries did, is to experience not only a clash of ideas but also a dynamic contrast of styles, forms and rhetorical techniques. The jousting match between these two remarkable writers is not just a contest between two political philosophies but also between two literary philosophies. There is common ground in the sense that both are ultimately using the same weapon, the English language, but they exploit its resources to opposite effect. Blake, in a famous aphorism in *The Marriage of Heaven and Hell*, writes that 'Without Contraries is no progression', a dialectic that the philosopher Friedrich Schelling sees also as constitutive of Romanticism: 'The essence of romanticism is that it arrives at its goal by means of contrasts.'[22] In political terms, the Burke–Paine confrontation is an example of progress by contraries – its effect was to raise Britain to a new level of political consciousness – but it can also be seen as a literary phenomenon with important implications for the development of British Romanticism.

NOTES

The author wishes to thank the University of Aberdeen for financial assistance with the cost of illustrations.

1 R. B. McDowell, *Irish Public Opinion 1750–1800* (London: Faber, 1944), p. 163.

2 *The Diary of the Right Honourable William Windham, 1784 to 1810*, ed. Mrs Henry Baring (London: Longmans, Green, and Co., 1866), p. 213.

3 *Diary and Letters of Madame D'Arblay 1778–1840*, ed. Charlotte Barrett, with Preface and Notes by Austin Dobson, 6 vols. (London: Macmillan, 1904–5), vol. IV, p. 435.

4 Samuel Parr, *A Sequel to the Printed Paper Lately Circulated in Warwickshire by the Rev. Charles Curtis* (London: Charles Dilly, 1792), p. 63.

5 Joel Barlow, *Advice to the Privileged Orders in the Several States of Europe, Resulting from the Necessity and Propriety of a General Revolution in the Principle of Government*, 2nd edn (London: Daniel Isaac Eaton, 1795), p. 6.

6 Cited by Gregory Claeys, *Thomas Paine: Social and Political Thought* (London: Unwin Hyman, 1989), p. 111.

7 This well-dressed female figure has previously been identified as either Hannah More or Mary Wollstonecraft. However, it is almost certainly Helen Maria Williams, whose *Letters Written in France* (1790) had made her famous in radical

circles, and who is pictured very similarly (again chastising Burke and in this case named) in *Don Dismallo Running the Literary Gauntlet*.

8 Edmund Burke, *An Appeal from the New to the Old Whigs, in Consequence of Some Late Discussions in Parliament, Relative to the Reflections on the French Revolution*, 3rd edn (London: J. Dodsley, 1791), p. 119.

9 Sir Brooke Boothby, *Observations on the Appeal from the New to the Old Whigs, and on Mr Paine's Rights of Man* (London: John Stockdale, 1792), pp. 5, 281.

10 John Thelwall, *The Tribune*, 3 vols. (London: John Thelwall, 1795–6), vol. III, p. 195; vol. II, p. 220.

11 Frank O'Gorman, 'The Paine Burnings of 1792–1793', *Past and Present* 193 (2006), 111–56.

12 *Sheffield Register*, 30 November 1792, quoted by E. P. Thompson, *The Making of the English Working Class* (1963; Harmondsworth: Penguin, 1984), p. 113.

13 For this and other propaganda items from the 1790s, see David Bindman, *The Shadow of the Guillotine: Britain and the French Revolution*, exhibition catalogue (London: British Museum Publications, 1989); the jug is entry no. 53 (p. 109).

14 Joel Barlow, *The Conspiracy of Kings; A Poem: Addressed to the Inhabitants of Europe, from Another Quarter of the World* (London: J. Johnson, 1792), p. 16 (lines 208–9).

15 Cited in Philip S. Foner, ed., *The Life and Major Writings of Thomas Paine*, 2 vols. (Secaucus, NJ: Citadel Press, 1948), vol. I, p. xlvi.

16 *Pennsylvania Packet*, 31 December 1778, quoted by Edward Larkin, *Thomas Paine and the Literature of Revolution* (Cambridge: Cambridge University Press, 2005), p. 75.

17 Boothby, *Observations*, p. 106.

18 *The Times*, 19 December 1792, p. 2.

19 Capel Lofft, *Remarks on the Letter of the Rt. Hon. Edmund Burke Concerning the Revolution in France, and on the Proceedings in Certain Societies in London, Relative to that Event* (London: J. Johnson, 1791), pp. 4–5.

20 *Miscellaneous Observations* (1797), no. 115, in Novalis (Friedrich von Hardenberg), *Philosophical Writings*, trans. Margaret Mahony Stoljar (Albany: State University of New York Press, 1997), p. 43.

21 For the notion of 'smooth-' and 'rough-mixing', and further comparison between Burke and Paine, see my *Romanticism and the Uses of Genre* (Oxford: Oxford University Press, 2009), pp. 187–91.

22 William Blake, *Complete Writings*, ed. Geoffrey Keynes (London: Oxford University Press, 1966), p. 149 (plate 3); F. W. J. Schelling, *The Philosophy of Art*, trans. Douglas W. Scott (Minneapolis: University of Minnesota Press, 1989), p. 223.

5

JANE RENDALL

Wollstonecraft, *Vindications* and *Historical and Moral View of the French Revolution*

In March 1794, when she was about to leave France, Mary Wollstonecraft wrote to her sister Everina: 'I certainly am glad that I came to France, because I never could have had else a just opinion of the most extraordinary event that has ever been recorded' (*MW Letters*, p. 249). In the five years between the outbreak of the Revolution in 1789 and her departure from France, the outlook and the politics of Mary Wollstonecraft, former governess, writer, reviewer and translator, were transformed by that 'extraordinary event'. In her published responses to the French Revolution and to its British critics, she engaged with its philosophical context, underlying principles and, eventually, its social and political history. She is known above all as a feminist writer, yet her feminism was integrally connected to her emergence as a leading radical commentator on, and historian of, the French Revolution.

After a varied and unhappy early life, in 1784 at the age of twenty-five, Mary Wollstonecraft, with her sister Eliza, opened a school at Newington Green, just north of London, the home of one of the leading academies for English dissenters.[1] There, although she herself remained formally within the Anglican church, she found a congenial circle of friends that included the dissenting minister, Richard Price, a campaigner for religious toleration and for the principles of the American Revolution.[2] Influenced by Price and by Hannah Burgh, the widow of James Burgh, author of *Political Disquisitions* (1774, 1775), she learned something of the 'commonwealth' outlook on British politics. 'Commonwealthsmen' saw the British constitution as corrupted by luxury and standing armies from its original purity, requiring an infusion of rational virtue.[3] In these years she began her writing career with her first publication, the relatively conventional *Thoughts on the Education of Daughters* (1787). The school failed, and in 1786 Wollstonecraft travelled to Ireland to take up a post as governess to the children of Lord and Lady Kingsborough. While in Ireland she completed her first novel, *Mary: A Fiction* (1788), in which she drew significantly on her own experience. Her heroine was a woman of considerable emotional feeling or 'sensibility', yet also one with wide-ranging intellectual ambition and a committed interest in philosophy and theology.

The meanings associated with 'sensibility' in the late eighteenth century drew on medical theories of the nervous system, and on sensational theories of knowledge associated with the philosophers John Locke and David Hume. Sensibility was linked to reactions to sensory stimuli, yet went far beyond the purely mechanical, since such reactions would be closely related to states of feeling and past associations, and might potentially be regulated by reason. Writers of the European Enlightenment explored the relationship between the senses, the emotions and reason. By the mid eighteenth century the gendered nature of sensibility came to be emphasized. Edmund Burke's early work, *A Philosophical Enquiry into the Origin of our Ideas of the Sublime and the Beautiful* (1757), described aesthetic perceptions and sensations in gendered terms, distinguishing the masculine experience of the sublime from perceptions of the beautiful associated with a particular kind of femininity. Beauty for Burke carried with it 'an idea of weakness and imperfection', with which women themselves colluded: 'they learn to lisp, to totter in their walk, to counterfeit weakness'.[4] Jean-Jacques Rousseau wrote, in his *Discourse on the Origin of Inequality* (1755), his novel, *La Nouvelle Héloïse* (1761) and his educational tract *Emile* (1762), of the need to recover the simplicity of an imagined 'golden' or 'natural' age in the past, in which women were the repositories of an instinctive moral sensibility in a purely domestic setting. In the work of popular novelists by the late eighteenth century, women were assumed to be more delicate and to have a greater capacity for sensibility than men.[5] In *Mary*, as in her early educational writing, Wollstonecraft used the conventional language of feminine sensibility as a guide to behaviour, but what is also apparent in the novel is the tension between that language and the heroine's desire for rational knowledge. That tension was to be central to her reaction to the French Revolution.

On returning to London, Wollstonecraft was fortunate enough to find employment as a reader, reviewer and translator for a new periodical, the *Analytical Review*, published from 1788 by the radical publisher Joseph Johnson and edited by a young Scot, Thomas Christie. Her work served as 'a partial replacement for the formal education she never really had'.[6] She read very widely and reviewed not only novels and educational works, but works of travel and philosophy, including publications by the historian Catharine Macaulay, the freed slave Olaudah Equiano, Richard Price and Jean-Jacques Rousseau. She also in these years learned French and German, to equip herself to earn money as a translator. In 1789 her published anthology, *The Female Reader*, demonstrated the breadth of her interests. In it she drew upon the liberal theorists of the dissenting English Enlightenment, whose idea of progress included constitutional reform, religious toleration and the improvement of education for men and women, though not necessarily radical social change. Though the *Female Reader* incorporated some highly conventional material, such as the extracts from the prescriptive writer John Gregory, whose *Father's Legacy to His Daughters* (1774) she was later to attack, there were also passages from religious writing by the dissenter Anna Letitia Barbauld which did 'honour to a female pen' (*MW Works*, vol. IV, p. 57), and poems by William Cowper on slavery and on the fall of the Bastille.

Wollstonecraft's reviews and the extracts published in the *Female Reader* indicate that she, like many of her dissenting friends and like Thomas Christie, was familiar not only with the English and European Enlightenments but with the writings of Scottish philosophers, historians and moralists.[7] David Hume, William Robertson, Henry Mackenzie and Hugh Blair all made an appearance in the *Female Reader*. The outlook of the Enlightenment was characterized by a stress on the power of sympathy and sentiment, and by a philosophical history which stressed the relationship between forms of production, manners and the newly developing concept of 'civilization'. Adam Smith had attempted to construct a social morality rooted in the sympathy which human beings feel when they attempt to put themselves in the place of another. Such a morality could only be developed to its fullest in the highest stage of 'civilization'. For according to the Scottish historians, virtually all peoples passed through a natural progress on the route from rudeness to refinement, a progress to be traced through four stages of development, from the nomadic to the pastoral, the agricultural and ultimately the commercial. Changing manners and forms of government were closely related to the stage of society reached. These writers were particularly concerned with the history of Europe, from the overthrow of the Roman Empire to the feudalism of medieval society and the transition to a modern commercial society. Most of them regarded the condition of women, or perhaps more accurately the attention which men paid that condition, as an index of the stage of society at which a people had arrived.[8] So William Robertson wrote of the coming in Europe of the age of chivalry, along with the extension of commerce, as signalling the beginning of a modern system of 'more gentle and polished manners', inculcating sensibility and humanity along with 'the refinements of gallantry'.[9] The Scots were to play an important role in elaborating and defending the manners and social relationships of what they viewed as the highest stage of society, the modern civilized and commercial world. That stage had been reached not by the willed changes of reformers and revolutionaries but by the gradual material improvements and advances in knowledge which shaped the political and social worlds.

We do not know when Mary Wollstonecraft first appreciated the full significance of events in France in the spring and summer of 1789. She would have watched with sympathy the successive attempts of dissenting campaigners to repeal the Test and Corporation Acts which denied them political equality; their second attempt failed in May 1789. This campaign strongly influenced the reformers' reception of the news from France. The opening of the Estates-General at Versailles in May, the fall of the Bastille in July, the proclamation of the Declaration of the Rights of Man in August, and the return of the royal family to Paris after the march of Parisian crowds to Versailles in October were all covered in very considerable detail in the London press. On 4 November 1789, Richard Price delivered his sermon on the anniversary of the revolution of 1688, *A Discourse on the Love of Our Country*, associating the dissenters' campaign with celebration of the French Revolution, emphasizing shared Enlightenment principles of religious toleration, an end to privilege and hierarchy, and reform of the church establishment in France. In reviewing that sermon in the *Analytical Review* for December, Wollstonecraft wrote of it as conveying 'the animated sentiments of ardent virtue', and of its expression of a true and rational patriotism (*MW Works*, vol. VII, p. 185).

In the course of the following year, she would have watched the political alliance being forged between the community of dissenters and the small group of MPs who followed the politician Charles James Fox, united in welcoming the French Revolution, and mused on the implications of the Revolution both for France and for Britain. When Edmund Burke's conservative *Reflections on the Revolution in France* appeared on 1 November 1790, Wollstonecraft published on 29 November one of the very earliest replies, her *Vindication of the Rights of Men*. In this she began to work out the connection between the vision of a more democratic and virtuous politics offered by the French Revolution and her own challenge to the existing gender order, defended by writers such as Adam Smith and Burke as characterizing a polished and civilized society. That project, continued in the *Vindication of the Rights of Woman*, was to culminate in her *Historical and Moral View of the Origins and Progress of the French Revolution; and the Effect It Has Produced in Europe* (1794), in which she finally assumed the character of a historian with a 'philosophical eye' (*MW Works*, vol. VI, p. 235). In these works she pursued a distinctive path. She shared with other Whigs and radicals a commitment to a progressively improving and increasingly democratic society, though not necessarily to the unrestrained commercial growth defended by Burke and Smith, and by the radical Thomas Paine.[10]

In her first *Vindication* Wollstonecraft was less concerned than other, later, contributors to the debate with Burke's detailed misrepresentations of the Revolution. From her first paragraph she signalled that her fundamental disagreements were not only with his account of events in France but also with his philosophical and moral framework. She was direct, hostile and witty in suggesting that his response to the Revolution was cast in the gendered terms of his first work, the *Philosophical Enquiry*, in which Burke identified the sublime with perceptions of greatness, terror and awe, but 'the beautiful' with qualities which appeared weak, sentimentalized and feminine. Wollstonecraft disdained 'the equivocal idiom of politeness' and 'flowers of rhetoric' arising from Burke's 'pampered sensibility', and used her first pages to associate his work with a fashionable world in which 'sensibility is the *manie* of the day' (*MW Works*, vol. v, pp. 7–9). She accused Burke of trying to convince his female readers 'that *littleness* and *weakness* are the very essence of beauty' (p. 45), encouraging them to counterfeit weakness and excluding them from the higher moral qualities informed by reason. And in association with her attack on sensibility, she challenged his 'gothic notions of beauty' (p. 10) which might appeal to emotion and prejudice concerning legitimate constitutions inherited from the past. Both style and substance were here linked, as Wollstonecraft opposed rational virtue to the language of sensibility and to a political morality based on an emotional predisposition towards the legacies of the past.

In defending Richard Price, Wollstonecraft restated the ideal of civil and religious liberty with which he and dissenting circles more generally were identified: 'such a degree of liberty, civil and religious, as is compatible with the liberty of every other individual with whom he is united in a social compact, and the continued existence of that compact' (*MW Works*, vol. v, p. 9). She set this view of liberty, which echoed that of John Locke in his *Two Treatises of Government* (1690), against Burke's appeal to past history as justifying the existence of hierarchical governments. Yet in writing of the encroachment of 'the demon of property ... on the sacred rights of men' (p. 9), Wollstonecraft went beyond Locke. She wrote of Burke as 'the champion of property' (p. 13), by which she primarily meant hereditary property, justified by the right of prescription. Here she first stated a position to which she was to remain committed: the civilization achieved so far in Europe was of a very partial kind, its progress hindered by the survival of the hereditary principle in a monarchical and aristocratic world.

For much of the *Vindication* Wollstonecraft denounced the way in which Burke applied this principle to Britain. However, towards the end of her work she turned her attention to the events of the Revolution. She defended the leaders of the National Assembly against Burke's ridicule, and against his continued assumption that they should have used the 'Gothic materials' of the past (*MW Works*, vol. v, p. 41) and should have learned from the model of the British constitution. Where he had defended the French church and its property against the new Civil Constitution of the Clergy, Wollstonecraft appealed to the natural principles of justice to defend the redistribution of wealth originally gathered to support 'idle tyrants' (p. 49): the French clergy could be better and more usefully employed than by living in such grandeur. Politeness was no substitute for a real humanity. 'Misery, to reach your heart, I perceive, must have its cap and bells'; Burke reserved his compassion for Marie Antoinette while ignoring the plight of poor, industrious mothers and their helpless children (p. 15). Throughout Burke's work, Wollstonecraft wrote, she was struck by his contempt for the poor. This was as clear in his denunciation of the fishwives of Paris in the October crowds as in his denial of any likely consolation for the hardworking labourer in this world. Wollstonecraft concluded her work with a vision of the possibilities of happiness for an industrious peasantry, living modestly but benefiting from education and domestic reform, enjoying its small property. Like Richard Price, she believed in the ultimately transforming power of enlightened reason to bring about a new and utopian society for all.[11]

The *Vindication of the Rights of Men* is marked by the same concerns that would come to dominate Wollstonecraft's later work: the moral failings of a modern commercial world still influenced by the hierarchies of the past; the association between sensibility and the moral corruption of women; the revolutionary possibilities of a truly rational virtue. The book was widely reviewed and went through a second edition. Reviewers were divided along party lines but almost all commented on Wollstonecraft's temerity as a woman in contributing to the debate in the masculine genre of the political pamphlet, with the *Gentleman's Magazine* mocking 'The *rights of men* asserted by a fair lady!'.[12] A dissenting admirer from Liverpool, William Roscoe, later a good friend, honoured her in his satirical ballad, *The Life, Death and Wonderful Atchievements of Edmund Burke* (1792):

> And lo! an amazon stept out,
> One WOLLSTONECRAFT her name,
> Resolv'd to stop his mad career,
> Whatever chance became.

In the course of 1791, in further reviews, Wollstonecraft occasionally expressed her support directly for the principles of the Revolution. So the political purpose behind a conservative moral tale, *Lindor and Adelaide* (1791), is described as, in the spirit of Burke, 'calculated to . . . make any exertion of reason to meliorate the wretched state of the poor, appear a lawless phrenzy' (*MW Works*, vol. VII, p. 343). Writing of David Ramsay's

History of the American Revolution (1791), she described that revolution as 'a new epoch in the history of mankind' (p. 375).

In the same year an increasing number of British Whigs and radicals contributed to the debate on the French Revolution. The first part of Thomas Paine's *Rights of Man* was published in March 1791. In May, Thomas Christie's *Letters on the Revolution* gave a detailed account of French revolutionary legislation and life in revolutionary Paris, and James Mackintosh's *Vindiciae Gallicae* offered a sharp and analytical rebuttal of Burke.[13] An American couple, Joel and Ruth Barlow, who had been friends of Christie and Paine in Paris, came to London with introductions from Thomas Jefferson; they rapidly entered radical circles and met Wollstonecraft. Like others returning from Paris, they brought with them a sense of optimism as to the future of the Revolution.

It was to William Roscoe, in October 1791, that Wollstonecraft first mentioned the book she was then writing, as one which would offer a transparent representation of her 'head and heart' (*MW Letters*, p. 190). The *Vindication of the Rights of Woman*, written in around three months and published in January 1792, is very little concerned with political rights. Its arguments rest on Wollstonecraft's broad perspective on the corrupt society in which she lived and the potential of revolutionary political action for transforming those conditions. She signalled both her hopes and her doubts in the dedication to Prince Talleyrand, Bishop of Autun, whose report on public education, undertaken for the constitutional committee of the National Assembly, argued that women's exclusion from all public positions would be for the general good, and recommended they should be educated accordingly, very much along the lines Rousseau had recommended. Wollstonecraft suggested, ostensibly to the leaders of the Revolution, now themselves acting as tyrants, that if women were not educated in the principles of a rational virtue, they would not share in the growth of a virtuous republic but would retard 'the progress of those glorious principles that give a substance to morality' (*MW Works*, vol. v, p. 65).

The second *Vindication* offered a detailed and highly critical analysis of the ways in which women were affected by the moral corruption of the contemporary world. Expected to be creatures of sensibility, dominated by feeling and taught to dissimulate and manipulate, they internalized the prescriptive advice addressed to them and narrowed their horizons. Yet that analysis was placed within a more positive, though often implicit, historical perspective and a framework for willed and progressive improvement, looking to the leadership of France. Wollstonecraft confronted not only the detailed educational prescriptions of Jean-Jacques Rousseau, but his arguments in favour of a state of nature. She did not reject the notion of civilization, or progressive improvement: 'Rousseau exerts himself to prove that all *was* right originally; a crowd of authors that all *is* now right; and I, that all will *be* right' (*MW Works*, vol. v, p. 84). She agreed with Rousseau's dismissal of the luxury and corruption of the contemporary world. In France even more than in Britain in spite of a general diffusion of knowledge, sensuality and 'a kind of sentimental lust' (p. 66) had corrupted manners. The principle of heredity, seen in the 'pestiferous purple' (p. 87) of the monarchy and aristocracy, and the immense inequalities of the *ancien régime* in France and Britain, meant that in spite of expanding knowledge, true progress was almost impossible. Yet Wollstonecraft did not accept Rousseau's dismissal of the idea of a progressive civilization: 'the citizen of Geneva . . . threw away the wheat with the chaff' (p. 84). She believed very strongly in the possibilities of intellectual and moral progress, not necessarily associated with unrestrained economic expansion.

Though she explored in considerable detail the ways in which women internalized social expectations of weakness, frivolity and vanity she also indicated how that might change through the transforming power of 'a revolution in female manners' (*MW Works*, vol. v, p. 114). From the first chapter of the second *Vindication* onwards she showed herself committed to the values of a rational Enlightenment: Reason, Virtue and Experience. Women were to be admitted to those values 'by leading them to observe the progress of the human understanding in the improvement of the sciences and arts; never forgetting the science of morality, or the study of the political history of mankind' (p. 249). Even if, as she commented, 'the science of politics is in its infancy' (p. 106), nevertheless France had demonstrated the potential of a revolutionary politics, however imperfect. It was to that 'enlightened nation' and to its system of national education, transformed through its extension to women, that she appealed: 'Let an enlightened nation then try what effect reason would have to bring them [women] back to nature, and their duty; and allowing them to share the advantages of education and government with man, see whether they will become better, as they grow wiser and become free' (p. 239). In August 1792 Wollstonecraft planned to go to France with the Johnson family and the married artist Henry Fuseli, with whom she was in love though her feelings were not returned. Though the group reached Dover, on the news of the violence involved in the Revolution of 10 August, they decided to abandon their journey. However, that autumn Wollstonecraft decided to travel independently to join Christie and other friends in Paris. In spite of further information on the prison massacres in September and the heightened dangers of life in Paris, Wollstonecraft's faith in the potential of the Revolution was not lessened.

Even so, on her first arrival she was a little disillusioned of her exalted hopes for the coming of Liberty and Virtue. Her first impressions, set out in the fragment remaining of her *Letters on the Character of the French Nation*, written in February 1793 and not published in her lifetime, were of 'the striking contrast of riches and poverty, elegance and slovenliness, urbanity and deceit' (*MW Works*, vol. VI, p. 443). She found familiar faces there among other British expatriates, including Christie and his wife Rebecca, Paine, the Barlows and the writer Helen Maria Williams and her lover John Hurford Stone. One young British observer frequenting this group later remembered that she remained optimistic: 'Miss Wollstonecraft was always particularly anxious for the success of the Revolution & the hideous aspect of the then political horizon hurt her exceedingly. She always thought, however, it would finally succeed.'[14]

Most of the Britons were sympathetic to the group then in power in the Convention, the Girondins. Perhaps surprisingly, Wollstonecraft does not appear to have met radical French women, even those associated with the more moderate politics of the Girondins, Madame Roland, Olympe de Gouges and Etta Palm d'Aelders. She might have encountered Madame Roland and the feminist philosopher, the Marquis de Condorcet, through the salon of Helen Maria Williams, though we have no evidence that she did. There may have been some recognition of Wollstonecraft's reputation. In February 1793 she wrote to Ruth Barlow that 'I am...writing a plan of education for the Committee appointed to consider that subject' (*MW Letters*, p. 221). Both Paine and Condorcet were members of the committee preparing the new constitution. However, when in May 1793 the Girondins were overthrown and arrested, the position of their British friends was threatened. Wollstonecraft, like others, went into hiding, at first to Neuilly-sur-Seine, just outside Paris, at a time when she was embarking on a new sexual relationship with Gilbert Imlay, an American radical and adventurer. In August he registered her as his wife at the American Embassy, giving her some protection against the revolutionary government, although they never married. By June 1793 she had started a 'great book' (*MW Letters*, p. 226), an ambitious new history of the French Revolution. In February 1793, in the *Letters on the Present Character of the French Nation*, she had indicated: 'I wish calmly to consider the stage of civilization in which I find the French, and, giving a sketch of their character, and unfolding the circumstances which have produced its identity, I shall endeavour to throw some light on the history of man, and on the present important subjects of discussion' (*MW Works*, vol. VI, p. 444). Now she turned again to the relationship between revolutionary transformation and the polished manners of a commercial and hierarchical society.

In the *Historical and Moral View* Wollstonecraft claimed to bring to the understanding of cause and effect in the Revolution a 'philosophical eye' (*MW Works*, vol. VI, p. 235), or the ability to analyse and generalize about patterns of individual and social behaviour across time. In the Preface she wrote that in doing so, it was important to 'guard against the erroneous influences of sensibility' (p. 6) and to take reason as the only safe guide to the progressive intellectual improvement of the present age. Here she was signalling the subversion of 'philosophical history' as a masculine genre; few women wrote history, and almost none claimed to be a philosophical historian in the mould of Willam Robertson or Edward Gibbon. Wollstonecraft's title echoed William Robertson's 'View of the Progress of Society in Europe', prefixed to his *History of the Reign of Charles V* (1769), and John Millar's *Historical View of the English Government* (1787). When the *Historical and Moral View* was published in late 1794, friendly reviewers recognized and praised her ambitions. The dissenting minister William Enfield noted in the *Monthly Review*: 'She writes this wonderful chapter in the history of the world not like an annalist, but like a philosopher.'[15] The *Analytical Review* called her 'our philosophical historian'.[16]

From the beginning she signalled the subject of her work as 'theoretical investigations' into 'the political effects that naturally flow from the progress of knowledge' (*MW Works*, vol. VI, p. 5), and promised further volumes, which never appeared. The first volume of the *Historical and Moral View* contained a detailed narrative of the history of the Revolution only as far as October 1789. It did so, of course, from the perspective of her experiences of 1793 and early 1794. Wollstonecraft attempted to explain the failure of radical expectations without abandoning her hopes for an ultimately more democratic society. And there were for her two main reasons why the Revolution failed.

The first lay in the partial nature of the civilization achieved by the 1790s. Following Robertson, she described modern European society developing as commerce, chivalry and science softened the harshness of the manners of medieval Europe. The growth of civilization was dependent on the arts and sciences and on industry and commerce; but progress in these areas was not necessarily accompanied by political change and could coexist with 'the remains of superstition, and the unnatural distinction of privileged classes' (*MW Works*, vol. VI, p. 16). In Britain after 1688 John Locke and others had made the case for religious toleration and civil liberties; the writers of the French Enlightenment echoed this, denouncing not only clerical oppression but also the despotism of the privileged classes and monarchy. British and French observers of the late eighteenth century had watched in North America the example of 'a government established on the basis of reason and equality ... [an] experiment in political science' (p. 20). In the United States, fortunately, such a government had not retained the legacies of a barbarian past, or any prejudice in favour of 'constitutions formed by chance, and continually patched up' (p. 20). In both France and Britain, though society had reached a very high level of polished manners, there still remained many obstacles to be overcome before a truly rational government and civilization might be achieved. Inherited institutions, including the monarchy, aristocracy and established churches had been too easily corrupted by wealth and luxury and turned to despotism, debauchery and oppression.

Wollstonecraft traced a disjunction between economic and material growth and political developments. On the one hand, the political system of the *ancien régime* had allowed court favourites like Calonne to sacrifice public credit to the extravagance of the crown in the last years of the monarchy. On the other hand, if economic growth was not accompanied by the expansion of an independent and principled middle rank, then the advantages of civilization were liable to be limited to an elite few. Wollstonecraft had further doubts, also, of the direction of such growth. Echoing Adam Smith, she wrote in her final pages of the dulling and repetitive effects of the division of labour in large-scale manufactures, in which 'every noble principle of nature is eradicated' (*MW Works*, vol. VI, p. 234).[17]

The second reason why the Revolution had not transformed the face of France was that its leaders were not sufficiently educated in political science, and were corrupted by the manners of their own society. In relating the political narrative of the Revolution, Wollstonecraft was critical of the judgement of those who sought 'to strike at the root of all their misery at once' in 'premature reforms' (*MW Works*, vol. VI, p. 45), while at the same time she condemned the absolute intransigence of the privileged classes. Her account of the growing conflict between the National Assembly and the court was deeply critical of the King and his advisers; yet there was a final sympathetic note from the year 1793 for royal supporters, as she wrote of fearing to meet 'some unfortunate being, fleeing from the despotism of licentious freedom, hearing the snap of the guillotine at his heels' (p. 85). Wollstonecraft called the leading patriots 'men without principles or political knowledge, excepting what they had casually gleaned from books, only read to while away an idle hour not employed in pleasure' (p. 142). The great reforms they were embarked upon, she argued, needed 'systematic management', and peaceful progress would depend upon 'the moderation and reciprocity of concessions made by the acting parties' (p. 144). The new constitution offered an opportunity for such moderation; Wollstonecraft suggested that agreement to allow the King an absolute veto on the legislation of the Assembly would have been an appropriate concession, and some compensation for his loss of absolute authority. Instead, she thought the plan adopted, for a single-chamber government with a suspensive veto for the monarch, was suitable only for a government in the highest stage of civilization, and utopian in the then circumstances of France. As she wrote, 'the revolutions of states ought to be gradual' (p. 166) and to facilitate peaceful alterations, but that did not mean that political endeavours should be abandoned.

Indeed, for Wollstonecraft one of the major errors of the leaders of the National Assembly was in failing to consolidate what had been achieved swiftly. In comparison, the new American states formed their separate constitutions within three months after the declaration of independence by Congress. The leaders of the National Assembly spent too long in aiming for political perfection. Once 'the natural, civil and political rights of man . . . the main pillars of all social happiness' (*MW Works*, vol. VI, p. 187) were established, then a government should have been built upon them. The delay in doing so encouraged counter-revolution and rumours of counter-revolution. Wollstonecraft's account of the October days in 1789, in which women took the lead, is of 'a torrent of resentment and enthusiasm' (p. 196) but also of bribery and corruption by the Duke of Orleans as inspiring a mob against the court. In this account Wollstonecraft demonstrates more sympathy for Marie Antoinette, threatened by the Parisian crowd, than she had done in the first *Vindication*, considering her here, she wrote, only as a woman and not as a queen (pp. 205–6). In her view it would have been appropriate for the leaders of the Assembly to have shown the people that they intended to adhere to the law, since 'in the infancy of society, and during the advancement of the science of political liberty, it is highly necessary for the governing authority to be guided by the progress of that science'. They should not have encouraged anarchy and 'licentious freedom' (p. 210.) The suddenness of political transformation had made it almost impossible for these political challenges to be handled with any experience, but Wollstonecraft believed it was the duty of the historian both to record and to comment. In these pages she is surely writing as much about the events she had witnessed in the subsequent years of the Revolution as a commentary on the events of October 1789.

Even if, under these circumstances, Europe had seen that the French had embarked upon a revolution which they were unable to guide 'with moderation and prudence', nevertheless there was reason to rejoice. The principles of the Declaration of the Rights of Man, 'a simple code of instruction, containing all the truths necessary to give a comprehensive perception of political science' (*MW Works*, vol. VI, pp. 219–21) were their achievement, which once made known, would, she believed, be generally acknowledged. If a republican government were ever to be consolidated in France it would bring with it an improvement in arts and manners. This might well entail the end of the riches and luxury of the urban world of Paris, as the population turned towards the greater frugality and domesticity of a rural existence, one which might offer 'that independent, comfortable situation, in which contentment is sought, rather than happiness' (p. 231). If the new system of national education were accompanied by the reformation of domestic manners, then it would produce a gradually ripening liberty and a more dignified national character.

Wollstonecraft sent her manuscript off to Joseph Johnson just before the birth of her daughter Fanny in Le Havre. Though preoccupied she was deeply shocked at the course of events in Paris, writing to Ruth Barlow on 8 July 'how many victims fall beneath the sword and the Guillotine! – My blood runs cold, and I sicken at thoughts of a Revolution which costs so much blood and bitter tears' (*MW Letters*, p. 255). It was an unhappy time, since it was becoming evident that Imlay was withdrawing from her. He left for London in August and she joined him there in the following April, leaving France behind her. But the relationship could not be mended, and after a failed suicide attempt, Wollstonecraft took the decision to go on a voyage to Scandinavia, to act as Imlay's commercial representative, in the hope of recovering a lost cargo ship.

The *Historical and Moral View* did not prove to be Wollstonecraft's final word on the theme of revolutionary change. On her journey she recorded her impressions of the peasant societies, ruled by absolute monarchs, that she observed in her last major work, *Letters Written during a Short Residence in Sweden, Norway and Denmark* (1796). And in that work also she emphasized the dangers of revolutionary transformation: 'An ardent affection for the human race makes enthusiastic characters eager to produce alteration in laws and governments prematurely. To render them useful and permanent, they must be the growth of each particular soil, and the gradual fruit of the ripening understanding of the nation, matured by time, not forced by an unnatural fermentation' (*MW Works*, vol. VI, p. 346).

If the *Historical and Moral View* did not explicitly address the feminist concerns at the heart of the *Vindication of the Rights of Woman*, Wollstonecraft's exploration of the nature of revolutionary change is nevertheless entirely consistent with and indeed deepens our understanding of her earlier works. The French Revolution provided the opportunity for her to relate fundamental political issues about the constitution of a rapidly changing society to the restructuring of gender relationships which she desperately wanted to see; on this subject she combined 'pragmatic reformism' with 'perfectibilist aspirations'.[18] She remained deeply hostile to all forms of hierarchy and privilege and challenged all those who sought to defend unlimited economic expansion and a commercial civilization characterized by polished manners. Wollstonecraft believed only a genuinely principled leadership, though one capable of compromise and concession, could create a truly progressive, democratic and virtuous society which brought equal benefits to all its members, a society in which women were full citizens and political agents.

NOTES

1 On Wollstonecraft's life, see Janet Todd, *Mary Wollstonecraft: A Revolutionary Life* (London: Weidenfeld and Nicolson, 2000), and Claire Tomalin, *The Life and Death of Mary Wollstonecraft* (London: Penguin, 1992).

2 On the politics of English dissenters, see Albert Goodwin, *The Friends of Liberty: The English Democratic Movement in the Age of the French Revolution* (London: Hutchinson, 1979), pp. 65–98.

3 G. J. Barker-Benfield, 'Mary Wollstonecraft: Eighteenth-Century Commonwealthwoman', *Journal of the History of Ideas* 50 (1989), 95–115.

4 Edmund Burke, *A Philosophical Enquiry into the Origin of our Ideas of the Sublime and the Beautiful*, ed. J. T. Boulton (London: Routledge and Kegan Paul, 1958), p. 110.

5 G. J. Barker-Benfield, *The Culture of Sensibility: Sex and Society in Eighteenth-Century Britain* (Chicago: University of Chicago Press, 1992).

6 Virginia Sapiro, *A Vindication of Political Virtue: The Political Theory of Mary Wollstonecraft* (Chicago: University of Chicago Press, 1992), p. 19.

7 Jane Rendall, ' "The grand causes which combine to carry mankind forward": Wollstonecraft, History and Revolution', *Women's Writing*, 4: 2 (1997), 155–72; Daniel O'Neill, *The Burke–Wollstonecraft Debate: Savagery, Civilization and Democracy* (University Park: Pennsylvania State University Press, 2007).

8 Mary Catherine Moran, ' "The Commerce of the Sexes": Gender and the Social Sphere in Scottish Enlightenment Accounts of Civil Society', in Frank Trentmann, ed., *Paradoxes of Civil Society: New Perspectives on Modern German and British History* (New York and Oxford: Berghahn, 2000), pp. 61–84.

9 William Robertson, *History of the Reign of the Emperor Charles V, with a View of the Progress of Society in Europe from the Subversion of the Roman Empire, to the Beginning of the Sixteenth Century*, in *The Works of William Robertson D.D.*, 12 vols. (London: Cadell and Davies, 1812), vol. IV, pp. 84–5.

10 For the nature of this debate, see Gregory Claeys, 'Introduction', in Gregory Claeys, ed., *Political Writings of the 1790s*, 8 vols. (London: Pickering and Chatto, 1995), vol. I, pp. xvii–lvi, and 'The French Revolution Debate and British Political Thought', *History of Political Thought* 11:1 (1990), 59–80.

11 Barbara Taylor, *Mary Wollstonecraft and the Feminist Imagination* (Cambridge: Cambridge University Press, 2003), p. 2.

12 The reviews of this work are reprinted in D. L. Macdonald and Kathleen Scherf, eds., *A Vindication of the Rights of Men: in a Letter to the Right Honourable Edmund Burke; Occasioned by his Reflections on the Revolution in France; and, A Vindication of the Rights of Woman: With Strictures on Political, and Moral Subjects; by Mary Wollstonecraft* (Peterborough, Ontario: Broadview

Press, 1997), pp. 417–30; *Gentleman's Magazine*, 61 part 1 (1791), pp. 151–4, rpt. *ibid.*, pp. 44–9.

13 For surveys of the contributions to this debate, see Claeys, 'Introduction', *Political Writings*, vol. I, pp. xvii–lvi; Gayle Trusdel Pendleton, 'Towards a Bibliography of the *Reflections* and *Rights of Man* Controversy', *Bulletin of Research in the Humanities* 85 (1982), 65–103.

14 I. B. Johnson to William Godwin, 13 November 1797, quoted in Todd, *Mary Wollstonecraft*, p. 210.

15 *Monthly Review* n.s. 16 (1795), 393–402; 394.

16 *Analytical Review* 20 (1794), 337–47; 343.

17 See Adam Smith, *An Inquiry into the Nature and Causes of the Wealth of Nations* (1776), ed. R. H. Campbell, A. S. Skinner and W. B. Todd, 2 vols. (Oxford: Clarendon Press, 1976), vol. II, pp. 781–8.

18 Taylor, *Mary Wollstonecraft*, p. 164.

6

PAMELA CLEMIT

Godwin, *Political Justice*

In the British controversy on the French Revolution, William Godwin's *An Enquiry concerning Political Justice* stood alone. Its format was significantly different from the mass of pamphlets which appeared in reply to Edmund Burke's *Reflections on the Revolution in France* (1790). They were designed as interventions in public debate, were published quickly and cheaply, and were likely to be read only once. *Political Justice*, by contrast, was a philosophical treatise published in two quarto volumes, written for posterity as well as for contemporaries. Its expansive typographical lay-out, frequent sub-divisions and marginal glosses, were meant for readers who would weigh its arguments carefully and often. Its high price of thirty-six shillings – not three guineas as stated in some early accounts – suggested that its intended readership was mainly confined to the educated middling and higher classes of society, and confirmed its distance from the 'dangerous portability' of the occasional pamphlet.[1]

Political Justice did not represent a decisive break with Godwin's intellectual past. When in 1789 his heart 'beat high with great swelling sentiments of liberty', he had already been 'for nine years in principles a republican' (though he always remained 'in practice a Whig').[2] *Political Justice* was no sudden outgrowth of revolutionary enthusiasm, but drew on longstanding traditions of British thought. Godwin was educated in the philosophical and theological traditions of eighteenth-century Protestant dissent, which had been extended to the secular sphere by the Rational Dissenters. By the early 1790s he had temporarily become a non-believer, but many of his values and structures of ordering experience remained indebted to the literature of nonconformity, in which the method of writing was as important as the content. In *Political Justice*, he set out to investigate the causes, effects and relations of government, and argued that the moral reform of individuals was a necessary prelude to social change. But his instructive design was not confined to philosophical statement. Godwin also aimed, in true dissenting style, to effect a moral transformation in his readers.

Godwin's dissenting upbringing meant that he was saturated in traditions of resistance to the established political, social and religious order. His father was an Independent (Congregationalist) minister who espoused the moderate Trinitarian dissent associated with Philip Doddridge and Isaac Watts. In 1773 Godwin began training for the ministry at Hoxton Academy, one of the leading progressive institutions of learning set up by dissenters, who were excluded by law from the ancient universities. Here he imbibed the principles of the Rational Dissenters, a group distinguished by their religious heterodoxy, their interest in advanced ideas and their belief in the possibility of moral regeneration, which paved the way for the English radicalism of the 1790s. Godwin's five years at Hoxton not only qualified him for his career of first choice – he spent five years as a candidate minister – but equipped him to change direction in 1783, when he abandoned the ministry and settled in London as a writer. The many works he produced over the next decade were written primarily to make money, but they also reveal his experimentation with an extraordinary variety of literary genres to comment on contemporary political affairs. He published a biography of William Pitt the elder, a collection of literary parodies, novels, political pamphlets and a history of the Dutch Patriot Revolution; but the mainstay of his work was political journalism. In 1784 he was appointed as writer of the 'British and Foreign History' section of the Whig *New Annual Register,* and in 1785 he became a contributor to the *Political Herald* (1785–6), a journal subsidized by the Foxite Whigs. By the end of the 1780s Godwin had become skilled in selecting the appropriate literary form to express what he wanted to say. In 1791 he gave up his work on the *New Annual Register* and negotiated with the publisher George Robinson a substantial advance for a book on 'Political Principles', which became *Political Justice.*

Political Justice was a late entrant into the debate on France. While Godwin was writing the book, from September 1791 to January 1793, public opinion turned sharply against the French Revolution and its British sympathizers. The first half of 1792 saw a rapid spread of Paineite radicalism, fuelled by the nationwide distribution of *Rights of Man* (1791–2) and the proliferation of working-class reform societies across the country. On 21 May, however, a Royal Proclamation against Seditious Writings and Publications was the first of a series of government measures to halt the spread of radicalism. In the autumn of 1792, conservative alarm at revolutionary violence in Paris, at the National Convention's decision to try Louis XVI for treason, and at the threat to British security posed by French aggrandizement in the Netherlands, led to the formation of loyalist associations to oppose the radical movement. In December 1792 Paine was tried *in absentia* for authorship of *Rights of Man, Part the Second.* Godwin attended the trial, and in February and March 1793 he published four letters in the *Morning Chronicle*, signed 'Mucius', protesting at the government's use of spies and informers to intimidate radicals.

Political Justice appeared on 14 February 1793, a fortnight after the French National Convention had declared war on Britain and Holland, urging the British people to rise against their oppressors, and three days after Britain declared war on France. 'It is the fortune of the present work', wrote Godwin in a last-minute addition to the preface, 'to appear before a public that is panic struck, and impressed with the most dreadful apprehensions of such doctrines as are here delivered' (*WG Writings*, vol. III, p. v). He hoped to avoid prosecution by presenting the work as 'by its very nature an appeal to men of study and reflexion', but it was probably the expensive format that persuaded the government not to prosecute.[3]

Political Justice is often regarded as a definitive statement of Godwin's intellectual views. Three decades later, William Hazlitt testified to its impact in *The Spirit of the Age*:

> No work in our time gave such a blow to the philosophical mind of the country as the celebrated *Enquiry concerning Political Justice*. Tom Paine was considered for the time as a Tom Fool to him; Paley an old woman; Edmund Burke a flashy sophist. Truth, moral truth, it was supposed, had here taken up its abode; and these were the oracles of thought. (*WH Works*, vol. XI, p. 17)

Hazlitt's irony is mainly directed against former members of the radical intelligentsia who, in their youth, embraced the theories of *Political Justice*, but rejected them in later life: 'Is [truth] at a burning heat in 1793, and below *zero* in 1814?' (p. 17). Godwin himself does not escape censure, in other parts of the essay, on the grounds of his excessive reliance on reason. Yet Hazlitt, whose background in Rational Dissent was similar to Godwin's and who was, from 1799 onwards, a personal friend, was better placed than most to understand the conceptual resonance of 'truth' in *Political Justice*. In the theological and philosophical traditions which the two men shared, truth was not the same thing as intellectual certainty. To commit oneself to following truth, 'whithersoever thou leadest' (*Thoughts on Man*, in *WG Writings*, vol. VI, pp. 173, 219), was to embark on an endless search for moral and spiritual enlightenment, 'still searching', in Milton's words, 'what we know not, by what we know, still closing up truth to truth as we find it'.[4] To arrive at a definitive conclusion would be to limit the possibilities for future growth and change.

That Godwin was 'still closing up truth to truth' in *Political Justice* is indicated by his extensive revisions and modifications in two further editions (1796, 1798), not to mention his writing of and successive revisions to the novel *Caleb Williams* (1794, 1796, 1797), which he later described as 'the offspring of that temper of mind in which the composition of my "Political Justice" left me' (Kegan Paul, vol. I, p. 78). He observed in *The Enquirer* (1797), 'When a man writes a book of methodical investigation, he does not write because he understands the subject, but he understands the subject because he has written' (*WG Writings*, vol. V, p. 93). Reviewing the project again in *Thoughts Occasioned by the Perusal of Dr Parr's Spital Sermon* (1801), a work which he planned to include as a preface to any future edition of *Political Justice*, he emphasized the experimental nature of the first edition:

> Every impartial person who knows me, or has attentively considered my writings, will acknowledge that it is the fault of my character, rather to be too sceptical, than to incline too much to play the dogmatist. I was by no means assured of the truth of my own system...I did not cease to revise, to reconsider, or to enquire. (*WG Writings*, vol. II, p. 171)

Godwin defends his intellectual mobility by reference to the dissenting belief in the duty of ceaseless enquiry: when further exploration reveals the inadequacies of one's professed views, revision becomes a moral duty.

Such statements, written with the benefit of hindsight, contain more than a hint of self-justification, but they also indicate the exploratory character of the first edition. Godwin set out to produce a comprehensive analysis of political principles in the manner of the learned compendia of the French *philosophes*. But in the process of writing, he rejected central aspects of French Enlightenment thought in favour of a secular elaboration of tenets drawn from the philosophers and theologians he had studied at Hoxton: John Locke, Samuel Clarke, Anthony Collins, David Hartley, Jonathan Edwards, Richard Price and Joseph Priestley. Such tenets, pursued to their logical conclusion, led him to adopt an anarchist position. He argued that individuals, by the exercise of reason and judgement, have the power to emancipate themselves from the false opinion on which government is based, and that this would lead to the gradual dissolution of the rule of law.

The air of provisionality surrounding some of Godwin's arguments was partly due to the circumstances of the book's production. In the preface, he explained that the decision to begin printing *Political Justice* long before its composition was finished, made for the sake of speed and efficiency, had resulted in apparent contradictions, notably concerning the nature of government, as he adjusted his arguments as he went along. Yet his observation that 'more has been gained than lost' (*WG Writings*, vol. III, p. v) by this method of production was not just a reference to the publishing schedule: it also expressed his view of the work as a contribution to public debate. His appeal to the 'candid reader' to 'make a suitable allowance' for inconsistencies, reflected his key philosophical principle that unrestricted discussion, either in speech or writing, affords the best scope for the exercise of private judgement. In this way, Godwin sought to create 'a work, from the perusal of which no man should rise without being strengthened in habits of sincerity, fortitude and justice' (p. iii), and which would actively promote social and political improvement.

Godwin's wish to renovate the reader's moral consciousness required an answerable style and method. Seeking to encourage the reader's capacity for rational judgement, he adopted a measured, lucid mode of exposition which provided a guarantee of his formal propositions. Mindful of the nonconformist ideal of stylistic plainness, he rejected the emotive techniques used by Burke to defend the existing aristocratic order in favour of an unadorned, logically conducted prose that would convey his arguments with clarity. Following the pedagogical mode of dissenting educational works, he adopted a deductive method, presenting the arguments for and against each proposition before drawing his own conclusion. Through the use of marginal glosses, he acted as the expositor of his own text and alerted the reader to his or her obligation actively to seek out the truth.

Yet if *Political Justice* was Godwin's most self-consciously abstract work, it also carried a strong tone of personal conviction. In rejecting the artifices of literary communication, Godwin sought to break down traditional barriers of social reserve, which he regarded as impediments to frankness and sincerity, and to speak directly to the reader. His understated use of biblical rhythms and imagery – notably that of the journey, wayfaring or warfaring – gives his philosophical account the insistent onward pressure and sense of yearning that are the hallmarks of nonconformist conversion-narrative. In putting the case for gradual reform rather than insurrection, Godwin observed: 'All human intellects are at sea upon the great ocean of infinite truth, and their voyage though attended with hourly advantage will never be at an end' (*WG Writings*, vol. III, p. 125). As well as mapping his own voyage of intellectual exploration and self-discovery, he invited the reader to embark on a similar journey.

In an autobiographical note for the year 1791, Godwin claimed that the chief stimulus for *Political Justice* was his disagreement with Montesquieu's comparative analysis of different forms of government, *De l'Esprit des lois* (1748, translated as *The Spirit of the Laws*, 1750), and his 'desire of supplying a less faulty work' (Kegan Paul, vol. i, p. 67). A refutation of Montesquieu's physical and geographical determinism was essential to his theory that human thought and action could, in time, be directed entirely by reason. Yet if Godwin originally planned a revision of Montesquieu, his work grew in the execution. Although he began by aligning himself with 'the most considerable French writers upon the nature of man', Holbach, Helvetius and Rousseau (*WG Writings*, vol. III, p. iv), he rejected central aspects of their theories as he went along. Simultaneously he built up his own political philosophy, based on the dissenting ideals of intellectual independence, benevolence and sincerity, to which were added arguments drawn from other sources, such as the republican tradition of the Commonwealth writers, the eighteenth-century advocates of land reform and Jonathan Swift's *Gulliver's Travels* (1726). *Political Justice* turned out to be a project of Blakean ambition as Godwin, like the blacksmith Los in *Jerusalem*, labouring to build Golgonooza, sought to create a system to avoid enslavement by another man's.

That Godwin was hammering out his arguments in the course of writing is especially evident in his change of opinion concerning the nature of government in books one and two. Having set out to enquire into the role of government in moral improvement, he first accepted that government was, in Paine's words, 'a necessary evil', and ended up arguing for its 'utter annihilation!' (*WG Writings*, vol. III, pp. 206, 311). The process by which Godwin came to reject government as an instrument for making men and women virtuous is as important as his conclusions. The fragmentary manuscript draft of *Political Justice* reveals that Godwin's initial plan was to explore the hypothesis that government may be 'the great desideratum for advancing mind to courage, justice, virtue and perfection' (*WG Writings*, vol. IV, p. 367), following Helvetius's belief in the power of good government to create virtuous citizens. But in the first chapter, Godwin adopted a more ambivalent stance towards government: 'If it could be proved that a sound political institution was of all others the most powerful engine for promoting individual good, or on the other hand that an erroneous and corrupt government was the most formidable adversary to the improvement of the species, it would follow that politics was the first and most important subject of human investigation' (*WG Writings*, vol. III, pp. 1–2). This equivocal statement reminds us that Godwin had accepted the principle 'That human depravity originates in the vices of political constitution', as early as 1782 or 1783.[5] In the event, Godwin did not merely analyze the vices of particular forms of government: he objected to the entire spirit of government as an impediment to freedom of thought. His growing dissatisfaction with government in books one and two is expressed through a series of contrasts between existing political institutions and an ideal realm of moral justice based on the unimpeded exercise of private judgement. This opposition is made explicit in the final chapter of book two, 'Of the Exercise of Private

Judgment'. Here Godwin highlights the inevitable tendency of political institutions to interfere with the exercise of private judgement, preparing for the
argument, developed in the rest of the work, for the gradual replacement of
the former by the latter.

Godwin, despite his loss of faith, was still writing within the moral
and philosophical framework of Rational Dissent. The objection made by
Samuel Taylor Coleridge in his religious lectures of 1795, that *Political Justice* 'builds without a foundation, proposes an end without establishing the
means',[6] and offers no proof for its propositions concerning the omnipo-
tence of truth and the progressive nature of man, would have made no
sense to Godwin. The objective validity of these concepts is presupposed
in his arguments, reflecting a theologically inspired concept of right reason.
His language retains much of its theological resonance. As well as declaring justice 'immutable', Godwin appealed to the 'standard of eternal truth',
proclaimed that virtue 'perpetually renovates itself', and opined, 'he is the
most useful soldier in this war, who accumulates in an unperishable form the
greatest mass of truth' (*WG Writings*, vol. III, pp. 87, 94, 134, 141). Even
so, Godwin was aware of possible objections to his thesis. He repeatedly
acknowledged the elements in human nature and society which obstructed
moral progress – while also insisting that such elements would, in time, be
governable by reason.

Having concluded that government could play no role in promoting virtue,
Godwin in books three and four developed the counter-argument that the
progress of moral and political truth required the least possible interference
by government. In book one, chapter four, he proposed 'three principal
causes' of moral improvement: literature, or 'discussion, whether written
or oral', education, and 'political justice, or the adoption of any principle
of morality and truth into the practice of a community' (*WG Writings*,
vol. III, p. 14). From book three onwards, however, he emphasized the
publication of truth as 'the grand instrument for forwarding the improvement of mind', and unreserved communication, as practised in dissenting
social circles, as the chief means by which moral improvement could be
achieved:

> Let us imagine to ourselves a number of individuals, who, having first stored
> their minds with reading and reflection, proceed afterwards in candid and unre-
> served conversation to compare their ideas, to suggest their doubts, to remove
> their difficulties, and to cultivate a collected and striking manner of delivering
> their sentiments. Let us suppose these men, prepared by mutual intercourse,
> to go forth to the world, to explain with succinctness and simplicity, and in a
> manner well calculated to arrest attention, the true principles of society. Let
> us suppose their hearers instigated in their turn to repeat these truths to their

companions. We shall then have an idea of knowledge as perpetually gaining ground, unaccompanied with peril in the means of its diffusion. Reason will spread itself, and not a brute and unintelligent sympathy.   (pp. 106, 121–2)

Godwin's vision of the replacement of political society by a discursive community of rational citizens indicates the extent to which his political conclusions were the outgrowth of his moral commitments. Thus he insisted on the gradual, inward nature of a just revolution: 'It can in reality scarcely be considered as of the nature of action. It consists in an universal illumination. Men feel their situation, and the restraints, that shackled them before, vanish like a mere deception' (p. 126). To counter the possible objection that this emphasis on mental revolution made social change a distant prospect, he invoked the example of France, as evidence that 'the work of renovation' – instanced by the writings of the *philosophes* – may produce unexpectedly swift and striking results.

In Godwin's own work of renovation, his quest for a social structure that could accommodate his belief in the supremacy of reason led to a searching critique of existing models. In books five and six, he analyzed the nature of monarchy, aristocracy and democracy, and traced their influence on manners and opinions, measuring their moral efficacy against the ideals of justice, benevolence, equality and sincerity established in the first half of the treatise. His strongest censure was reserved for monarchy and aristocracy, which, he concluded, barricaded the road to truth by encouraging 'implicit faith, blind submission to authority, timid fear, a distrust of our powers, an inattention to our own importance and the good purposes we are able to effect' (*WG Writings*, vol. III, p. 268). While democracy offered less of an impediment to private judgement than other forms of government, it too failed to fulfil Godwin's demand for the elimination of political supervision of opinion. Thus he rejected the procedures of democratic government – permanent representative assemblies, decisions by voting, parties or societies, and the secret ballot – as based on a specious notion of collective wisdom, which inhibited sincerity and rational judgement. In place of these morally flawed types of government, Godwin proposed a simplified mode of social organization modelled on the Independent religious communities of his youth, made up of small, self-governing parishes, and subject to no disciplinary authority except for ad hoc juries.

In books seven and eight, Godwin expanded his account of an ideal future society governed by reason. In arguing for the gradual dismantling of existing systems of law and property, he simultaneously developed a new model of society which harmonized his twin requirements for complete intellectual independence and mutual moral accountability. As men and women became more fully rational, he suggested, even juries would be abolished, since vice would be 'sufficiently checked by the general discountenance and sober condemnation of every spectator' (*WG Writings*, vol. III, p. 391). Godwin further argued for the equalization of property, placing himself in a long tradition of writers, including Plato, Sir Thomas More and Swift, who had advocated common ownership of land. Such a longing for a simplified society is also present in the writings of the eighteenth-century Scottish republicans Robert Wallace and William Ogilvie, from whom Godwin drew support for a series of related arguments for rejecting the luxuries of commercial society, reducing professional specialization and minimizing labour. More controversially, Godwin condemned marriage as 'an affair of property, and the worst of all properties' (p. 453), and argued for its abolition in favour of relationships between the sexes based on free choice and mutual affection.

This single-minded commitment to the goal of intellectual autonomy could lead to potentially absurd conclusions, as when, for example, Godwin condemned co-operative ventures such as musical concerts and plays. That Godwin was deliberately pushing his theoretical commitments to their limit in book eight is evident from his final 'deviation into the land of conjecture' (*WG Writings*, vol. III, p. 460). Pursuing Benjamin Franklin's speculation, reportedly made in conversation with Richard Price, that 'mind will one day become omnipotent over matter', he conjectured that humanity would gradually acquire the power to defeat physical illness and even prolong human life. Thus he envisaged a future society in which

> the men... will perhaps be immortal. The whole will be a people of men, and not of children. Generation will not succeed generation, nor truth have in a certain degree to recommence her career at the end of every thirty years. There will be no war, no crimes, no administration of justice as it is called, and no government... Every man will seek with ineffable ardour the good of all. (p. 465)

Godwin ended this excursion into pure theory by reminding the reader that it was based on a 'matter of probable conjecture' (p. 465): his broader arguments for a simplified social system were to stand independently of his vision of the remote future.

Even leaving aside this digression, Godwin's arguments concerning a future egalitarian society have often been read as evidence of an utopian cast of thought. Yet he sought to counter the objection that his views were 'visionary and theoretical' (*WG Writings*, vol. III, p. 428) by arguing that the error lay in supposing a system based on justice and equality to be impracticable. The fact that society could not be transformed immediately did not lessen the value of the idea. On the contrary, exposure to such a notion, 'as one of the great objects towards which we are tending... will impress us with a just apprehension of what it is of which man is capable... and will fix our ambition and activity upon the worthiest objects' (pp. 476–7). Godwin's aim, in pursuing his theoretical commitments as far as they would go, was to establish a set of values by which present-day society could be judged, and according to which progress could be measured. In this way, he argued, theory and practice were 'essentially connected' (p. 474).

While theory and practice were connected, Godwin was anxious that they should not be confused with each other. In the chapter, 'Mode of Effecting Revolutions', he cautioned against premature attempts to transform society: 'There are two principles... which the man who desires the regeneration of his species ought ever to bear in mind, to regard the improvement of every hour as essential in the discovery and dissemination of truth, and willingly to suffer the lapse of years before he urges the reducing his theory into actual execution' (*WG Writings*, vol. III, p. 116). Even so, Godwin in his final chapter insisted on the practical significance of his speculative undertaking. However distant the prospect of social change, he observed, 'there are high duties incumbent upon every branch of the community' (p. 469). He divided his imagined community of educated readers into three groups – 'those cultivated and powerful minds, that are fitted to be precursors to the rest in the discovery of truth', 'the rich and great' and 'the now increasing advocates of equality' (pp. 469, 470, 473) – and offered advice to each concerning their respective duties in furthering the spread of truth.

The double thrust of Godwin's conclusion is entirely in keeping with the dual character of the work. Throughout *Political Justice*, his abstract arguments concerning the gradual progress of truth and benevolence are accompanied by a practical concern with the renovation of social conduct. In book four, chapter four, for example, his philosophical disquisition concerning the nature of truth, virtue and sincerity is brought home to the reader by appendices discussing the opportunities for practising truthfulness, virtue and sincerity in everyday life. Such a concern with 'the improvement of every hour' reflects Godwin's familiarity with the nonconformist tradition of practical divinity, in which readers were encouraged to monitor all aspects of their daily experience for its spiritual significance. In a secular rewriting of injunctions to spiritual watchfulness, Godwin urged his readers to be vigilant to the possibilities for moral improvement in everyday life: 'There is no situation in which we can be placed, no alternative that can be presented to our choice, respecting which duty is silent' (*WG Writings*, vol. III, p. 373). In this way, *Political Justice* presented a new model of political engagement outside institutions. Godwin encouraged his readers not merely to familiarize themselves with moral principles as inspiring ideals, but to accelerate the spread of truth and justice by putting those principles into immediate practice in the real world.

Godwin's synthesis of theoretical and practical concerns in *Political Justice* was the key to the work's phenomenal success. According to John Fenwick, Godwin's first biographer, *Political Justice* 'was scarcely published when it was every where the theme of popular conversation and praise. Perhaps no work of equal bulk ever had such a number of readers; and certainly no book of such profound enquiry ever made so many proselytes in an equal space of time.'[7] It had a special appeal for educated readers sympathetic to the principles of the French Revolution, whose political optimism was being tested by the deteriorating situation in France. William Wordsworth's reported statement to a lawyer friend – 'Throw aside your books of chemistry . . . and read Godwin on Necessity' – indicates one of the ways in which *Political Justice* offered intellectual stability at a time of historical flux (*WH Works*, vol. XI, p. 17). In adopting the principle that all events were determined by necessary and universal laws, and applying it to human action and thought, Godwin presented a view of humanity as inevitably overcoming the vices, errors and prejudices that obstructed reason and advancing towards a greater understanding of morality. Since 'no mind can be so far alienated from truth, as not in the midst of its degeneracy to have incessant returns of a better principle' (*WG Writings*, vol. III, p. 19), violence in France could be seen as no more than a temporary setback on the road to general improvement. Thus Godwin encouraged readers to regard 'all things past, present and to come as links of an indissoluble chain', and to 'reflect upon the moral concerns of mankind with the same clearness of perception, the same unalterable firmness of judgment, and the same tranquillity as we are accustomed to do upon the truths of geometry' (p. 173).

For many readers, engagement with *Political Justice* was not just a matter of intellectual assent to a set of abstract propositions: it also led them to re-evaluate their lives. For Robert Southey, then a student at Oxford reluctantly preparing for a career as an Anglican priest, reading *Political Justice* involved a political awakening. He wrote to his friend Grovesnor Bedford on 2 December 1793: 'I am studying such a book! . . . democracy, real true democracy is but another word for morality – they are like body & soul.'[8] In a subsequent letter, Southey applied Godwin's analysis of the corrupting effects of hierarchy to his own upbringing and education. Writing to Horace Walpole Bedford on 12 December 1793, he described 'the wretched debasement of society' in Godwinian terms: 'Sin is artificial – it is the monstrous offspring of government and property. The origin of both was in injustice.'[9] Although by October 1795, Southey had rejected *Political Justice* as a guide to action, he acknowledged the role played by the work in his moral and intellectual development. In a letter to Grosvenor Bedford, dated 1–10 October, he wrote: 'my mind is considerably expanded, my opinions are better grounded, and frequent self-conviction of error has taught me a sufficient degree of scepticism on all subjects to prevent confidence. The frequent and careful study of Godwin was of essential service. I read, and all but worshipped . . .'[10]

A generation later, another young radical uncertain of his *métier*, Percy Bysshe Shelley, was similarly led by a reading of *Political Justice* to a critical reappraisal of his personal history. In a letter of introduction to its author, dated 10 January 1812, he reconstructed his aristocratic upbringing in terms of Godwin's analysis of political imposture. A childhood of 'passive obedience', in which 'coercion obviated its own intention', had given way to adolescent withdrawal from the world, fuelled by 'extravagant romances' and 'ancient books of Chemistry and Magic' (*PBS Letters*, vol. I, p. 227). However, these youthful fantasies had now been overtaken by a sense of duty to humanity, and the catalyst for this transformation, Shelley declared, was a reading of Godwin's 'inestimable book on "Political Justice"': 'till then I had existed in an ideal world; now I found that in this universe of ours was enough to excite the interest of the heart, enough to employ the discussions of Reason' (pp. 227–8). This self-dramatizing account is in part a reflection of the writer's wish to present himself as an exemplary reader of *Political Justice* and as a worthy student of Godwin's teachings. Yet Shelley was not isolated, or exceptional, in viewing *Political Justice* as a turning-point in his development.

As well as prompting readers to take stock of their lives, *Political Justice* gave them a new sense of public responsibility. Godwin's emphasis on writing and discussion as the best means of reform had a special appeal for those drawn to a literary career. 'Does not writing hold the next place to colloquial discussion in eliciting and classing the powers of the mind?' (*PBS Letters*, vol. I, p. 231) wrote Shelley to Godwin, defending his early publications, on 16 January 1812. A generation earlier, the American playwright William Dunlap was among those who found in the arguments of *Political Justice* a convincing justification of authorship. 'Your political justice is my Gospel', he wrote to Godwin on 1 October 1795: 'I read in it daily, I weigh its arguments and trace its doctrines to all their consequences. To aid the progress of these truths, I conceive to be a duty incumbent on me both by writing and acting.'[11] But it was Wordsworth, a later critic of philosophical abstraction, who responded most directly to Godwin's call for the 'true philanthropist' (*WG Writings*, vol. III, p. 468) actively to engage in the publication of truth. On 8 June 1794 Wordsworth wrote to his friend William Mathews describing his plan for a journal, to be called the *Philanthropist*, and declared it the duty of 'every enlightened friend of mankind' to 'diffuse by every method a knowledge of those rules of political justice, from which the farther any government deviates the more effectually must it defeat the object for which government was ordained'.[12]

As well as encouraging readers to employ their talents in the service of truth, Godwin sought to inculcate a broader concept of duty to live a life based on his moral principles. Sympathetic readers adopted *Political Justice* as a guide to action. For example, Henry Crabb Robinson, then an articled clerk in Colchester, had followed the much-travelled path from Trinitarian dissent to Unitarianism and was thus especially attuned to Godwin's view of morality as 'the perpetual associate of our transactions' (*WG Writings*, vol. III, p. 373). In his reminiscences, Crabb Robinson recalled his first reading of *Political Justice* in 1795:

> No book ever made me feel more generously. I never before felt so strongly, not have I ever since, I fear, felt so strongly the duty of not living to one's self and that of having for one's sole object the welfare of the community. His idea of justice I then adopted and still retain. I was not alarmed by the declamations so generally uttered against his opinions on the... duties arising out of the personal relations of life. I perceived then the differences between principles as universal laws, and maxims of conduct as prudential rules.[13]

Shelley, too, found Godwin's moral vision a catalyst to feeling as well as thought, observing on 3 June 1812: 'I did not truly *think* & *feel*...until I read Political Justice' (*PBS Letters*, vol. I, p. 303). And, like Crabb Robinson, Shelley recognized that the importance of Godwin's theoretical principles lay in the effect they had on human actions. He defended Godwin to his friend Elizabeth Hitchener on 25 July 1811: 'You say that equality is unattainable, so will I observe is perfection; yet they both symbolize in their nature, they both demand that an unremitting tendency towards themselves should be made' (p. 125). While Shelley concurred with Godwin's most extreme speculative conclusions, he shared his commitment to moral renovation as an essential preliminary to social change: 'Every error conquered, every mind enlightened is so much added to the progression of human perfectibility' (p. 162).

Political Justice did not remain the property of an elite. According to Fenwick, 'pirated editions were published in Ireland and Scotland; and people of the lower class were the purchasers. In many places, perhaps some hundreds in England and Scotland, copies were bought by subscription, and read aloud in meetings of the subscribers.'[14] The radical publishers Daniel Isaac Eaton and Thomas Spence printed extracts from *Political Justice* in their respective periodicals for working people, with Godwin's chapter, 'The Education of a Prince', together with extracts from his hostile analysis of aristocracy, appearing in the first volume of Eaton's *Hog's Wash, or A Salmagundy for Swine* (1793–5), and his criticisms of monarchy in volume two of Spence's *Pigs' Meat; or, Lessons for the Swinish Multitude* (1793–5). In 1796, when over 3,000 copies of the first edition had been sold, George Robinson issued a second edition in octavo, priced fourteen shillings, to appeal to a broader market, and a third edition appeared in 1798.

These later editions modify the rationalist and individualistic stance of 1793. In the second edition, Godwin reaffirmed his central belief in private judgement but also acknowledged a moral role for pleasure, feeling and the private affections. In the third edition, he further emphasized the role of feeling and sympathy in moral judgements. In his acknowledgement of the human need for sympathy and social regard, he was influenced by David Hume and Adam Smith – especially Smith.

The first edition of *Political Justice* gave the purest expression of Godwin's philosophical anarchism. His intellectual position was first articulated prior to the French Revolution, but the political debates of the early 1790s provided a catalyst for his distinctive fusion of dissenting principles and Enlightenment rationalism. The same association with the French Revolution led to the marginalization of his theories, towards the end of the decade, when he became the victim of a popular campaign to discredit his teachings, which associated him in the public mind with sedition, atheism and sexual immorality. Critics of Godwin have often argued that he retracted his progressive views as he grew older, pointing to the apparent contradiction between his rational philosophy and his fictional explorations of the flawed character of human motivation. Yet while Godwin modified his philosophy, he never abandoned his first principles. Hence his appeal to reformers in the nineteenth century, when *Political Justice* was widely discussed and read by Ricardian Socialists, Owenites and Chartists, and Godwin was declared by Friedrich Engels 'almost exclusively the property of the proletariat'.[15]

NOTES

1 Kathryn Sutherland, ' "Events... have made us a world of readers": Reader Relations 1780–1830', in David B. Pirie, ed., *The Penguin History of Literature, Vol. V: The Romantic Period* (Harmondsworth: Penguin, 1994), p. 45. Burke's *Reflections* was priced at three shillings; part one of Thomas Paine's *Rights of Man*, initially priced at three shillings, was reprinted when part two was published in 1792, both selling at sixpence (*ibid.*, p. 19).

2 Godwin, autobiographical note for 1789, in C. Kegan Paul, *William Godwin: His Friends and Contemporaries*, 2 vols. (London: Henry S. King, 1876), vol. I, p. 61 (corrected from the manuscript); Godwin to Caroline Lamb, 25 February 1819, *ibid.* vol. II, p. 266.

3 Mary Shelley, 'Life of William Godwin', in Nora Crook, gen. ed., *Mary Shelley's Literary Lives and Other Writings*, 4 vols. (London: Pickering and Chatto, 2002), vol. IV, p. 86.

4 John Milton, *Areopagitica*, in *Complete Prose Works of John Milton*, gen. ed. Don M. Wolfe, 8 vols. (New Haven and London: Yale University Press, 1953–82), vol. II, p. 551.

5 Godwin, manuscript list of political principles, cited in Mark Philp, 'Introduction', *Political and Philosophical Writings of William Godwin*, gen. ed. Mark Philp, 7 vols. (London: Pickering and Chatto, 1993), vol. I, p. 17.

6 Samuel Taylor Coleridge, *Lectures 1795 on Politics and Religion*, ed. Lewis Patton and Peter Mann, vol. I in *The Collected Works of Samuel Taylor Coleridge* (Princeton, NJ: Princeton University Press, 1971), p. 164.

7 [John Fenwick], 'Mr Godwin', in *Public Characters of 1799–1800* (London: R. Phillips, 1799), pp. 373–4.

8 Bodleian MS. Eng. Letters c. 22.

9 *New Letters of Robert Southey*, ed. Kenneth Curry, 2 vols. (New York: Columbia University Press, 1965), vol. I, p. 40.

10 *The Life and Correspondence of Robert Southey*, ed. Charles Cuthbert Southey, 6 vols. (London: Longman, Brown, Green and Longmans, 1849–50), vol. I, p. 247.

11 Bodleian MS. Abinger c. 2, fol. 120.

12 *The Letters of William and Dorothy Wordsworth: The Early Years, 1787–1805*, ed. Ernest de Selincourt, rev. Chester L. Shaver (Oxford: Clarendon Press, 1967), pp. 124–5.

13 *Henry Crabb Robinson on Books and Their Writers*, ed. Edith J. Morley, 3 vols. (London: J. M. Dent, 1938), vol. I, p. 3.

14 [Fenwick], 'Mr Godwin', p. 374.

15 Friedrich Engels, *The Condition of the Working Class in England*, ed. Victor Kiernan, intro. Tristram Hunt (Harmondsworth: Penguin, 2009), p. 245.

7

NANCY E. JOHNSON

Wollstonecraft and Godwin: dialogues

According to William Godwin's *Memoirs of the Author of a Vindication of the Rights of Woman*, he and Mary Wollstonecraft did not particularly like each other when they met for the first time at the publisher Joseph Johnson's on 13 November 1791. After dinner, Godwin recalled, 'Mary and myself parted, mutually displeased with each other' (*WG Novels*, vol. 1, p. 112). However, a subsequent meeting at the home of the novelist Mary Hays on 8 January 1796 was more successful. By April they were in social contact, by August they were lovers, and on 29 March 1797 they married. When their relationship began, both Wollstonecraft and Godwin were already accomplished authors. Godwin had published his influential book of political philosophy, *An Enquiry concerning Political Justice* (1793), and his novel *Things As They Are; or, The Adventures of Caleb Williams* (1794). Wollstonecraft had published her first novel, *Mary, A Fiction* (1788), and her groundbreaking texts of political and social theory, *Vindication of the Rights of Men* (1790) and *Vindication of the Rights of Woman* (1792). Both authors were well ensconced in the radical circles of the 1790s, supporting the French Revolution (until the increasing violence persuaded them otherwise) and engaging in reform efforts at home in Great Britain.

Wollstonecraft and Godwin were intimate partners for only a short period of time. Wollstonecraft died on 10 September 1797 from complications following childbirth; thus, they had less than two years together. Yet, despite the brevity, their relationship was a significant one not only for the authors themselves but also for the trajectory of radical writing in the 1790s. In a series of texts we might consider 'in dialogue', we see an extended discussion of a key component of British writing on the French Revolution: the relationship between the personal and the political, the intimate and the public. Once the heady days of the early Revolution had passed, authors entered a reflective period in which they had to come to terms with the egregious violence of the Revolution and the personal toll of a mass political movement. Social and political reform, which remained the goal of radical writing from the mid to later 1790s, became intimately bound up with sympathy, sensibility and the forces of emotion. The abstract principles that dominated early written responses to the French Revolution were complicated by the humanizing of those principles in literature. One of the results was narrative representations of the private, intimate world infused with politics and, correspondingly, political structures supported by domestic foundations. The private and the public, the emotional and the political, were intricately and intimately bound.

The texts I will examine in this chapter are all examples of literature in dialogue. Wollstonecraft's *Letters Written during a Short Residence in Sweden, Norway and Denmark* (1796) is a travelogue, but it is comprised of letters to her estranged lover, Gilbert Imlay. The genre of the letter is both private and public. As Bruce Redford notes, letters are an 'intimate conversation', yet they were also a popular vehicle of political discourse in the latter part of the eighteenth century.[1] Godwin's *Caleb Williams* and Wollstonecraft's *The Wrongs of Woman: or, Maria* (1798) constitute an example of intertextuality, another form of dialogue. Wollstonecraft engages with Godwin's novel to explore the politics of domestic tyranny as it pertains to women. The final text, Godwin's *Memoirs of the Author of a Vindication of the Rights of Woman* (1798), makes a private life public to show the reciprocity of the personal and the political. In dialogue with Wollstonecraft's *Wrongs of Woman*, Godwin addresses the role of sentiment and sensibility in social and political reform. He celebrates a single life – that of Mary Wollstonecraft – to honour her but also to instruct the public in the value of the individual contribution to national transformations.

Letters: fusing the private and the public

Wollstonecraft's *Letters Written during a Short Residence in Sweden, Norway and Denmark* are a compilation of letters that Wollstonecraft prepared for publication shortly after returning from her travels in Scandinavia on a business mission for Gilbert Imlay, her former lover and the father of her daughter Fanny. Imlay, an American author and business entrepreneur, asked Wollstonecraft to pursue financial compensation for the loss of a ship, the *Maria and Margaretha*, which was carrying a load of silver. Imlay suspected that the ship had been stolen by Peder Ellefsen, a Norwegian shipmaster with whom Imlay had concocted a scheme to circumvent the British embargo on trade between Scandinavia and France.[2] Wollstonecraft was to meet with Imlay's partner, Elias Backman, in Gothenburg, Sweden, as well as merchants, agents, lawyers and judges in Sweden and Norway. Her travels also took her to Denmark, where she met with the statesman Count

Bernstorf, seeking legal help with the Danish courts. Wollstonecraft's trip was an act of independence (a woman travelling alone and conducting business), but it was emotionally fraught for reasons that had little to do with Imlay's entrepreneurial dilemmas and everything to do with Wollstonecraft's personal, social and political concerns.

By the time Wollstonecraft sailed from Hull in June 1795, her relationship with Imlay was in disarray. After the birth of their daughter in Le Havre in 1794, Imlay left France for England, never to return to a stable domestic situation with his 'wife' and daughter.[3] When Wollstonecraft moved back to London, after months of waiting for Imlay to return to France, he had already taken a new lover. Wollstonecraft's romantic turmoil is a subtext of her published *Letters Written in Sweden*. Wollstonecraft looks for solace in sensibility and the Romantic sublime. The golden age that she and her fellow radicals located in political reform, she also finds in picturesque landscapes, benevolence and sympathy. Engaging with the aesthetic theories of her political rival, Edmund Burke, Wollstonecraft indulges in images of the sublime and beautiful. In her first letter, which is from Gothenburg, she notes the 'picturesque beauty' of '[r]ocks piled on rocks, forming a suitable bulwark to the ocean' and 'little patches of earth, of the most exquisite verdure, enamelled with the sweetest wild flowers, [which] seemed to promise the goats and a few straggling cows luxurious herbage'. She is 'delighted with the rude beauties of the scene; for the sublime often gave place imperceptibly to the beautiful, dilating the emotions which were painfully concentrated'. That evening, she contemplates 'all nature at rest'; even the rocks seemed to 'recline' and 'repose', along with her sleeping child. The scene, which melds humanity and nature, triggers a mental query about 'these imperious sympathies' (*MW Works*, vol. VI, pp. 247, 248–9).

While the picture Wollstonecraft paints seems to be a Romantic retreat into the emotional self, abandoning the social and political world, it is not. In this scene, we see how Wollstonecraft fuses her personal turmoil with the world at large. The image of the '[r]ocks piled on rocks', forming a 'bulwark', is a reminder of war, never far from the minds of Wollstonecraft and her peers in the wake of the French Revolution. But the image is also a reminder of commerce in the age of war – and thus of Imlay and his missing ship. The rocks, representing war and commerce (but also Imlay himself), are then juxtaposed with the domestic scene of wild flowers, goats and cows. The line between public and private becomes blurred when Wollstonecraft elaborates on the scene: 'Come no further, they [the rocks] emphatically said, turning their dark sides to the waves to augment the idle roar. The view was sterile.' In this description, Wollstonecraft moves Imlay from his public role as a businessman to his private role as Wollstonecraft's estranged lover. Ever since her final months in France, Wollstonecraft was frustrated by Imlay's 'rock-like' silences in response to the 'roar' of her pleas to return. Furthermore, the rocks are then juxtaposed with 'the sweetest wild flowers', an image Wollstonecraft frequently uses to represent herself and her daughter. She is 'heart's ease', which 'peeped through the rocks', while her daughter sleeps 'innocent and sweet as the closing flowers' (pp. 247–8).

As Wollstonecraft moves on to her discussion of sympathy, her thoughts are triggered by the now 'sleeping' rocks. 'What . . .' she ponders, 'is this active principle which keeps me still awake? – Why fly my thoughts abroad when every thing around me appears at home?' Thoughts abroad presumably refer to thoughts of Imlay, which in turn generate '[s]ome recollections, attached to the idea of home', and are then 'mingled with reflections respecting the state of society'. This movement of thought from the personal to the social returns to the personal when her reflections 'made a tear drop on the rosy cheek I had just kissed' but then shifts back again to the public when she embraces sympathy. The force of 'some involuntary sympathetic emotion, like the attraction of adhesion', makes her feel 'still a part of a mighty whole, from which', she explains, 'I could not sever myself' (pp. 248–9). This immersion into romantic (however troubled) and maternal love leads her to universal love, which pulls her back from the brink of melancholy and misanthropy. The message to Imlay about the value of domestic happiness is unmistakable in her ruminations on the sublime, the beautiful and the power of sympathy – but so is her philosophical position on universal love and the significance of social bonds, which are reciprocally dependent on domestic bonds.

Another aspect of Wollstonecraft's travels that blends the private and the public was her role as a business envoy. Involvement in Imlay's business could not have been a comfortable venture for the woman who wrote so harshly of 'the iron hand of property' in *Vindication of the Rights of Men* (*MW Works*, vol. v, p. 24). As she travels through Norway, Wollstonecraft re-invokes her classical image of a golden age – an era marked by 'independence and virtue; affluence without vice; cultivation of mind, without depravity of heart; with "ever smiling liberty"; the nymph of the mountain' (*Letters Written in Sweden*, in *MW Works*, vol. VI, p. 308).[4] The image sits in direct contrast to her portrayal of England and America as nations dependent on commerce. 'England and America owe their liberty to commerce', she notes, 'which created a new species of power to undermine the feudal system. But let them beware of the consequence; the tyranny of wealth is still more galling and debasing than that of rank' (p. 309). The 'tyranny of wealth' was a persistent concern of Wollstonecraft, and a prescient one.

Given her strong views on commerce, Wollstonecraft stays far afield from the details of her business in Scandinavia. It may very well be because Wollstonecraft, as Mary Favret has suggested, was herself engaged in the business of writing and was perhaps wrestling with her own transformation of 'the imaginative self' into 'commercial property' in writing these letters for publication.[5] However, Wollstonecraft does protest against commerce, and in one of her final letters, from Altona, Germany, she presents commerce as the enemy to the picturesque. Attempting to find a pleasant prospect of the river Elbe, Wollstonecraft is assaulted by the industrial smell of glue, and complains that 'to commerce every thing must give way; profit and profit are the only speculations'. Rather than the sound of a modulated wind, she hears only 'an account of the tricks of trade, or listen[s] to the distressful tale of some victim of ambition' (*Letters Written in Sweden*, in *MW Works*, vol. VI, p. 343).

One of those tales is a very personal one. Despite acting as his business emissary, Wollstonecraft is forthrightly critical of Imlay's personal business activities. 'Ah! shall I whisper to you', she writes in *Letters Written in Sweden*, 'that you – yourself, are strangely altered, since you have entered deeply into commerce – more than you are aware of.' She urges him to 'shake off the vile dust' of commerce that impedes his thinking and keeps him in 'a continual state of agitation' (*MW Works*, vol. VI, pp. 340–1). However, this rather gentle 'whisper' gives way to a much harsher indictment of his role in business in one of her later letters. 'The interests of nations are bartered by speculating merchants. My God! With what *sang froid* artful trains of corruption bring lucrative commissions into particular hands, disregarding the relative situation of different countries – and can much common honesty be expected in the discharge of trusts obtained by fraud? But this, *entre nous*' (p. 344). Knowing that she was preparing these letters for publication, there is nothing '*entre nous*' (between us) about her condemnation of Imlay's scheme with Ellefsen, a design by two 'speculating merchants', to defy the British embargo and thereby disrupt the political and military strategies of nations. For Wollstonecraft, the workings of individual business transactions have global implications and are answerable to universal moral demands.

In addition to commerce, the state of France is one of the international concerns informing Wollstonecraft's *Letters*. Wollstonecraft's trip to Scandinavia followed quickly on the heels of her time in France. She had travelled to Paris in December 1792 to witness first-hand the events of the Revolution. After a move to Neuilly in 1793, she wrote the *Historical and Moral View of the Origin and Progress of the French Revolution* (1794). Wollstonecraft left France in April of 1795, and by June of the same year, she was on her way to Sweden. While she viewed the trip as a restorative one – some relief from her troubled relationship with Imlay and her recent suicide attempt – the spectre of France haunts her letters. The picturesque scenes that Wollstonecraft enjoys are relief from 'the horrors [she] had witnessed in France' (*Letters Written in Sweden*, in *MW Works*, vol. VI, p. 247).

Still, Wollstonecraft reaffirms her beliefs in the principles of the Revolution. Among her assessments of Norwegian sea-captains is puzzlement at their devotion to their families and their lack of 'public spirit'. The captains' 'exertions', she writes, 'are, generally speaking, only for their families'. But she trusts that this situation will change when 'politics, becoming a subject of discussion, enlarges the heart by opening the understanding' (*MW Works*, vol. VI, p. 274). Moreover, she is confident that this very enlightenment will be one of the consequences of the French Revolution. Characteristic of Wollstonecraft's approach in her *Letters* is her insistence that the heart plays a role in political development. Here politics is the catalyst for enlarging the heart; elsewhere, it is the heart that feeds the understanding: 'we reason deeply, when we forcibly feel' (p. 325). Wollstonecraft also comments on the state of French émigrés. She describes Adrienne de Noailles, marquise de Lafayette, as a woman, characteristic of her class, who suffered from nervous disorders that one might attribute to '*ennui*' (boredom); however, her recent troubles have restored her health. By way of finding some good in her displacement, Wollstonecraft argues that 'adversity and virtuous exertions put these ills to flight, and dispossessed her of a devil' (p. 341). Throughout *Letters Written in Sweden*, Wollstonecraft remains committed to the early visions of the French Revolution and her own goals of reform: 'to carry mankind forward, and diminish the sum of human misery' (p. 346).

Novels: unveiling domestic despotism

Wollstonecraft broaches the politics of domestic tyranny in *Letters Written in Sweden* when she observes a welcome 'interregnum' for young women 'between the reign of the father and husband' (*MW Works*, vol. VI, p. 325). Both she and Godwin make this topic a central focus of their novelistic inquiries into 'things as they are' and the need for reform. Through novels that frame themselves as memoirs, Godwin and Wollstonecraft both write 'private histories' of those who have been traditionally dispossessed by political systems and remain in danger of further dispossession in the emerging social contract. They warn that vestiges of patriarchalism, which rendered the king the father of the nation and the father the king of the household, persist in the constitutional monarchy now in place. Only an acknowledgement of inalienable rights (those rights that cannot be violated by a government) can protect individuals from the insidious workings of government in the home and in political institutions.

In a preface that was withheld from publication in the first edition of *Caleb Williams*, Godwin articulates his rationale for turning to the novel to examine how 'the spirit and character of the government intrudes itself into every rank of society'. Godwin had already presented his theories of government in his philosophical *Enquiry concerning Political Justice*, but the novel provided the opportunity to move beyond 'refined and abstract speculation' into a detailed, material study of 'things passing in the moral world'. Moreover, the novel was an advantageous form, according to Godwin, because it would reach those people who were unlikely to read philosophy and science, and it could serve as 'a valuable lesson' while maintaining 'interest and passion'. In *Caleb Williams*, those 'things passing' are the conditions of oppression in the home: 'the modes of domestic and unrecorded despotism, by which man becomes the destroyer of man' (*WG Novels*, vol. III, p. 279).

For Godwin, the 'private' world of the family is thoroughly infused with politics, and a study of the family is an examination of power relationships between persons in authority and their subordinates. Likewise, an investigation into political tyranny requires a study of the family because therein lies a source of the perpetuation of inequalities and oppression. The specific subject of Godwin's novelistic inquiry into domestic tyranny is the relationship between the servant Caleb Williams and his master Falkland, who is also a justice of the peace and therefore a representative of the law. Godwin's choice of subject is a significant one because a servant embodies the intersection of the private domestic world and the public realm of employment. In addition, servants are in a precarious position, sitting on the margins of the familial unit; they are neither securely in a family nor are they independent of the family. Godwin also investigates the emotions that pervade relationships of power. In *Political Justice*, familial loyalties come second to concern for the general good; however, in *Caleb Williams* we see just how strong these loyalties can be and how destructive their outcomes.

The conflict of the novel results from an intensification of the relationship of power between Caleb Williams and Falkland. As a servant, Caleb is already subservient to Falkland. As an orphan, Caleb is also emotionally vulnerable to the chivalric tendencies of his master. However, these more acceptable forms of deference and obedience give way to assertions of ownership. The critical moment is when Caleb, driven by an 'ungoverned curiosity' and a 'boiling passion', opens a locked trunk that he suspects contains the secrets of Falkland's past life. Discovered by Falkland (and nearly killed by him), Caleb is cast into a world of fear, chaos and uncertainty;

'[o]ne short minute', he observes, 'had effected a reverse in my situation' (*WG Novels*, vol. III, p. 120). Caleb's shift from mere servitude to imprisonment is secured by Falkland's confession of murder. He requires that Caleb hear his confession and thereby forces him into a Faustian bargain. 'Do you know what it is you have done?' Falkland asks Caleb. 'To gratify a foolishly inquisitive humour you have sold yourself' (p. 123). As his master, Falkland already 'owned' Caleb, but the proprietorship was softened by the feudal relationship that required Falkland to act with paternal protection and temperance. But the harsh reality of their relationship, not in a feudal era but in an age of revolution, is now in full view: Caleb has 'sold' himself, and Falkland owns him outright.

The extent of Caleb's imprisonment becomes clear when he suggests leaving Falkland's service and becoming 'master of my own actions' (*WG Novels*, vol. III, p. 137). Falkland denies him his request and reminds him: 'I have dug a pit for you; and, whichever way you move, backward or forward, to the right or to the left, it is ready to swallow you' (p. 138). Caleb escapes, but from that point on, he is an 'outlaw' and Falkland pursues him as his property, demonstrating that liberty is a function of property. As long as an individual cannot claim the Lockean right of property – that is, owns the property in oneself – then one is subject to ownership by another. Caleb's momentary enjoyment of freedom when he boasts, 'you [Falkland] shall neither make prize of my liberty, nor sully the whiteness of my name' (p. 308) yields to his loss of liberty as he becomes a hunted man.

As a man of talent and merit, Caleb should be a character of hope; he should be the positive alternative to the dissipated figure of inherited privilege. 'I was not born indeed to the possession of hereditary wealth;' he writes of himself, 'but I had a better inheritance, an enterprising mind, an inquisitive spirit, a liberal ambition.' But unaware of 'the power which the institutions of society give to one man over others', and the consequent destruction of talent and merit, Caleb finds himself 'shut up, a deserted, solitary wretch'. He begins to feel the loss of the self that is the very foundation of liberty and confesses '[m]y life was all a lie. I had a counterfeit character to support. I had counterfeit manners to assume' (*WG Novels*, vol. III, pp. 318–19). This move towards a negation of the self is fulfilled when in the manuscript ending of the novel Caleb declares himself one of 'the living dead'. 'True happiness', he declares, 'lies in being like a stone – Nobody can complain of me – all day long I do nothing – I am a stone – a GRAVE-STONE! – an obelisk to tell you, HERE LIES WHAT WAS ONCE A MAN!' (p. 340). Similarly, but less dramatically, in the published ending of the novel, Caleb concludes 'I began these memoirs with the idea of vindicating my own character. I have now no character that I wish to vindicate'

(p. 277). In both instances, an utter loss of self is the price Caleb pays for his loss of self-ownership.

While Caleb is clearly a victim in his relationship with Falkland, he is also complicitous in his imprisonment because he is entrapped by his own emotions – the love and loyalty a servant can feel for his master.[6] The confession scene described above is prefaced by a garden scene in which Caleb begins to suspect that Falkland is the murderer of Barnabas Tyrrel. He describes 'the tumult of his thoughts' as his 'blood boiled' within, but he also experiences 'a kind of rapture' that leads to 'the most soul-ravishing calm'. This latter state results from Caleb's realization that 'it was possible to love a murderer' (WG Novels, vol. III, p. 117). Even when threatened by Falkland, Caleb asserts, 'I will never injure my master' and admits 'I still continued to pity, rather than hate my persecutor' (pp. 124, 201).

Caleb is a complex character as he variously dons the roles of servant, wife and beggar, all of whom suffer from disenfranchisement. In his capacity as Falkland's secretary, Caleb is a servant; in his thoroughly subordinate position sealed by love, Caleb replicates a wife; when he is an outlaw and outcast, Caleb becomes a beggar.[7] But also important to Caleb's story is the subplot of Emily Melvile and her cousin Barnabas Tyrrel in volume I, which prepares us for our reading of Caleb's story. Emily is paradigmatic of female figures in novels of the mid to later eighteenth century. Unprotected by status or the right of property, she is subject to the brutalities of family members who regard her as their property. When Emily falls in love with Falkland, her tyrannical cousin (and guardian) Tyrrel tries to force her into a marriage with a brutish labourer, Grimes; when she resists, he imprisons her in an apartment and plots her abduction and rape. Emily is saved by Falkland, but Tyrrel has her arrested for debt and she soon falls ill and dies.

Emily's story foreshadows Caleb's demise, but it also serves as a model for the fate of women in a state where domestic tyranny is reciprocally supported by political despotism. Mary Wollstonecraft takes on this paradigmatic woman and, in her unfinished novel, Wrongs of Woman, which is cast as a memoir, begins a comprehensive study of women's relationship with the law.[8] Like Godwin, Wollstonecraft examines the emotional component of domestic relationships: the love and the loyalty that keep women in subservient roles, but also the bond of friendship that supports those victims of oppression. While Godwin broaches the significance of communities in Caleb Williams, in the domestic scenes with Laura and the criminal community of thieves, Wollstonecraft makes community a central part of her inquiry in Wrongs of Woman.

The novel is largely comprised of narratives in dialogue: the caretaker Jemima and two of her inmates in the madhouse, Maria Venables and Henry

Darnford, tell their stories to each other, and in the case of Maria, also to her daughter, in the form of a memoir. In Maria's and Jemima's stories, Wollstonecraft delineates the disadvantages women face as subjects of the law. Jemima, who is born an illegitimate child, is at birth placed outside the law and the family unit. Her life continues at the margins of society, and, unable to claim property in herself (because she owns no property), she is easily commodified by others; she is 'a slave, a bastard', and, ultimately, 'a common property' (*MW Works*, vol. I, p. 112). Maria's story is that of the middle-class woman who brings property into a marriage only to see it dissipated by an irresponsible husband. An attempt by her uncle to circumvent the law that transfers a woman's property to her husband leaves the largest part of his fortune to Maria's daughter. But this attempt at liberation leads only to Maria's imprisonment. When she flees her abusive husband with her daughter, her husband has her abducted and imprisoned in a madhouse – and his actions are fully sanctioned by the law. Maria has no right to take her daughter because children are the property of their father, and a husband has the right to retrieve a deserting wife as well as have her committed to a madhouse. Denied the 'rights of man', Jemima and Maria are both delivered into the legal 'wrongs of woman'.

The memoir that Maria writes to her daughter is the only form of property that Maria can claim as her own and bequeath to her daughter because under laws of *coverture* the property a woman brings into a marriage belongs to her husband, unless it is protected in a trust. According to the jurist Sir William Blackstone, in *Commentaries on the Laws of England* (1765–9), when a man and woman marry they become 'one person in law'. The 'very being or legal existence of the woman', he continues, 'is suspended during the marriage, or at least is incorporated and consolidated into that of the husband: under whose wing, protection, and *cover*, she performs every thing'.[9] In the court scene at the end of the novel, we see how the alignment of property and the law works to the advantage of men. Maria's husband is able to charge Darnford with seduction because his wife is his property and he can argue that she was 'stolen' by Darnford. Furthermore, Maria is unable to testify against her husband because they are one under the law. Blackstone explains that '*nemo in propria causa testis esse debet*' ('no one is allowed to be a witness in his own cause'); likewise, '*nemo tenetur seipsum accusare*' ('no one shall be bound to accuse himself').[10] If a wife were to testify against her husband, she would be testifying against herself. The political and social implications of a woman's dependent status in the law were fundamental: she could not enter into a civil covenant; she could not participate in the social contract and enjoy the individual rights given to full citizens.

Wollstonecraft's inquiry into the emotions that perpetuate domestic tyranny in *Wrongs of Woman* focuses on the romantic couple and the delusional tendencies of love. When Maria falls in love with George Venables, her future husband, she describes it as a 'revolution' of feelings (not unlike Caleb Williams's experience in the garden). 'My fancy', she continues, 'had found a basis to erect its model of perfection on' (*MW Works*, vol. I, p. 131). Although we do not have a conclusion to Maria's relationship with Darnford, Wollstonecraft hints at perils as their romance unfolds. They initiate their acquaintance on the terrain of Jean-Jacques Rousseau's *Julie ou la nouvelle Héloïse* (1761), a text that Wollstonecraft criticizes in her *Vindication of the Rights of Woman*. Barbara Taylor notes the similarities between the two novels – in both, characters enter into a 'land of chimeras', fuelled by an 'inflamed' literary imagination.[11] Maria constructs Darnford as 'an ideal lover' before she meets him and while in a state of heightened imagination, just as St Preux casts Julie as his romantic ideal in *Héloïse* (*MW Works*, vol. I, p. 96). Moreover, Darnford, as a man who engaged in 'commercial speculations' (p. 101) and resided for a time in America, clearly resembles Wollstonecraft's former lover Gilbert Imlay. Still, as Taylor also notes, Wollstonecraft's approach to sensibility, and to Rousseau, was a complex one. While warning of the hazards of romantic fantasies, she clearly saw in female sensibility and the imagination a source of liberation – as evidenced by her letters from Scandinavia.[12]

Romantic love is suspect in *Wrongs of Woman*; however, friendship thrives. Friendship as a form of *fraternité* proves to be a vital source of solace and strength for those in the madhouse. They instruct each other with their stories, building a community that is an important alternative for those who cannot claim individual rights and self-directing lives. The narrative conversations in *Wrongs of Woman* propel the characters into action. Jemima is moved to help Maria locate her baby, and Darnford and Maria resolve to seek their own liberation. The discovery of the baby's death and Darnford's and Maria's inability ultimately to escape the law underscore the need for systemic political reform.

Memoirs: making the private public

The dialogues within Wollstonecraft's novel reflect the discourse of texts circulating in the 1790s, and within this milieu the memoir was becoming increasingly important. Along with autobiography and biography, the memoir had been used for social, political and religious reform in the seventeenth and eighteenth centuries. Puritans and dissenters saw an opportunity in literature for personal accounts to model figures of historical development and social change through stories of both ordinary and extraordinary people. History, according to J. Paul Hunter, was embedded in these genres. History was to be found in lives, and the stories of these lives were seen to be an 'effective kind of didactic tool'.[13] Forms of personal biography were especially popular at the end of the eighteenth century. Renowned Revolutionary figures in France, as well as prominent radicals who were charged with treason in Great Britain, wrote stories about their ordeals and used the occasion to clarify their political positioning and justify their actions.[14] For William Godwin, in particular, biography became a vital mechanism for achieving reform. Pamela Clemit and Gina Luria Walker note that Godwin's *Memoirs of the Author of a Vindication of the Rights of Woman* is 'the first of several philosophical biographies, in which he aimed to foster gradual social change by transforming the moral consciousness of his readers'.[15]

Godwin's vision of the memoir as a didactic opportunity and vehicle for reform reflects Wollstonecraft's representation in *Wrongs of Woman*. In a memoir, Godwin writes, '[t]he justice which is thus done to the illustrious dead, converts into the fairest source of animation and encouragement to those who would follow them in the same career'. The people, he continues, are 'interested in this justice, as it teaches them to place their respect and affection, upon those qualities which best deserve to be esteemed and loved' (*WG Novels*, vol. I, p. 87). In addition, Godwin's acknowledgement of the workings of sympathy echoes the emphasis on the social bond of friendship and the value of compassion in Wollstonecraft's novel. 'I cannot easily prevail on myself to doubt', he writes, 'that the more fully we are presented with the picture and story of such persons as the subject of the following narrative, the more generally shall we feel in ourselves an attachment to their fate, and a sympathy in their excellencies' (p. 87). Attachment and sympathy become critical components in educating the public.

Godwin's vindication of Wollstonecraft is infused with his defence of sensibility. While both authors embrace reason as crucial to their political agenda, including the ideal of private judgement and an expansion of the franchise, by the mid to later 1790s, they were considering the usefulness of sentiment in bringing about change. When Godwin critiques Wollstonecraft's *Vindication of the Rights of Men*, he is critical of her 'too contemptuous and intemperate treatment' of Edmund Burke (*WG Novels*, vol. I, p. 108). In his comments on her *Vindication of the Rights of Woman*, he remarks on its 'somewhat amazonian temper' and notes its deficiency in 'method and arrangement' (pp. 109, 110). However, while condemning her 'burst of indignation', he admires and values her 'luxuriance of imagination' and 'trembling delicacy of sentiment', and, most important, he sees the 'eminence of genius' in her political doctrines (pp. 107, 109, 110). He attributes to Wollstonecraft the ideal of 'exquisite sensibility' balanced with 'soundness of understanding' (p. 88). Moreover, he shows the reader how sensibility is manifest in action – a critical step for an argument that sensibility is valuable to social and political reform. Godwin tells a story of Wollstonecraft's heroism on a ship returning from Lisbon, where she was visiting her friend Fanny Blood. Their ship encountered another ship in distress. When the captain refused to help, Wollstonecraft, driven by an intense compassion, insisted they help and threatened the captain until he complied. Godwin suggests that Wollstonecraft may have saved the lives of those on board.

The life that Godwin writes in the *Memoirs* is one in which the public and private are inextricably bound. Godwin does not hesitate to tell us about the romantic traumas of the author who so stridently warns women about unchecked passions in *Vindication of the Rights of Woman*. He celebrates her emotional life while he admires her intellectual life – and both are manifest in private and public domains. Wollstonecraft wrote to expose the social and political principles that dominated women's private lives, and in turn, to reveal how the constructs of women's private lives, especially within the family, were a foundation for patriarchal politics. Godwin writes in admiration of Wollstonecraft's politics, but it is her passions that seem to captivate him. He attributes her appeal to her expression of emotion and her ability to evoke sympathy in the reader, when he comments on her Scandinavian letters.

> If ever there was a book calculated to make a man in love with its author, this appears to me to be the book. She speaks of her sorrows, in a way that fills us with melancholy, and dissolves us in tenderness, at the same time that she displays a genius which commands all our admiration. Affliction had tempered her heart to a softness almost more than human; and the gentleness of her spirit seems precisely to accord with all the romance of unbounded attachment.
>
> (*WG Novels*, vol. 1, p. 122)

Arguably, one of Godwin's goals in the *Memoirs* is to redeem the value and appeal of emotion that Wollstonecraft wrestles with in *Wrongs of Woman*. The attention that he gives to sentiment in the *Memoirs* indicates an interest in Godwin, himself, in the power of sensibility as it might advance reform.

In the final chapter of the *Memoirs*, after describing Wollstonecraft's death, Godwin assesses their relationship and creates a paradigm of a complementary couple. 'We had cultivated our powers... in different directions', he writes, 'I chiefly an attempt at logical and metaphysical distinction, she a taste for the picturesque.' Godwin saw in himself an intellectual deficiency. He could not claim 'an intuitive perception of intellectual beauty'. While he enjoyed 'a strong and lively sense of the pleasures of the imagination', he explains, only by 'dint of persevering examination, and the change and correction of [his] first opinions' could he be 'right in assigning to them their proportionate value'. According to Godwin, his deficiency was Wollstonecraft's strength. He credits her 'intuition' as the source of her insights, the foundation for her intellectual endeavours. 'Her religion, her philosophy... were, as I have already said, the pure result of feeling and taste. She adopted one opinion, and rejected another, spontaneously, by a sort of tact, and the force of a cultivated imagination.' Godwin suggests that 'she reasoned little' and that 'there is a kind of witchcraft' in 'a robust and unwavering judgment of this sort'; however, he recognizes in her means of inquiry the possibility of 'produc[ing] a responsive vibration in every ingenuous mind' when it 'decides justly' (*WG Novels*, vol. I, pp. 140–1).

Godwin's account of Wollstonecraft's intellectual activities is important not so much for its accuracy as for what it reveals about Godwin's own reflections on the process of reform in civil society. Wollstonecraft was a significant political theorist, as Virginia Sapiro, among other contemporary critics, has argued.[16] Her *Vindication of the Rights of Men* was one of the first responses to Edmund Burke's *Reflections on the Revolution on France*, and it clearly articulates one of the central disputes that occupied political discourse in the 1790s: the constitution and distribution of rights. Wollstonecraft's *Vindication of the Rights of Woman* is regarded as a seminal feminist text. Employing both reason and passion, she delineates the forces that have infantilized, and impeded the progress of, women and elucidates the changes that must take place in education, marriage and society at large for women to achieve a state of rational virtue.

Thus, Godwin's depiction of Wollstonecraft's intellectual strength as intuition, feeling, taste and an innate sense of the picturesque is a limited one. However, what it reveals about Godwin and the trajectory of radical thinking towards the end of the 1790s is significant. It indicates that Godwin, so often portrayed as the leading proponent of rational thought, has broadened his thinking and sees in intuition a valid form of judgement. Such a view supports his advocacy of private judgement, and it provides women with an opportunity to use a quality, so often attributed to women, to claim the same rights to private judgement as men. Godwin concludes the *Memoirs* with a sentence that credits Wollstonecraft with improving him as a philosopher and confirms that his definition of 'intellectual' is now a more inclusive one: 'While I have described the improvement I was in the act of receiving, I believe I have put down the leading traits of her intellectual character'

(*WG Novels*, vol. I, p. 141). While we might read 'intellectual' as 'reason,' given the 'leading traits' that Godwin has just described, we as readers must broaden our own interpretation of the term. The passion that was so suspect as a result of the 'madness' of the French Revolution and the emotion that seemed an impediment to women was being reconstituted by British writers contemplating reform in the wake of the French Revolution.

Conversation between texts was a phenomenon that marked the body of British writings responding to the French Revolution. Burke's *Reflections* was a letter to a Parisian gentleman, and 'the letter' itself generated a wave of written responses. Novels between so-called Jacobin and Anti-Jacobin authors embarked on a debate over the individual's relationship to government. In the particular case of Wollstonecraft and Godwin, the dialogues they carried on with each other, with the public, and for Wollstonecraft, Gilbert Imlay as well, are significant for the shift they reveal in radical thinking in the 1790s, a decade dominated by revolution. Improvement based on reason alone was no longer sufficient. Reformers had to consider human emotion – the workings of sympathy, compassion, loyalty and love. Intimate relationships, they found, were infused with politics, and political relationships were secured by personal bonds. The relationship between Wollstonecraft and Godwin embodied the inseparability of the personal and the political, the private and the public. Through their exchanges, they became a model of the 'humane investigator' and 'benevolent reformer' that Wollstonecraft invokes at the end of her Scandinavian letters (*MW Works*, vol. VI, p. 346). As such, they were poised to become an effective alternative to the revolutionaries of France.

NOTES

1 Bruce Redford, *The Converse of the Pen* (Chicago: University of Chicago Press, 1986), p. 1.
2 Janet Todd, *Mary Wollstonecraft: A Revolutionary Life* (London: Weidenfeld and Nicolson, 2000), pp. 258–9, 274.
3 Imlay and Wollstonecraft never legally married, though Imlay had registered Wollstonecraft as his wife at the American embassy in France because British expatriates were in danger. Wollstonecraft enjoyed a certain degree of safety and freedom of movement in France as the 'wife' of an American. *Ibid.*, 239.
4 Carol Poston suggests that Wollstonecraft borrows Milton's image of liberty as a mountain nymph from 'L'Allegro,' lines 35–6; see Mary Wollstonecraft, *Letters Written during a Short Residence in Sweden, Norway, and Denmark*, ed. Carol Poston (Lincoln: University of Nebraska Press, 1976), p. 128 n. 4. Marilyn Butler and Janet Todd attribute the quotation 'ever smiling liberty' to Handel's *Judas Maccabeus* (words by Thomas Morel) (1746); see *The Works of Mary Wollstonecraft*, ed. Janet Todd and Marilyn Butler, 7 vols. (London: Pickering and Chatto, 1989), vol. VI, p. 308 n.

5 Mary Favret, *Romantic Correspondence: Women, Politics and the Fiction of Letters* (Cambridge: Cambridge University Press, 1993), pp. 97, 99, 110.

6 See Alex Gold Jr., 'It's Only Love: The Politics of Passion in Godwin's *Caleb Williams*', *Texas Studies in Literature and Language* 19 (1977), 135–60.

7 In the Preface to the 'Standard Novels' edition of Fleetwood (London: R. Bentley, 1832), Godwin explains that he was 'tracing a certain similitude' with the story of Bluebeard. Falkland was his Bluebeard and Caleb Bluebeard's wife (p. 449).

8 Mary Wollstonecraft died before finishing the novel. It was published posthumously in 1798 by William Godwin.

9 Sir William Blackstone, *Commentaries on the Laws of England*, 4 vols. (1765–9; Chicago: University of Chicago Press, 1979), vol. I, p. 430.

10 *Ibid.*, p. 431.

11 Barbara Taylor, *Mary Wollstonecraft and the Feminist Imagination* (Cambridge: Cambridge University Press, 2003), pp. 75, 74.

12 *Ibid.*, pp. 72–4.

13 J. Paul Hunter, *Before Novels: The Cultural Contexts of Eighteenth-Century English Fiction* (New York: W. W. Norton, 1990), p. 345, p. 403 n. 12.

14 See Pamela Clemit and Gina Luria Walker, 'Introduction' to William Godwin, *Memoirs of the Author of a Vindication of the Rights of Woman* (Peterborough: Broadview Press, 2001), pp. 20–1. For an example of a 'memoir' by a British radical charged with treason, see Thomas Holcroft's *A Narrative of Facts, relating to a Prosecution for High Treason* (London: Symonds, 1795).

15 Clemit and Walker, 'Introduction', p. 13.

16 See Virginia Sapiro, *A Vindication of Political Virtue: The Political Theory of Mary Wollstonecraft* (Chicago: University of Chicago Press, 1992).

8

JON MEE

Popular radical culture

This chapter approaches the British radical movement in the 1790s as a cultural and not simply a political phenomenon. Inspired by events in France in 1789, many Britons certainly hoped that their country would become a more enlightened nation, even if opinions differed as to what might constitute enlightenment. Across these differences, there persisted an aspiration to participate in a new literary and political culture, especially among many of those who had previously been excluded. Over the previous few decades the spread of print culture, the rise of literacy, and the development of a tessellation of societies, clubs and urban entertainments had produced what might be termed a popular enlightenment across Britain and Ireland. Debating clubs and newspapers habituating those excluded from the franchise to the discussion of political and public matters fed into the official meetings and penumbra of debating clubs and other groups surrounding the London Corresponding Society and its older and more respectable ally the Society for Constitutional Information.

Given the focus of this Companion on writing about the French Revolution, my account of radical culture will have an emphasis on print, but on print as part of this larger aspiration to social and political participation represented by the interacting careers of a selection of radical writers and publishers. Circulation was central to the meaning of writing in this context (and key to whether it was prosecuted or not), and printers, booksellers and readers were as important as writers. Without wishing to overlook the importance of the English provinces, not to mention the quite distinctive responses to the French Revolution in Ireland, Scotland and Wales, this chapter concentrates on the formation of a radical culture in London, partly out of the exigencies of space and partly because the capital and its bookshops, newspapers and coffee houses acted as such a magnet for many of those wishing to rewrite the republic of letters. Exciting and attractive this world may have been for its participants, but it was far from being an open public sphere. The spectres of surveillance, incarceration, bankruptcy (a method often preferred by government to relying on juries) and even execution loomed over popular radicalism, conditioning its sense of the range of political possibilities open to participants, including what and how they might write and publish.

The causes of the emergence of popular radicalism in the 1790s were diverse and complex, with no single point of origin. Thomas Paine's *Rights of Man* (1791–2) aimed to convince a broad audience of readers that they had a right to consider themselves part of the political nation and encouraged them to participate in discussion, debate and organization. In the world of political events, the French Revolution provided the most obvious stimulant for the emergence of a movement committed to reform of Parliament and deeper changes in British society, but many of those involved, including, for instance, the 'gentleman radical' John Horne Tooke, had already been schooled in the Wilkesite radicalism of the 1760s, opposition to the American War, and the parliamentary reform movement of the 1780s. The Society for Constitutional Information, founded in 1780, played a key role in the last, especially through the distribution of reformist tracts, but it was revivified and its character altered by the French Revolution. Ably led by Horne Tooke and his lieutenant the solicitor John Frost, allying themselves with Paine at various of the Society's meetings in 1792, the SCI committed itself to making *Rights of Man* widely available at a cheap price and soon looked to collaborate with the LCS (whose delegates attended some SCI meetings).[1] The sense of excitement produced by this collaborative energy across a range of new political societies is palpable in much of what survives from the writing of 1792.

The attraction of the LCS for its members was that it didn't just offer 'jam tomorrow', as John Barrell puts it, but 'a sense of immediate, present participation, to whoever would join it and engage in its activities and debates'.[2] The meeting of Thomas Hardy and his friends in a London tavern in January 1792 may have proposed to set up the LCS as the first ever political society open to all, but it was also continuous with and attractive to an expanding popular culture of reading and debate. Co-ordinating the activities of various societies across the country, the first of which seems to have been the Sheffield Constitutional Society, set up in November 1791, the LCS quickly developed into the major clearing house for radical opinion. Although the government became obsessed with insurrectionary plots, the primary 'official' business of the LCS, consonant with the original objectives of the SCI, was the dissemination of political knowledge. Most LCS publications, therefore, are devoted to putting ideas into circulation rather than stabilizing a particular programme.[3] Although it remained firmly committed to the core demands of universal suffrage and annual parliaments, no single stable ideology emerges behind its publications or the wider culture of radicalism that the LCS played a key role in sustaining. Indeed, as Mark Philp and James Epstein have argued, the ideology of reform in the period was 'fragmented', most obviously in shifting between appeals to the idea of a 'British' constitutional politics and 'French' ideas of universal political rights, associated with Thomas Paine.

The publication of Paine's *Rights of Man* did have a direct influence on the decision of Hardy and others to set up the LCS, although Hardy's account of the origins of the society stresses the importance of the Duke of Richmond's letter of 1780 on parliamentary reform (widely circulated by the SCI, and republished by the LCS in 1795). The history of the society Hardy provided in his autobiography suggests that early on there was an expectation that men from within the political elite would come forward as leaders, although he also insisted that the people needed to exert themselves in their own cause.[4] When the LCS emerged, Paine had published only part one of *Rights of Man*. It was while writing part two, published early in 1792, that he began to see the possibilities of a genuinely popular movement. Paine's republicanism was certainly not the official programme of the LCS, whose publications rarely use *Rights of Man* as a reference point, but the example it gave of the dissemination of political knowledge was crucial. From exile in Paris, later in 1792, Paine wrote to the Attorney-General Archibald Macdonald: 'I have gone into coffee-houses, and places where I was unknown, on purpose to learn the currency of opinion, and I never yet saw any company of twelve men that condemned the book' (*Trials*, vol. 1, p. 99). Producing Paine's letter in court, Macdonald scoffed at the idea that 'the sense of this *nation* is to be had in some pot-houses and coffee-houses in this town' (p. 85). Radical culture in the 1790s was in part an attempt to argue and demonstrate that those who frequented such places did have a right to participate in articulating 'the sense of this nation'.

Once the Royal Proclamations of May and December 1792 against seditious writings had begun to bite, especially after John Reeves and his counter-revolutionary Association for the Preservation of Liberty and Property against Republicans and Levellers came into play, the LCS was already being pressured towards a defensive posture that regularly insisted on the constitutionalism of its politics and the respectability of its proceedings more generally.[5] Fixing one's colours to *Rights of Man*, declared a seditious libel after Paine's trial, would have been foolhardy, and the strategic nature of the LCS's official line ought to be distinguished from the opinions held and expressed by its members. Moreover, the use of the constitutionalist idiom often found in LCS documents was not necessarily – as Epstein, Philp and others have pointed out – a reflection of the conservatism of the political ideas espoused by the LCS. Where the constitution that was being invoked went back long before the settlement of 1688 and current parliamentary arrangements, placing weight, for instance, on an ancient Anglo-Saxon precedent, the effect could be much the same thing as an appeal to natural rights.

If many of the LCS's official publications have an emphasis on orderliness and respectability, they are concerned mainly with procedural matters involved in setting up any new organization, but perhaps also with 'proving' the LCS to be worthy of a place in political society. Men such as Thomas Hardy and Francis Place, looking back on the 1790s, both stressed sobriety and self-improvement as one of the legacies of the popular radical movement to nineteenth-century working-class culture. Elite resistance to the extension of the franchise assumed that the people 'out-of-doors' could or would not know how to exercise freedom properly. Such attitudes permeated even relatively sympathetic groups such as Grey's Society of the Friends of the People, set up from those within the parliamentary Whig party, in April 1792, with pretensions to being the natural leaders of the people.

Increasingly, such groups were alarmed at developments inspired by Paine. Good order may have been on display in official LCS publications, but it would be misleading to accept accounts of 'rational' self-improvement as the sole or even dominant mode of the popular radical movement. Gatherings within the broader culture of radicalism did sometimes have the saltier flavour of tavern free-and-easies than the civicism stressed in the official publications would suggest. Numerous spy reports give accounts of seditious toasts and convivial songs. Significantly, this picture emerges more clearly in print when one looks at what else was being published by radicals beyond the official publications of the LCS and SCI, even by their members. Here one sees a picture that is much more brazenly involved in testing the limits of respectability, and even throwing off the kind of behaviour that is easily glossed in terms of a rational public sphere. Nor are its participants always easy to assimilate to the idea of an emergent working-class consciousness of the sort E. P. Thompson influentially identified with radicalism in the 1790s.

Early on at least, the government seemed most alarmed at the prospect of men of talents within the elite coming forward as the leaders of the popular movement. There were several gentlemen associated with the movement, many of whom, like Joseph Gerrald, who drafted the LCS's petition for parliamentary reform in 1793, conceived of themselves as part of a wider transatlantic process of political and moral revolution.[6] The poet Robert Merry provides an example of someone who stayed close to events in France as they developed after 1789, travelling backwards and forwards between London and Paris over 1791–2, eager for the British societies to co-operate with French republicans. Merry seems to have become a member of Grey's Friends of the People in April 1792, but he had already joined the revived SCI in June 1791, proposed by Tooke, and its meetings seem to have taken up most of his political attention in Britain. In France he urged the National Assembly to set up a republic and defended the overthrow of Louis XVI in the English press.[7] His poetry had developed along with his journalism towards the celebration of a popular republic. *The Laurel of Liberty* (1790) rejoiced at the early stages of the Revolution and his *Ode for the 14th of July* (1791), written and performed for a meeting of 'The Friends of Liberty' in the Crown and Anchor tavern in 1791, urged others to join in with his enthusiasm. Merry may have been the anonymous author of *A Circumstantial History of the Transactions at Paris on the Tenth of August; plainly Shewing the Perfidy of Louis XVI and the General Unanimity of the People, in Defence of their Rights* (1792). He was announced as the author of a forthcoming pamphlet on a very similar topic in *The Times*, 11 September 1792. Eventually Merry was to be accused of losing the character of a gentleman by sacrificing his social status to his politics. In the summer of 1793, unable to live in aristocratic Britain, he tried to depart for Switzerland with another radical, Charles Pigott. The military campaigns on the continent thwarted their plans and they turned back at Harwich. Merry went into internal exile in Yorkshire, Pigott returned to London, where he was arrested for uttering seditious words after an incident at a coffee house.

Pigott was another child of the gentry who played an important early role in encouraging the radical movement to divest itself of the notion that the aristocracy were born to rule. He too was accused of class betrayal for his pains. Having moved in social circles associated with Foxite Whigs in the 1770s and 1780s, he published *Strictures on the New Political Tenets of Edmund Burke* (1791). Ostensibly attacking Burke for abandoning his erstwhile Whig political friends and allies, as its argument develops so does the pamphlet's constitutionalist rhetoric begin to be reoriented towards praise of Paine and Rousseau. Possibly Pigott's knowledge of developments in French thinking was mediated through his brother, Robert, who was actively involved in the Jacobin Club, but, whatever its origins, his next publication represented a major repudiation of Whiggism, making full use of personal information and newspaper reports to expose the private lives of the aristocracy and royal family, including Pitt and even the King, but especially the high-rolling gambling circles surrounding the Prince Regent. *The Jockey Club* (1792) was published in a series of expanded editions over the course of the year, exploiting a growing taste for scandal in the press and turning it to political account, explicitly calling for a republic to sweep away the corruption of British political life. Its irreverent and scurrilous content would have lent itself to being read aloud in tavern free-and-easies and debating societies, including division 25 of the LCS, which Pigott himself joined.

Pigott represents a side of the radical movement that we might call free-thinking, tending even towards a kind of Jacobin libertinism, certainly alive to new French ideas. This freethinking aspect of radical culture found perhaps its most energetic advocate in the bookseller Daniel Isaac Eaton, another member of division 25, who kept up the circulation of radical ideas through his journal *Hog's Wash*, later known as *Politics for the People* (1793–5), and a slew of challenging pamphlets, a heady mix of radical politics and anti-clericalism, some written by himself, but also including Paine's *The Age of Reason* (1794–5), Pigott's posthumous *Political Dictionary* (1795) and Volney's *The Law of Nature* (1796). Although he had run a stationer's shop in Hoxton, an area of London notorious for religious dissent, Eaton seems to have become interested in radical political publishing only in 1792, starting with the physician James 'Old Hubert' Parkinson's *The Budget of the People* (1792). Early in the same year, Eaton had joined 'The Friends of the Liberty of the Press,' set up by the Whig politician and barrister Thomas Erskine, along with other radical publishers, such as James Ridgway and H. D. Symonds, and writers Merry and Parkinson, but Eaton's pamphlets and, especially, *Hog's Wash* were increasingly designed for wide dissemination, certainly beyond the world imaginable by most of Erskine's more Whiggish associates. The weekly format of *Hog's Wash* allowed for a quick response to events, its reprints of classic political texts leavened by the kind of topical squibs eighteenth-century journalism excelled at. The result was boisterous and accessible: the whole atmosphere of the journal a challenge to traditional patterns of deference. In 1793 the government tried to round up Eaton with the other publishers associated with Paine and Pigott, most notably Ridgway and Symonds, but he was acquitted three times over 1793–4. The last trial in February 1794, for publishing John Thelwall's allegory of the decapitation of a royal gamecock, 'King Chanticleer', was greeted as a landmark verdict for the radical movement, reversing the series of convictions for printers and publishers.

Given the concerns about respectability in the LCS, it is little wonder that Pigott was never mentioned in any of its official documents, nor that Hardy later complained that Eaton was a man who published 'freely, perhaps too freely.'[8] Pigott's *Political Dictionary* (1795), which Eaton published after its author's death, offered ribald and irreverent revisions of the language of politics, including, for instance, a description of the church as 'a patent for hypocrisy; the refuge of sloth, ignorance and superstition, the corner-stone of tyranny'. Some editions came with a preface made up of what purport to be Pigott's own words, uttered while suffering in gaol from the fever that ultimately killed him.[9] Eaton's presentation of Pigott as a man of feeling may seem hard to square with the scurrility of *The Jockey Club*, but others – whatever they thought of Pigott – were far from seeing a contradiction between a materialist perspective hostile to religious morality and the language of sentiment. John Thelwall offers a case in point, although not one from the same mould as Pigott or even Eaton. Thelwall was not a member of the elite, although he was certainly committed to self-improvement and even self-promotion. He had been articled as a lawyer's clerk, tried his luck as a tailor and an actor, despite a stammer, before attempting to support a family through literary work in the 1780s. Even the judge at his trial for treason recognized him to be 'a man of letters, associating with the company of gentlemen' (*Trials*, vol. VIII, p. 105). Thelwall had been a friend of Horne Tooke's, dining regularly at his home in Wimbledon, with other members of the SCI, but from early 1792 he was active in the Southwark Society of the Friends of the People before being introduced to the LCS by Gerrald late in 1793.

Thelwall's political activities were matched by progressive scientific interests. He composed an *Ode to Science* (1791) for the Philomathian Society, a group William Godwin later attended, and also participated in the Physical Society at Guy's Hospital. His contribution to the vitalism debate there, published as *An Essay towards a Definition of Animal Vitality* (1793), made an implicit case against the Christian notion of the soul. These scientific interests ran alongside a taste for sentimental literature. Showing remarkable energy and commitment, Thelwall managed to produce the arresting prose oddity *The Peripatetic* (1793), which blends Sterne's sentimentalism with democratic politics, while doing all he could do to stop the government suppressing debating societies around the metropolis. By early in 1794 he had transformed himself into the most brilliant speaker possessed by the LCS, despite repeated attempts by Reeves to close down his lectures at Beaufort Buildings on the Strand. The government finally intervened itself when the LCS began to co-ordinate the efforts of the radical societies into the calling of a British Convention, arresting Thelwall with the other radical leaders in May, but persisting with his trial even after Horne Tooke and Hardy were acquitted.

Thelwall emerged from prison after his own acquittal a hero and cast himself as a martyr in *Poems Written in Close Confinement* (1795), a collection published by Eaton, Ridgway and Symonds:

> WITHIN the Dungeon's noxious gloom
> The Patriot still, with dauntless breast,
> The cheerful aspect can assume –
> And smile – in conscious Virtue blest![10]

The collection also reveals how integral his sentimentalism was to his materialism and to his politics, for he represented the whole universe as bound up by physical principles of sympathy that even while in the Tower connected him to his colleagues in the LCS. Thelwall anticipated Samuel Taylor Coleridge's description of 'Philanthropy' as 'a thing of *Concretion*' in a letter of July 1794 to Robert Southey (*STC Letters*, vol. I, p. 86), but the materialism in Thelwall's version of sympathy never sat easily with Coleridge's Christianity, even while the two men were close over 1796–7. Soon after his acquittal Thelwall left the LCS for some months, but he remained a very important figure within the larger radical movement. He continued to write political pamphlets, including *The Natural and Constitutional Rights of Britons* (1795), the defence he prepared for himself, but was wisely dissuaded from giving in court, *The Rights of Nature* (1796) and *Sober Reflections* (1796), developing the political aspects of his thinking to include questions of social and economic rights. But it was as an orator that Thelwall made his most powerful contributions to radical culture. His speeches frequently preached restraint to his listeners, but he always insisted on the importance of the people acting for themselves. The idea of popular sovereignty was at the heart of his 'universal moral revolution'.[11]

Thelwall's success as a speaker at the LCS mass meeting in October 1795, which preceded an attack on the King's coach, played a major part in the government's decision to introduce the Two Acts or Convention Bills. Even so, not everyone in the movement saw Thelwall as sufficiently pressing the rights of the multitude. For some, he was too close to figures like Horne Tooke, whose evasive conduct at Thelwall's trial was pilloried in the wonderfully acerbic *John Horne Tooke Stripped Naked and Dissected, and his Political Anatomy Exposed* (1795). Addressing Horne Tooke directly, the anonymous author condemns him for failing to aid the man who 'fluttered around you for advice, your prototype, if not your disciple'.[12] Possibly written by angry elements within the LCS, the pamphlet is an expression of confidence in its ability to prosper without the aid of gentlemen like Horne Tooke. New men had come to the fore of the movement. When Hardy retired from the LCS after his trial, another shoemaker, John Ashley, took over as Secretary. John Gale Jones emerged as a formidable speaker who matched Thelwall at the mass meetings of 1795. Nowhere is the self-confidence of the movement in 1795 more apparent than in the material that issued from 'The Tree of Liberty', the shop superintended at its various addresses by Richard 'Citizen' Lee. Short satires like *The Happy Reign of George the Last* and the broadsheet *King Killing*, for instance, joined Eaton's edition of Pigott's *Dictionary* in implying the need for a revolution in the very language of politics. Lee issued his own anthologies, made up of extracts from Pigott and other republican writers, for a penny a time. When these were freely distributed at the LCS mass meetings, the government claimed it had to act and started the movement of the Convention Bills through Parliament. The government spy James Powell claimed that Lee had become popular in the movement for his efforts raising subscriptions on behalf of the imprisoned radicals in 1794. Meeting him frequently at Eaton's shop, Powell encouraged Lee to join the convivial gathering he had begun at his home in imitation of one inaugurated by Thelwall after his acquittal.[13] In the optimism of the early weeks of 1795, even William Godwin seems to have attended, once at least, despite his reservations about popular political associations.[14] Lee, like Thelwall, harboured literary ambitions: both men had expressed a desire for cultural participation by writing poetry for the periodical press, but what may make their conjunction over 1794–5 seem odd for modern readers is that Lee's poetry first appeared in *The Evangelical Magazine* and the religious emphasis continued in his political pamphlets and poetry. Other radicals had fuelled their politics with religious convictions. Hardy's Presbyterianism could take on millenarian overtones, and he had been close to Lord George Gordon, although he claimed not to have been a supporter of his 'wild schemes'.[15] Religion in his case, and that of Lydia, his wife, seems to have fed into a commitment to abolitionism and radical politics. Several significant publishers of radical material, J. S. Jordan, Benjamin Crosby and Arthur Seale, among them, also met London's eager market for sermons and religious writings of all kinds, but within the LCS this religious current did not always receive a warm welcome. The hatter Richard Hodgson, for instance, seems to have been hostile to any expression of religious sentiments with the LCS as inimical to his idea of rational enlightenment. His views were echoed by Thelwall's insistence that the enlightened spirit of the French Revolution had nothing in common with the Inner Light that drove on the English revolutionaries of 1642, a point of view that echoes through his disagreements with Coleridge on religion and poetry. Hodgson and Thelwall were certainly taking a very different line on religion from Lee. Given this potential for conflict, no wonder that religious matters were banned from LCS meetings, although men such as Lee and John Bone seem to have rebelled against the ruling as an unwarranted restriction on free speech.

Broadsheets such as Lee's *King Killing*, from which the LCS tried to dissociate itself, betray a millenarian enthusiasm that for some commentators seemed to look back to the Gordon Riots of 1780. Unsurprisingly, the LCS insisted that Lee was no longer a member when *King Killing* was debated in Parliament. Yet Lee himself was unapologetic in claiming a religious basis for his politics. A note to his poem in praise of Hardy's 'Tribute of

Civic Gratitude' made it quite clear that Lee regarded him as a specifically 'CHRISTIAN HERO': 'Let the infidel candidly investigate (if Infidelity can possibly be candid)... this illustrious Character, and then lift his audacious Front to the Heavens and tell the ALMIGHTY, that pure Christianity is inimical to the Cause of Freedom.'[16] Lee does seem to have left the Society some time in 1795 along with Bone, perhaps joining him in the short-lived London Reforming Society, but his case shows that those who disavowed the French infidelism associated with Volney and Paine's writings were not, as the modern reader might assume, necessarily those who were the most moderate in political terms. J. S. Jordan, who first published Paine's *Rights of Man*, was also the original publisher of *The Brazen Trumpet* (1798), a cheap weekly journal which regularly adopted a fiercely prophetic register, closing its sixth and final number with a ringing condemnation of 'the chief booksellers who have been too timid, or ill disposed to the cause it has taken up'. The whole prophetic idiom is very different from the emphasis on manners often found in the pages of LCS's own *Moral and Political Magazine* (1796–7).[17]

Where the idiom does often appear is in the publications associated with Thomas Spence. Like many others discussed in this chapter, Spence was not a product of the French Revolution or even of reading Paine, but of the intellectual and political awakening offered by the popular enlightenment in the English provinces. One source of his radicalism was his minister James Murray, a Calvinist who preached in support of the American colonists, but Spence was also interested in spelling reform and based his politics on the question of the redistribution of landed property. He first expounded his theories in a lecture called 'The Rights of Man' in 1775, for which he was expelled from the Newcastle Philosophical Society. After a period schoolteaching, Spence moved to London in 1788 and became an active member of the LCS early on, promoting its commitment to the diffusion of knowledge through his remarkable journal *Pig's Meat*, a heady blend of freethinking and millenarianism, and the first radical journal to bring out Lee's poetry. In *The End of Oppression* (1795), Spence even attacked Paine, for failing to realize that the distribution of land rather than monarchical government was the real source of the wrongs the LCS ought to right. *The Rights of Infants* (1797) argued for female equality, a cause treated more positively in the popular radical movement than is sometimes allowed.

Like all the writers discussed in this chapter, Spence's activities in the 1790s were overshadowed by the threat of imprisonment. He was arrested at least eight times, and imprisoned for two lengthy periods. He was picked up with Thelwall and the others for treason in May 1794. Although never brought to trial, he was effectively removed from circulation for months.

In 1801–2, he was imprisoned again, this time for seditious libel after publishing *The Restorer of Society to its Natural State*. From this period until his death in 1814, his name was increasingly linked to insurrectionary movements, one path followed by radicals forced underground after the passing of the Two Acts. For many of those mentioned in this chapter, the Two Acts marks the end of the culture of popular radicalism in the 1790s. Thelwall continued lecturing, but by the end of 1796 he had withdrawn to Wales. Arrested as the bills made their way through Parliament, Lee escaped from custody and fled to America early in 1796 (with the wife of the spy Powell). A more celebrated exile, Robert Merry, followed him later in the same year, to the disappointment of his friend Godwin. Eaton also fled to Philadelphia, but, unlike Lee and Merry, who both died in the United States, returned to Britain. His ideas, like Spence's, fed into the wave of radicalism that swept through Britain after 1815.

The LCS continued to be active until it was outlawed in 1799, but despite continuing the resistance to the Convention Bills, it was effectively ended as a broad-based political culture by their passing. Those who are apt to chastise the movement more generally for its lack of a coherent political programme perhaps underestimate the difficulties facing the LCS in terms of persecution and precedent. What is more striking is the political energy and creativity that flourished under the umbrella of the LCS in these years when it had to deal with state repression as well as the contingencies of events to forge a space for itself in the public sphere. Focusing on these radical careers and on the way they interacted and unfolded in the 1790s may help us to get away from thinking of the politics of the period in terms of pre-packaged languages of radicalism or republicanism. The rapid journey of 'Citizen' Lee from *The Evangelical Magazine* to *King Killing* in just two short years from 1793 to 1795 suggests just how far could be travelled in a short space of time by those who became enthused by the culture of popular radicalism. Yet the trajectory ended with a crash and exile in the United States, as it did for Eaton, Merry and many others. Original writing and thinking about politics is hard enough, but thinking it under the conditions of repression made it peculiarly difficult in the 1790s. The achievement, then, is all the more remarkable, not least because the culture of popular radicalism provided such an important example for the next wave of radicalism in the early years of the nineteenth century.

NOTES

I am grateful to the Leverhulme Trust for the award of a Major Research Fellowship which allowed me the time to research and write this essay.
1 See the SCI Minute Books at the National Archives, London, TS 11/961–2.

2 John Barrell, *The Spirit of Despotism: Invasions of Privacy in the 1790s* (Oxford: Oxford University Press, 2006), p. 57.

3 Nearly all of these publications are usefully collected in Michael T. Davis, ed., *London Corresponding Society, 1792–1799*, 6 vols. (London: Pickering & Chatto, 2002).

4 Thomas Hardy, *Memoir of Thomas Hardy* (London: James Ridgway, 1832), p. 100.

5 For a discussion of Reeves and the Association, see Kevin Gilmartin's essay in this volume (chapter 9).

6 Albert Goodwin, *The Friends of Liberty: The English Democratic Movement in the Age of the French Revolution* (London: Hutchinson, 1979), p. 279.

7 See Merry's *Reflexions politiques sur la nouvelle constitution qui se prepare en France, adressees à la republique* (Paris, 1792). I am grateful to Rachel Rogers for calling this pamphlet to my attention.

8 SCI Minute Books, TS 11/963/3509.

9 Charles Pigott, *A Political Dictionary: Explaining the True Meaning of Words* (London: D. I. Eaton, 1795), p. 9. In editions with the preface, it appears at pp. i–iv.

10 John Thelwall, *Poems Written in Close Confinement in the Tower and Newgate, Under a Charge of High Treason* (London: J. Ridgway, 1795), p. 9.

11 *The Tribune* (18 April 1795), pp. 155–6.

12 *John Horne Tooke Stripped Naked and Dissected, and his Political Anatomy Exposed to the Electors of Westminster* (London, 1795), p. 6.

13 See Powell's letter to his spymaster James Ford in the National Archives at PC 1/23.

14 See William Godwin, diary, Bodleian MS. Abinger e. 6, fol. 46v, entry for 17 January 1795, which records that he had tea at Powell's with a group including Lee and the recently acquitted Thelwall.

15 Hardy, *Memoir*, p. 8.

16 Richard Lee, *Songs from the Rock, to Hail the Approaching Day, Sacred to Truth, Liberty, and Peace* (London: Richard Lee, 1795), p. 111.

17 See *The Brazen Trumpet* 6 (17 March 1798), 126. For the LCS magazine, see Davis, *London Corresponding Society*, vols. III and IV.

9

KEVIN GILMARTIN

Counter-revolutionary culture

The early 1790s witnessed Britain's emergence as the leading counter-revolutionary power in an age of revolution, a position it held through the Napoleonic era and into the post-Waterloo restoration of legitimate continental regimes. The deployment of British troops against the threat of French republicanism abroad was accompanied by ideological mobilization at home, with profound consequences for literature and the arts as well as the press and public opinion. Yet scholars have not always looked closely at the way a conservative defence of the crown, the established church and the unreformed constitution shaped public expression. The fact that Romanticism has guided British literary studies in the period has itself narrowed the range of attention. The rubric for this volume, the 1790s, indicates a shift in conceptions of literary history. Yet to understand how counter-revolutionary culture has been overlooked it is worth setting out from the framework that Romanticism long provided.

In *Romantics, Rebels, and Reactionaries*, one of the few surveys to attend closely to conservatism, Marilyn Butler observed the way Romantic studies connected 'changes in the arts of the 1790s with change in politics', yielding the language of 'Romantic Rebellion' and 'Romantic Revolution'. Challenging this reductive equation of political and aesthetic upheaval, Butler instead identified the *preceding* decades (1760 to 1790) with liberal developments in the arts, notably primitivism and neo-classicism, and then argued that after 1792 there was a 'marked political reaction, towards a conscious conservatism, which in the next decade made itself felt deeply and decisively in the arts'.[1] Yet even Butler goes on to treat the 1790s primarily as a matter of reformist sentiment under pressure. It is clear that progressivist tendencies, legacies of the Protestant Reformation, and the Enlightenment, have remained deeply embedded in our assumptions about literary history, especially where the spread of print culture and literacy are concerned. Looking back on the 1790s in his *Life of Napoleon* (1828–30), William Hazlitt proposed that 'the French Revolution might be described as a remote but inevitable result of the invention of the art of printing', a claim he linked with the corrosive effect of vernacular translations of the Bible upon 'the feudal system', and the emergence of a dissident 'public sense' that was 'free from slavish awe' (*WH Works*, vol. XIII, pp. 38, 41).

As a veteran of later decades of political warfare, Hazlitt was hardly naïve about the inevitability of reform through print expression. In *A Letter to William Gifford*, he identified William Gifford, editor of the Tory *Quarterly Review*, as an instance of 'the *Government Critic*, a character nicely differing from that of a government spy – the invisible link, that connects literature with the police' (*WH Works*, vol. IX, p. 13). Once a solvent of feudalism, print culture had instead become involved in securing legitimate power from the threat of revolution, and Hazlitt would have known that Gifford was an important 'link' as well with the conservative culture of the 1790s. Before taking on the *Quarterly* in 1809, Gifford helped to inaugurate counter-revolutionary criticism as editor of the *Anti-Jacobin; or, Weekly Examiner* (1797–8). His two Juvenalian verse satires, *The Baviad* (1791) and *The Maeviad* (1795), assaulted the liberal excesses of Robert Merry, Mary Robinson and the Della Cruscans. Lord Byron joined others in judging these 'the first satires of the day'.[2] If their reputation has waned, Gifford's identification of radical politics with a literary fashion for simplicity, sensibility and coterie intimacy helped establish a critical framework for anti-Jacobinism throughout the 1790s and beyond. As Gary Dyer has argued, by overlooking Gifford modern critics have risked 'underestimating or neglecting the persistence and the intellectual rigor of monarchist, Anglican thought in this period'.[3]

In identifying Gifford as 'the oracle of Church and State' (*WH Works*, vol. IX, p. 15), Hazlitt qualified the progressivism that often guided his sense of literary history. Yet he still seemed to regard the existence of a '*Government Critic*' as a perversion of the natural course of things. The 'unmanageable claims of literature and philosophy' had startled 'the great and powerful' into mobilizing the likes of Gifford to 'restore the taste of the public to its legitimate tone' (pp. 33–4). And in linking the government critic with the government spy, Hazlitt registered a pervasive tendency to identify conservative expression with repressive state power. Certainly there was a close association between counter-revolutionary print culture and the state in the 1790s. Yet far from being inevitable, this was a matter of difficult negotiation, with compromises on both sides. To acknowledge the complex history of counter-revolutionary culture is to see the limits of any simple identification of conservatism with a repressive outer limit on free expression. The campaign against revolution and radical reform in Britain was a complex and enduring hybrid of innovation and tradition, of civic enterprise and state power, with new forms of expression brought to bear upon the desire to contain alarming innovations in speech and print.

There is a simpler way of accounting for the critical neglect of conservative culture, one as firmly lodged in Romantic studies as the image of the rebel artist. This is the notion that genius, embodied in the visionary company of Blake, Wordsworth, Coleridge, Byron, Shelley and Keats, occupied the liberal side of the question. Yet even on its own terms there are difficulties with this argument. Prose fiction arguably weighs on the conservative side of the question, and the Tory sensibilities of Walter Scott and Jane Austen have no doubt been a factor in Romanticist neglect of the novel. For poetry, the identification of genius with radicalism is also problematic. There will always be debate about precisely when Coleridge, Wordsworth and Southey shed their youthful radicalism for mature conservatism. Yet whatever the timing, their literary achievement cannot simply be identified with the radical cause. Wordsworth's *Prelude* records a profound and early inner struggle between reformist and conservative impulses. In the *Biographia Literaria* (1817) and elsewhere, Coleridge developed his influential theories of the creative imagination alongside a conservative approach to mobilizing intellectual labour as a way of securing social order.

As the acknowledged Romantic-period figure of conservative genius, Edmund Burke remains the principal exception to a neglect of conservative expression. His *Reflections on the Revolution in France* (1790) has been considered prophetic both for its warning that the Revolution would become more violent and destructive, and for the way it anticipated the recoil of British elites from an initial sympathy with events in France. With Thomas Paine's *Rights of Man* (1791, 1792), it frames the polar terms for a 'Revolution Controversy' in the 1790s. For Romantic studies, the *Reflections* offers a benchmark of the conservative temperament that has long been used to map a range of cultural developments. So for example Burke's stress on customary transmission has been found to work its way through gothic revaluations of Anglo-Saxon inheritance, and his sexualized rendering of a mob assault on Marie-Antoinette's chambers can be taken to shape the terms for patriarchal romance in the novel.

Yet while Burke did become a foundational figure for Anglo-American conservatism, his immediate impact may have been less pivotal. The *Reflections* was arguably more productive of hostile radical responses than of sympathetic conservative expression. J. G. A. Pocock reminds us that Burke 'remained a lonely and distrusted figure' through his last decade, and that counter-revolutionary activists in the 1790s 'relied less on Burke for their polemics than on William Paley, Hannah More, and other authoritarian elements lying deep in Whig and Tory tradition'.[4] Though the term 'Burkean' often names a conservative attachment to inherited tradition, the way the *Reflections* worries over how the past should condition the present suggests that Burke was wrestling with his earlier Whig and reformist commitments, rather than providing the bearings for High Church and Tory positions that came to dominate reactionary Britain. And if Burke's extravagant style made the *Reflections* a difficult model, its form as an ostensibly private letter imperfectly suited for the press betrays a certain reluctance about counter-revolutionary public expression. This rhetorical nervousness is reinforced by Burke's attack on 'the political Men of Letters' in France as a rootless 'literary cabal' committed to 'something like a regular plan for the destruction of the Christian religion' (*EB Writings*, vol. VIII, p. 160).

For Burke, a lack of attachment to available institutions and sentiments encouraged the revolutionary spirit of innovation for its own sake. 'When I hear the simplicity of contrivance aimed at and boasted of in any new political constitutions', he complained, 'I am at no loss to decide that the artificers are grossly ignorant of their trade, or totally negligent of their duty.' Against abstract natural rights, he urged a more 'practical science' of government and a respect for existing social relations:

> These metaphysic rights entering into common life, like rays of light which pierce into a dense medium, are, by the laws of nature, refracted from their straight line. Indeed in the gross and complicated mass of human passions and concerns, the primitive rights of men undergo such a variety of refractions and reflections, that it becomes absurd to talk of them as if they continued in the simplicity of their original direction. The nature of man is intricate; the objects of society are of the greatest possible complexity.
>
> (*EB Writings*, vol. VIII, pp. 111–12)

This concern for the sheer resistance of complex lived experience to speculative adjustment advanced a strand of conservative social thought that had important consequences for the later nineteenth century. Raymond Williams makes this point in *Culture and Society*, when he pairs Burke with the radical journalist William Cobbett as the conservative avatar of a response to social change that condemned new developments 'in the terms and accents of an older England'. Williams finds in Burke's insistence upon 'the necessary complexity and difficulty of human affairs' an organic principle of common inheritance that would 'by the end of the nineteenth century... be called a national "culture"'.[5]

What is often striking about the counter-revolutionary movements of the 1790s, however, is how little they worried over the organic complexity of inherited social forms. Conservatives no doubt shared a broad commitment to existing institutions and a suspicion of radical innovation. Yet far from trusting the sure ground of inheritance, many were convinced that longer eighteenth-century trends towards scepticism, infidelity and immorality had actually laid the groundwork for Jacobin subversion. Where the 'dense medium' of common life was already compromised, the point became to intervene and renovate in ways that Burke might consider rash. And given the sharp sense of crisis precipitated by the war and the threat of French invasion, there was a pragmatism about conservative enterprise, a willingness to undertake whatever needed to be done to prevent revolution.

The institutional framework for counter-revolutionary public organization and expression took shape in late 1792 with the establishment of John Reeves's Association for the Preservation of Liberty and Property against Republicans and Levellers. Announced by Reeves and his collaborators in the London press in November and December, against a backdrop of vigorous radical activism by the London Corresponding Society, the Association movement spread throughout Britain in the early months of 1793, reaching perhaps a thousand regional affiliates, all committed to the counter-revolutionary work of corresponding with other societies, issuing loyal addresses, circulating conservative literature and assisting the legal campaign against subversion. From the outset the London committee distinguished itself from party and government:

> We do, as private men, unconnected with any Party or description of persons at home, taking no concern in the struggles at this moment making abroad, but most seriously anxious to preserve the true Liberty, and unexampled prosperity we happily enjoy in this kingdom, think it expedient and necessary to form ourselves into an ASSOCIATION for the purpose of discouraging, in every way that lies in our power, the progress of such nefarious designs as are meditated by the wicked and senseless Reformers of the present time.[6]

Alongside an essential repressive aim ('the purpose of discouraging'), there is a vivid sense here of the way loyalism developed out of the longer eighteenth-century tradition of private men associating freely to advance public purposes. This kind of expansive energy has generally been identified with liberal Enlightenment developments. However, the loyalist activism of the 1790s was consistent with more disciplinary strands in the history of British public life, notably the rise of moral reform movements and prosecution societies after 1688. Where controlling enterprise had long met with resistance because it seemed inconsistent with English liberty, the new Jacobin threat offered an opportunity for its effective revival.

The loyalist Association initially extended its professions of independence from party to government. 'None of the King's Ministers knew or heard of this Association, till they saw the first advertisement in the public prints.'[7]

Reformers had their doubts about this claim, and John Reeves's career in a series of government offices was typical of counter-revolutionary civic leadership, suggesting at least informal ministerial affiliation. In any case the Pitt ministry soon took a direct interest in the movement. The Prime Minister found in Reeves's initiative 'a Spirit and Disposition to Activity which if We give it at the outset a right Direction may be improved to very important purposes'.[8] Among changes the government made to Reeves's original scheme was a more hierarchical and centralized committee structure, with less frequent public meetings. 'In this Way', Pitt explained, 'We hope to avoid the Inconvenience of much public Discussion at Numerous Meetings, and yet have the Impression and Effect of Numbers on our Side.'[9] As the Association movement developed, committee membership tended to be dominated by elites – clergymen assisted by the gentry in the countryside, and by commercial and professional men in towns.[10]

The process by which Reeves and government ministers negotiated the form of loyalist Association, so as to reinforce rather than erode central government, suggests some important post-Revolutionary developments in British civic enterprise. Directives from the London committee continued to articulate a *negative* mission with respect to radical organization. This was reinforced in the Association's pamphlet version of Justice William Ashhurst's November 1792 charge to a Middlesex grand jury, urging support for the 'coercive power of the State' in its campaign against 'seditious and unconstitutional' doctrines.[11] At the same time, the Association contributed signally to what Mark Philp has called 'vulgar conservatism', an effort to combat popular radicalism on its own terms by engaging directly in loyalist print appeals to ordinary readers. In Philp's incisive account, this kind of vernacular counter-revolutionary address violated Burke's assumption that 'the vulgar were the object of conservative thinking, not intended participants in it', and risked opening out upon democracy by including disenfranchised English subjects in a public debate about political affairs.[12]

The development of a quasi-official pamphlet and broadsheet literature of popular conservatism, subsidized by elites in order to secure the subordination of ordinary readers, was among the more striking features of counter-revolutionary culture in the 1790s. In exchange for their loyalty, the Association offered common Britons a range of native advantages to French revolutionary promises: the virtues of honest labour, cottage domesticity and innocent popular recreation; unquestioning faith in God in this world, and due reward for it in the next; equal protection under British law, and the mild authority of benevolent elites; access to charity in times of need, and freedom from the violence and disorder of French republican government. To be sure, most of this came in a relentlessly didactic literature, with titles that adequately convey a limited substance: for example, *An Antidote against French Politics*, and *To the Mistaken Part of the Community, Who Assemble in Seditious Clubs for the Purpose of Obtaining a Redress of What They Suppose Grievances*. Yet the Association catalogue did contain publications that were more engaging in their rhetorical development, and these offer a revealing glimpse of the way British elites facing the threat of revolution envisioned popular contentment.

The 'John Bull' series of broadsheet tracts, written by the Anglican clergyman William Jones and circulated by Reeves's Association, unfolded as a heartily vernacular sequence of letters, typically between John Bull and his brother Thomas Bull. They exposed the horrors of French Jacobin innovation, and recommended instead the material advantages of the British constitution. Circumstantial social detail tended to be limited by the figural dimensions of the main correspondents and their fellow countrymen, who included Parson Orthodox, Sir John Blunt and the steward David Trusty. This tightly knit allegorical world enforced a range of hierarchical relations meant to secure social obligation, and in this way the tracts prescriptively modelled the terms of their own transmission. Thus in *John Bull's Answer to His Brother Thomas's Second Letter*, John dissuades his daughter from radical aspiration with the warning that 'Industry is fortune enough for us – we help the rich, and the rich help us.'[13] Presumably, a daughter will defer to her father where a man of modest means himself defers to men of property. And in *One Penny-worth More, or, A Second Letter from Thomas Bull to His Brother John* (fig. 9.1), Thomas explains his own surprising stock of information with an account of the Parson's regular practice of taking 'us all now and then, rich and poor, to dine with him' in convivial assemblies that culminate in an instructive harangue. Here allegory interpolates allegory, as Parson Orthodox relates a tale of a flock of sheep and their good shepherd king beset by French wolves and '*Wolf-Principles*'.[14] Throughout the series, this kind of figurative tale was interspersed with didactic treatments of law, history and political economy, and with vivid reports of French atrocities.

Where subversion did menace the closely knit society of John and Thomas Bull, it entered through a cast of shadowy outsiders, and was so easily neutralized as to leave one wondering about the need for a loyalist popular literature. The rhetorical work of counter-revolution seemed reducible to bluster about native contentment. 'Does [Paine] and his brothers think that we shall be as easily gulled as the French? And that Britons, who enjoy more liberty and property, than any nation under Heaven, will change it for their foolish equality?'[15] And yet rare interludes of Jacobin incursion offer some of the series' most vividly rendered episodes, indicating how Association pamphleteers understood the rhythms of ordinary life as a potential hedge

One Penny-worth more,

O R

A ſecond Letter from *Thomas Bull* to his Brother *John*.

Dear Brother,

SO kindly as you have received my former Letter, I feel as if I ſhould be much wanting in my Duty; if I did not ſend you a few more of my Thoughts, at this critical Time. The Hand of Providence, Brother John, is very manifeſt: all my Neighbours ſee it, and talk about it. The French, they ſay, are as great an Example of *Puniſhment* as of *Perfidy*. They tried to ruin *Old England*, by ſending their Soldiers to fight againſt our Government in *America*; and in ſo doing they taught them the evil Leſſon of Fighting againſt their *own* Government at Home. They came back with *the Itch* of Rebellion upon them, and gave it to their old Comrades: while our honeſt Fellows, who took the other Side, brought Home as much Loyalty, or more, than they carried out, and have kept it ever ſince. The boundleſs Expences of that wicked Attempt, by Land and by Sea, brought the French Nation to *Beggary*: and from *Beggars* they turned into *Thieves*: like the *Gypſies*, who are either the one or the other as it ſuits their *Convenience*: and ſo they have got a *Gypſie Government*. Their famous *Fayette* is fallen, with all his Money, into the Hands of the Enemy: and may forfeit his Head if he comes Home. Such is the Fate of their noble General. The poor King, when he ſet his Hand to that vile Treaty with *America*, did not foreſee that he was ſigning his own *Death-Warrant*. The Queen, who perſuaded him (becauſe ſhe never *loved the Engliſh*) is in Priſon with him: both of them in Danger of being murdered (if they are not already) by a *Mock-Trial*, like our *King Charles*. Theſe are ſtrange Things, Brother John, and almoſt make my Hair ſtand on End! Many People ſaid, Years ago, it would come Home to them; and now their Words are fulfilled beyond all that could have been thought of: for the French are at this Time the moſt diſtracted Nation under Heaven; and, what is worſe, they are the moſt wicked. Was not their Good-Will to this Country the ſame as ever, when they picked out two famous Engliſhmen, *Thomas Pain* and the *Birmingham Doctor*, to ſit in their new Aſſembly, and aſſiſt them in the Work of teaching *John Bull* to eat *Revolution-Soup*, diſhed up with human Fleſh and French Pot-Herbs? I love Liberty *with Law*, ſuch as we have in England, as well as anybody does; but that Liberty *without Law*, which makes Men *eat* one another, can come only from the Devil, who would eat us all. I thought thoſe frightful Stories that came from France were paſt Belief: but a Gentleman of our County, who was there laſt Summer, ſays he will take his Bible-Oath before any Juſtice, that he ſaw the Blood of People they had killed run out of the Mouths of their Murderers.—When they had ſhut up three hundred and ſifty poor helpleſs Prieſts in a Pound, and where putting them to Death as one would kill Hogs for the Navy, an Engliſh Gentleman was walking along the Street, and heard a Soldier ſay, as the Muſkets were firing in that bloody Maſſacre, "*Aha! they are ſhewing the Prieſts fine Sport there.*" A Man will ſtand at his Door, and ſee his next Neighbour dragged out of his Houſe, to have his throat cut by Villains in the Street, and take no more Notice, than if the Pariſh-Officers had called upon the Man for a Poor's Rate or a Window-Tax! When an Engliſh Gentleman, ſeeing a raw Head carried along, and the Corpſe ſhamefully dragged after it, only adviſed them to bury it, they ſeized him, and cut off his Head and threw it among the Mob. This is French Liberty, my Boy. Our King (God bleſs him) is contented if a Man pulls his *Hat* off: but to theſe new Tyrants of France, he muſt pull his *Head* off; and even then they are not ſatisfied: they ſell his Houſe and Land from his Family, and put the Money into the Purſe of the *Nation*, that is of *themſelves*. What think you of an impudent Whore of Babylon, riding along the Streets on Horſeback, at the Head of a Troop, with a long Sword by her Side, and Piſtols in her Belt, like the *Goddeſs of Liberty*; and if ſhe did but point with her Finger at any Perſon going along the Street, his Head was off in a Moment. There's *Petticoat Government* for you! *John Bull*. "France and England, ſays the Birmingham Doctor, as the Repreſentative of this Kingdom) have now diſcovered the Secret that it is their *Intereſt* to be *Friends*." It may be *his* Intereſt, and it may be *their* Intereſt; but it will never be *our* Intereſt, till *Tom Bull* turns into *Tom Fool*, and Engliſhmen are changed into a Nation of Villains. It would, no Doubt, be a pleaſant Sight to ſome Folks, if we were to pull down King Charles and his Horſe at Charing-Croſs, and ſet up the Idol of Liberty (that She-Devil of the French) for Fools to dance about, and ſing *Hymns* with *Tom of Bedlam* for their *Clerk*. This would bring People together; and when they were together, they would take Heat, juſt as Horſe-Dung does, when it is laid in a Heap. This is the Uſe of your *Liberty-Trees*, Popular *Clubs*, and *Revolution-Dinners*, &c.

When we talk about *Kings* it reminds me of what happened here very lately. A Man, like a London Rider, thruſt himſelf in amongſt us at a Public Houſe. He talked at a high Rate about French Liberty, and the Tyranny we live under at Home: he laughed at the *Nonſenſe* and *Blaſphemy* of Kings having Authority from Providence: what, ſaid he, are we ſuch Fools as to believe that Kings are ſent down *booted* and *ſpurred* from the Clouds to *ride* Mankind? Some of the Company ſtared at him, and looked as if they felt the Spurs in their Sides: but, ſays I, hold a little, Mr. Londoner, you don't put that Caſe quite right. You know, we muſt all be ridden by *ſomebody*; for we cannot ride upon *ourſelves*. When a *good* Horſe carries a *Gentleman*, he is as well pleaſed as his Maſter: but ſuppoſe, Mr. Londoner, ſaid I, ſuppoſe he ſhould take it into his Head to throw his Maſter, that he might be ridden by *his Equals*! then in that Caſe, you know, Mr. Londoner, he will have a *Horſe* upon his Back inſtead of a *Man*; aye, Twenty, or a Hundred Horſes, all clambering upon his Back at once, till they break him down, and he is fit for Nothing but the Dogs. This is my Way of underſtanding *Liberty* and *Equality*. And now, go and aſk your Birmingham Doctor how much that Horſe will *better himſelf*. This is the Way they have *bettered* themſelves in France. They that will not carry a *King*, ſhall have the *Beaſts of the People* upon their Backs; and the poor Fools are pleaſed, becauſe they think it will be their Turn to ride next. Every Body can ſee how bad it would be for Horſes to carry Horſes; and it is always the ſame Thing when the People carry the People.

After this Londoner was gone, we found he was one of thoſe Fellows who are hired to go about with *Tom Pain*'s Books: but he did not think proper to produce them: if he had, we ſhould have put them into a *Pitch-Kettle*, and ſtirred them about well, and then burned the Pitch and the Books together: this being the proper End of that *black Doctrine*, which ſome Men put into others to *ſet the World on Fire*.

And now, *Brother John*, if you find I am a little better taught than you expected, I will tell you how it happened. Our Miniſter takes us all now and then, rich and poor, to dine with him. One Day after Dinner, when we had lighted our Pipes, and Neighbours were talking to one another about common Things, he gave a Rap upon the Table to call our Attention, and when he ſaw we were all ready, he began as follows:

"My dear Friends,

"Wicked People are at Work to corrupt your Minds with a frantic Affection for *unlawful Liberty*, by giving *falſe* and *nonſenſical* Notions of *civil Society*. I will therefore ſhew you, in a plain Way which you can eaſily underſtand, the Danger to which all Governments are now expoſed from the Arts of deſigning People.

"In Countries where they feed their Flocks a little differently from what we are uſed to, four Parties are concerned; the *Sheep*, the *Shepherd*, the *Dogs*, and the *Wolves*. Once upon a Time, the Wolves wanted to have the Sheep to themſelves; and thought it would be beſt if they could eat them with their own Conſent. So they ſent Meſſages to them privately, wondering how Sheep, in *theſe enlightened Times*, ſhould have no more Spirit, than to live under that Tyrant the Shepherd; and telling them how happy they would all be if *he* were out of the Way; and how they hoped ſoon to ſee all thoſe Ruffians the Shepherds, worried out of the World. But how to get at the Shepherd they did not know, becauſe of the Dogs: ſo they ſent another Meſſage to corrupt the Dogs; telling them how ſorry they were to ſee them living upon *ſtale Cruſts* and *ſour Butter-Milk*, when there would ſoon be Mutton enough for them all, if they would but come over to their Intereſt. So they got the Dogs to their Side; made the Shepherd fly for his Life; and then began to kill the Sheep: of which when the Sheep complained, they told them it was *all for their Good*; that a great *Improvement* had taken Place, which muſt coſt a great many Lives; but that all would be right ſoon. Thus the poor Sheep were in a miſerable Caſe. The Dogs, their old Guardians, were now turned traiterous and blood-thirſty: and no Juſtice could be had by complaining of one Wolf to another Wolf: ſo they were either worried to Death at Home, or ſcattered over the Mountains, in hourly Danger both from Dogs and Wolves, and with no Shepherd to protect them.

"The Wolves having ſucceeded ſo well, ſent to their Brethren in other Countries: and the *Wolf-Principles* grew ſo faſt, that the Species of Sheep were nearly extinct, and there was now a new World of Wolves; who, when there are no Sheep left, muſt fall upon the Dogs whom they uſed for their Convenience, and at laſt devour one another.

"Neighbours, continued he, you have heard and read ſo much lately, that you will want little of my Help in applying the Story to what has happened in a neighbouring Country. The Shepherd is the *King*; driven from his Throne, and in Danger of his Life from his traiterous Subjects; whoſe hearts were firſt poiſoned by the Enemies of all Religion, permitted to corrupt the People, and ſpread their atheiſtical Opinions without Controul. The Wolves are the pretended Patriots and Democrats, who have got the Nation into their own Clutches, and can kill whom they pleaſe, without Law, Judge, or Jury: there being now no Law but their own ſavage Will; and ſo the vileſt of Murderers go without Puniſhment. The *Dogs*, thoſe faithful and warlike Animals, are the French Army; once the Guardians of the King and the People; and kept for their Security againſt Thieves, Rebels, and Invaders; but now, bribed with Plunder; with no Senſe of Honour left; and carrying about War, to levy Contributions from innocent People, and ſpread their new *Liberty*, as *Mahomet* did his *Fools-Paradiſe*, by the Terrors of the Sword: and they are aſſiſted in all this by an Infatuation peculiar to this Time, and never heard of before in the World. The poor ſilly Sheep are the Bulk of the People; firſt gulled into vile Opinions, and then devoured by their unmerciful and inſatiable Fellow-Subjects. The Country of France has of late taken up a new *political Slang*, or Cant-Language, accommodated to their new Monſter of a Government, and put it into a Catechiſm for Women and Children; while the Chriſtian Catechiſm is kicked out of Doors. Hitherto they have murdered and plundered with as little Difficulty as a Gang of Wolves devour Sheep and Lambs. They have made Money of the Poſſeſſions of the Church; they have robbed their King of all his Treaſures to an immenſe Value; they have ſeized and ſold the Eſtates of their Countrymen, for not approving their Proceedings, which no Man of Senſe or Humanity can endure. But all this is not ſufficient, without plundering and taxing the Cities and Countries round about them. Where this will end, God knows! A Proſpect of their devouring one another, when their Supplies of Plunder ſhall be drained and waſted, is all that appears at preſent. Before which, infinite Miſchief may be done; and we ourſelves may ſuffer; unleſs the *Shepherd*, the *Sheep*, and the *faithful Dogs* ſhall all hold together againſt the *Wolves*."

A few ſuch Diſcourſes as this, Brother John, would ſave our Country from all the Perils of the preſent Times, and as ſoon as I learn more, you may expect to hear farther from your loving Brother,

December 12, 1792. THOMAS BULL.

Printed by Norman and Carpenter, No. 14, *Fetter-Lane*, *Fleet-Street*: Where may be had, *Thomas Bull*'s firſt Letter to his Brother *John*.

[Entered at Stationers-Hall.]

Figure 9.1 William Jones, *One Penny-worth More, or, A Second Letter from Thomas Bull to His Brother John*, London, 1792.

against subversion. In *One Penny-worth More*, Thomas Bull relates how loyal tavern conversation was interrupted by a suspicious 'London Rider', who 'thrust himself in amongst us' to talk 'at a high Rate about French Liberty, and the Tyranny we live under at Home'. A hearty round of refutation follows, with a warning that if the Jacobin outsider had dared to produce his stock of Paine's *Rights of Man*, 'we should have put them into a *Pitch-Kettle*, and stirred them about well, and then burned the Pitch and the Books together'.[16] Loyalist violence of this kind was typically threatened rather than enacted. *John Bull's Second Answer to His Brother Thomas* recalls a similar tavern episode. John shares a pipe with David Trusty until their patriotic conversation is interrupted by 'an ill looking' stranger, who 'began talking about Liberty and Equality', and winds up proposing a toast to Tom Paine. The gathered community once again refutes the interloper and pledges God and country instead, while avowing their own 'peaceable behaviour' up to the point where they may be roused against a 'common enemy'.[17] In the published catalogue of the Association, these visions of festive loyalism were supported with a host of patriotic ballads and songs.

The same rough didacticism and argument by allegory that found epistolary expression in the John Bull letters was elsewhere shaped as fictional conversation. Vertical development of the dialogue form reinforced social hierarchy, as in *A Dialogue Between Mr. T –, a Tradesman in the City, and His Porter, John W –*, and William Paley's *Equality, As Consistent with the British Constitution, In a Dialogue between a Master-Manufacturer and one of His Workmen*. Again, fictional rendering of didactic content tended not to be vividly circumstantial, nor was there a sharp sense of the threat of revolution from below. In *A Dialogue Between a Labourer and a Gentleman*, the 'stranger' who has given the labourer John a copy of Paine's *Rights of Man* is no match for the immediate authority of the gentleman. Familiar conversation simultaneously unravels Paine's alien challenge and weaves a tight fabric of linked social hierarchies: master and servant, parent and child, employer and employee, governor and governed. The reader is invited to follow John through a series of ritual concessions that lead inexorably back to contentment: 'Yes, Master,' 'No Master, to be sure not,' 'I believe you are right, Master,' 'Why that's true, Master,' 'Good day, Master; and thank you for all you have said, which has made me quite easy again.'[18] Deployed in this restrictive fashion, the dialogue form could easily degenerate into catechism, and the Association did produce an *Englishman's Political Catechism*.

Hannah More's *Village Politics. Addressed to All the Mechanics, Journeymen, and Day Labourers, in Great Britain* (1792) represents a striking exception to the way loyal conversation tended to unfold within the constraining play of social hierarchy.[19] This vividly realized conversation between the loyal blacksmith Jack Anvil and the deluded Painite mason Tom Hod was the most enduring popular loyalist pamphlet of the 1790s, appearing again in later episodes of unrest. The author shared a loyalist propensity for allegory, so there was no accident about the way character was reduced to labouring function – Anvil the blacksmith and Hod the mason. Against the supposed primitivism of Paine's levelling principles, *Village Politics* offered a defence of specialization that hewed closely to allegorical identity within the dialogue format. 'Now, Tom, only suppose this nonsensical equality was to take place', Jack complains, to the point where the entire village was reduced to raising potatoes. In a village of Spades, no one would be left at the particular tasks for which they were properly trained:

> As every other man would be equally busy in raising potatoes for *his* family, why then you see if thou wast to break thy spade, I should not be able to mend it. Neighbour Snip wou'd have no time to make us a suit of clothes, nor the clothier to weave the cloth; for all the world would be gone a digging.
>
> (*Political Writings*, vol. III, p. 4)

From here it was a short step to another piece of loyalist ideology for the poor, the argument that the tricky business of governing was best left to the governing classes. 'Every one in his own way', Jack argues, 'I am a better judge of a horse-shoe than sir John; but he has a deal better notion of state affairs than I' (p. 5). As in the John Bull series, allegory interpolates allegory. The conversation includes an embedded Burkean parable of Sir John's resistance to his wife's reckless desire to rebuild 'yonder fine old castle' (p. 4) along French lines, and a homely retelling of Livy's cautionary tale of the stomach and its rebellious members.

Village Politics is more credibly vernacular and circumstantial than the typical Association tract. At the same time, Hannah More is sophisticated about the play of language and literacy within her imagined world of plebeian conversation. The dialogue opens upon a primal scene of radical reading, as Jack confronts Tom poring over Paine's *Rights of Man*, and wonders at his apparent dejection. '*Looking on his book*', Tom explains that 'I find here that I'm very unhappy, and very miserable; which I should never have known, if I had not had the good luck to meet with this book.' Jack responds sensibly enough to this burlesque distortion of the radical challenge. 'A good sign, tho'; that you can't find out you're unhappy without looking into a book for it' (*Political Writings*, vol. VIII, p. 2). The dramatic situation accords with a loyalist pressure away from political reading and speculation, and towards the unmediated material comforts of life under the British constitution. More's sympathy for an argument from palpable experience is evident too in Jack's claim that the French Jacobin 'gibberish' of '*civism*, and *incivism*, and *equalization*' is only a way of 'making ourselves poor when we are getting rich' (p. 9). Yet Jack's initial discovery of a 'good sign' in the book as a source of discontent registers a more complex countervailing strategy. With its network of figural characters and embedded allegories, *Village Politics* is a densely mediated exercise in counter-revolutionary persuasion, incorporating everything from a charity-school tale and the local sayings of Sir John to a seventeenth-century work of devotion, Richard Allestree's *Whole Duty of Man*. And for the Evangelical author, scripture remained the essential discursive authority. 'Your book tells you that we need obey no government but that of the people', Jack complains, 'but *mine* tells me, "Let every one be subject to the higher powers, for all power is of God"'' (p. 6). In the end *Village Politics* is structured as much by this battle of the books as by a reductive contest between English roast beef and French revolutionary jargon.

When Hannah More moved on from *Village Politics* to develop her own Cheap Repository tracts (1795–8), she integrated a monthly series of subsidized tales, ballads and devotional works with a Sunday school project already underway in the parishes around her home at Cowslip Green in Somerset. And she remained committed to a mediated form of vulgar conservative expression. The ideological complexity, and even ambiguity, of her work was reinforced by an intense Evangelical Anglicanism, since this joined her with a tradition of pious enterprise that had developed in the decades before the French Revolution, under the leadership of William Wilberforce and others. Like other moral reformers, she criticized the excesses of the rich as well as the vices of the poor, and risked charges of an insufficient respect for established authority. Alert to the pitfalls of her own enterprise, More filled her tracts with assurances that (for example) the newly acquired reading habits of the lower orders would not distract them from working for their superiors. At the same time, she benefited from a shift in the climate of opinion after 1789, as elites who might otherwise have been suspicious of Puritan meddling found reason to support morally improving initiatives that promised a more subordinate populace. The success of the Cheap Repository was impressive, with More reporting a million tracts circulated within the first year, a figure clearly driven more by elite subsidy than by demand from ordinary readers.

By infusing counter-revolutionary culture with Evangelical fervour, More helped shift the terms of a conservative intervention in the life of ordinary British subjects, and arguably put manners and morals ahead of constitutional matters. In a challenge to narrowly political interpretations of the Cheap Repository, Susan Pedersen has argued that these tracts were less concerned with the new political threat of Tom Paine than with the long-standing moral irregularities of popular culture, as evinced in the chapbook literature of the eighteenth century.[20] Certainly More emulated this available popular literature in the format and content of her Cheap Repository tracts. Titles such as *The History of Tom White the Postilion* and *Black Giles the Poacher* extended the familiar promise of roguish misadventure, but delivered instead cautionary tales about the hazards of crime, gambling, drunkenness, brawling, superstition and impiety. And particularly where she extended her narrative designs out through multi-part series – as in *The Way to Plenty; or, The Second Part of Tom White* (fig. 9.2) – More embellished core didactic material with reflexive treatments of her own activity as an enterprising moral reformer. This reflexivity is epitomized where characters within the Cheap Repository tracts read and recommend Cheap Repository tracts. In this sense, the real subject of More's work became a network of mutually reinforcing relationships among generous elites, enterprising middling sorts and the contented poor. Taken together, her tracts offer one of the period's most comprehensive and detailed literary representations of social reform, envisioning the transformation of everything from labour and recreation to domestic habits, learning and communal piety.

If Hannah More's case for popular subordination was distinctly Evangelical, its moral tenor was consistent with wider trends. Robert Hole has suggested that by the end of 1793 the debate triggered by the French Revolution 'switched from predominantly political, constitutional, philosophical arguments to predominantly social ones of control and social cohesion, of morality, individual belief and restraint'.[21] Such a shift was not of course absolute. In the earliest debate over events in France, anxieties about the constitutional position of the church involved moral and spiritual concerns. And even with a shift away from constitutional issues later in the decade, conservative argument remained attentive to matters of government and social hierarchy. John Bowles, a member of Reeves's original London committee and a fierce Association pamphleteer, brought together both strands of counter-revolutionary argument in 1800 in his *Reflections on the Political and Moral State of Society at the Close of the Eighteenth Century*. According to Bowles there could be no security for Britain until atheist and republican principles were rooted out at home and abroad. To the ancient threat of luxury, the late eighteenth century had added the 'two systems of Modern Infidelity and Modern Philosophy' that were 'corrupting the heart of Europe, and thence diffusing their poison to every part of the civilized world'. Where vulgar conservative pamphleteering sometimes seemed to discount the Jacobin threat, Bowles escalated it to harrowing proportions. 'The cultivation of their talents, the extent of their knowledge, their advancements

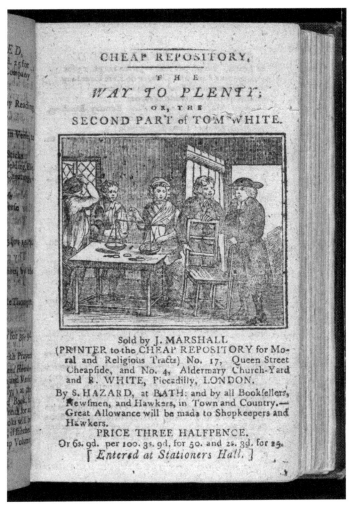

Figure 9.2 Title page to Hannah More, *The Way to Plenty; or, The Second Part of Tom White*, London and Bath, 1796.

in science, only enable them the better to pursue their projects of destruction, more effectually to attack Religion, Government, and Social Order, and to establish more firmly their horrid sway of impiety and vice.' Bowles's language here indicates just how fully the threat of revolution was felt to involve intellectual and moral concerns. Where subversion relied on 'cultivation' and 'science', the counter-revolution could not risk being narrowly political. 'In a great Moral contest – in a struggle involving the existence of all the Religious and political Establishments of the World, where can any adequate defence be found, but in the mass of Religion and Virtue still remaining in Society?'[22]

Bowles became such a fierce campaigner against vice and obscenity that he wound up alienating many of his allies. Yet he was hardly singular in his belief that manners had become a key terrain in the struggle against political subversion. Indeed, the tendency for conservative activists to make their case for social cohesion in the language of cultivation, literature and knowledge can be considered a distinctive anti-Jacobin contribution to the emerging nineteenth-century idiom of national culture. Interestingly, conservatives drew this insight into the importance of national culture as much from the terms of a radical threat as from the nature of existing 'Establishments'. *The Spirit of Anti-Jacobinism for 1802* offered the following comprehensive definition of its enemy:

> JACOBINISM ... is not merely a political, but an anti-social monster, which, in pursuit of its prey, alternately employs fraud and force. It first seduces by its arts, then subdues by its arms. For the accomplishment of its object it leaves no means unemployed which the deep malevolence of its native sagacity can devise. It pervades every department of literature and insinuates itself into every branch of science. Corruption is its food, profligacy its recreation, and demolition the motive of its actions, and the business of its life.[23]

The annual volume in which this harrowing passage appeared was brought out by the publishers of the monthly *Anti-Jacobin Review*, founded in 1798. In both these publications, and in their immediate predecessor, the weekly *Anti-Jacobin; or, Weekly Examiner* of 1797 and 1798, counter-revolutionary culture struggled to combat the monstrous threat of revolution with adequately comprehensive and resourceful print vehicles. If pamphlet warfare shaped the initial debate over the French Revolution, the decade closed with a fuller conservative development of the periodical review as an instrument of literary expression and critical surveillance.

The first *Anti-Jacobin* was a raucous weekly miscellany, distinguished by its slashing critical manner and by the satirical poetry of George Canning, John Hookham Frere, George Ellis and William Gifford. Its coterie sensibilities may seem too idiosyncratic to have inaugurated a sustained conservative periodical tradition. In this sense the earlier and more plodding monthly *British Critic*, launched in 1793 by two Anglican clergymen, was perhaps more typical of later eighteenth-century conservative reviewing practices. Yet both periodicals shared one crucial feature, a negative critical orientation towards other liberal or radical periodicals. The *British Critic* was established (with ministerial support) as a way of countering the likes of the dissenting *Analytical Review*, while the *Anti-Jacobin* offered Gifford's savage weekly editorial commentary on 'the Jacobin Daily Papers of the Metropolis'.[24] And it was this contrarian mission that the monthly *Anti-Jacobin Review* looked to in 1798 when it invoked the earlier weekly *Anti-Jacobin* as a model for its own campaign 'to counteract the pernicious effects' of the monthly reviews.[25] The treason trials of 1794 and the subsequent 'gagging acts' did much to suppress radical organization and relieve acute fears of political insurrection from below. Counter-revolutionary activists could therefore afford to shift their policing energies from Jacobin clubs and debating societies to the wider arena of print culture. Conservative periodical reviewing became a form of surveillance, a way to manage print expression at its crucial point of transmission, the critical review itself. In this sense, counter-revolutionary periodical reviews became (like More's Cheap Repository tracts) surprisingly reflexive forms, notably in 'The Reviewers Reviewed' section of the *Anti-Jacobin Review*. This critical reflexivity, and the sense of canny surveillance it involved, was a striking legacy of the counter-revolutionary reviewing of the 1790s. Major nineteenth-century conservative periodicals such as the *Quarterly Review* and *Blackwood's Edinburgh Magazine* can seem remote from the first wave of anti-Jacobinism. Yet they were established with a familiar sense of resentment about the supposed dominance of liberal or radical periodical reviewing, and a similar desire to make criticism a synoptic form of cultural surveillance.

NOTES

This chapter draws on arguments developed more fully in my book, *Writing Against Revolution: Literary Conservatism in Britain, 1790–1832* (Cambridge: Cambridge University Press, 2007).

1 Marilyn Butler, *Romantics, Rebels, and Reactionaries: English Literature and Its Background, 1760–1830* (Oxford: Oxford University Press, 1981), pp. 4, 15.

2 *Lord Byron: Selected Poems*, ed. Susan J. Wolfson and Peter J. Manning (Harmondsworth: Penguin Books, 1996), p. 37 n. 4.

3 Gary Dyer, *British Satire and the Politics of Style, 1789–1832* (Cambridge: Cambridge University Press, 1997), p. 47.

4 J. G. A. Pocock, Introduction to Edmund Burke, *Reflections on the Revolution in France*, ed. Pocock (Indianapolis, IN: Hackett, 1987), p. xl.

5 Raymond Williams, *Culture and Society, 1780–1950* (New York: Columbia University Press, 1983), pp. 3, 7, 11.

6 Association for the Preservation of Liberty and Property against Republicans and Levellers, *Association Papers* (London, 1793), Part I: *Proceedings of the Association*, Number 1, p. 5.

7 Preface, *ibid.*, p. iv.

8 Quoted in Michael Duffy, 'William Pitt and the Origins of the Loyalist Association Movement of 1792', *Historical Journal* 39 (1996), 943–62; 953. I draw

here on Duffy's careful account of the government's role in the development of the loyalist Association movement.

9 *Ibid.*, p. 957.

10 Austin Mitchell, 'The Association Movement of 1792–3', *Historical Journal* 4 (1961), 64–5.

11 *Mr Justice Ashhurst's Charge to the Grand Jury for the County of Middlesex*, in Gregory Claeys, ed., *Political Writings of the 1790s*, 8 vols. (London: Pickering and Chatto, 1995), vol. VII, pp. 215–18.

12 Mark Philp, 'Vulgar Conservatism, 1792–3', *English Historical Review* 110 (1995), 44–5.

13 *John Bull's Answer to His Brother Thomas's Second Letter* (1792). BL 648.c.26. (25).

14 *One Penny-worth More, or, A Second Letter from Thomas Bull to His Brother John* (London: Norman and Carpenter, 1792).

15 *John Bull's Second Answer to His Brother Thomas*, in Association for the Preservation of Liberty and Property Against Republicans and Levellers, *Association Papers* (London, 1793), Part II, *A Collection of Tracts*, number 2, pp. 6–7.

16 *One Penny-worth More.*

17 *John Bull's Second Answer to His Brother Thomas* (1792), *Association Papers*, Part II, number 2, pp. 7, 9.

18 *Association Papers*, Part II, number 3, pp. 8–12.

19 See Philp, 'Vulgar Conservatism', pp. 60–1.

20 Susan Pedersen, 'Hannah More Meets Simple Simon: Tracts, Chapbooks, and Popular Culture in Late Eighteenth-Century England', *Journal of British Studies* 25 (1986), 84–113.

21 Robert Hole, *Pulpits, Politics and Public Order in England, 1760–1832* (Cambridge: Cambridge University Press, 1989), p. 102.

22 John Bowles, *Reflections on the Political and Moral State of Society, at the Close of the Eighteenth Century* (London: F. & C. Rivington, 1800), pp. 123, 128, 149–50.

23 *The Spirit of Anti-Jacobinism for 1802* (London, 1802), p. iv.

24 *The Anti-Jacobin; or, Weekly Examiner* 27 (May 14 1798), 210.

25 *Anti-Jacobin Review and Magazine* 1 (1798), 3.

10

GINA LURIA WALKER

Women's voices

After the fall of the Bastille in July 1789, British women took to their pens. They were already writing novels, lyric poetry, conduct books – genres dominated by women and the ones to which they had been historically relegated. Now urgent political concerns surfaced in their domestic tales. Women tried their hands at historical writing, traditionally a male preserve, and experimented with a variety of unladylike genres: proto-journalism, polemic and life-writing in the form of memoirs. They all wrote letters which they deployed for purposes beyond personal communication. As a result, through the 1790s a 'women's war' took shape in print in which their reactions to momentous events across the English Channel kept pace with those of their male contemporaries.

Like men, women expressed a range of complex positions on the religious and political issues of the day. But a curious thing happened: in joining the debate, women writers found themselves and what they wrote becoming enmeshed in the French Revolution quarrel. Writing about politics, they risked being viewed as suspect agents of a cross-Channel movement to radicalize Britain. In the extended crisis during the 1790s, women's intrusion into the male republic of letters signalled momentous changes in gender dynamics. The ancient question of the nature of woman was now debated against the backdrop of impending reforms in education, and the possibility of reform of laws concerning women. There was no more explosive topic for women to write about than the 'woman question' itself. The Revolution debate became even more contentious as it incorporated competing views on women's nature, roles and education.

The most complex aspect of the 'women's war' was the moral sphere of reputation. Bluestocking women had earlier ventured beyond the circum-scribed private modes of writing sanctioned for women. Even such elite women were occasionally judged guilty of unladylike intrusion into the republic of letters that suggested a lack of decorum which itself hinted at sexual impropriety. In reacting to the French Revolution debate, women now seemed to infringe on the territory between the genteel domestic sphere in which they were supposed to dwell and the robust public sphere reserved for men. This raised alarms that female intellectuals might perceive themselves as equals in the fraught climate of opinion. The idea of the equality of the sexes was already in circulation since the seventeenth century, when the Catholic-turned-Protestant Huguenot François Poullain de la Barre, strongly influenced by the philosophical principle of Descartes, *cogito ergo sum* ('I think, therefore I am'), had matter-of-factly argued that the 'mind has no sex.' In the Revolution debate, the idea of sexual equality posed a particular danger. What appeared on the face of it to be a simple matter of asking men to be generous and include women in the benefits of natural rights, grant them the potential of intellectual equity and therefore the right to comparable education, was quickly recognized as a subversive political demand that would change the balance of power between women and men. The idea of gender equality was itself the subject of heated conversation in learned circles throughout Europe, especially in France. The French Revolution debate accelerated the impact of an idea whose time was at hand.

British women read reports in periodicals and pamphlets of the exciting, frightening roles that French women played as the Revolution unfolded. In the October Days of 1789, Parisian women mobilized to make the successful march on Versailles to demand that the King and Queen return to Paris with them. Women's political clubs quickly assumed heady power; in 1793 the Society of Revolutionary Republican Women was formed, 'the first political interest group for common women known in western history'.[1] Some women made radical proposals for transforming women's roles in every sector of French life. For example, Marie Madeleine Jodin's *Vues Législatives pour les Femmes* (*Legislative Views for Women*) (1790), addressed to the French National Assembly, opened with the assertion, 'et nous, aussi, nous sommes citoyennes' ('we are citizens, too') and sounded the call for women to demand republican rights.

Paralleling such activity, Olympe de Gouges's stirring *Declaration of the Rights of Woman* (1791), and her trial and execution in November 1793, thrilled, horrified and threatened to infect British female contemporaries. The execution of Girondist Manon Roland in the same month as de Gouges and posthumous publication of Roland's memoirs, *An Appeal to Impartial Posterity*, in English translation in 1795, provided another model of female civil activism to existing ones, and displayed the powerful political implications of life-writing. Unlike French women, British women did not generally marshal their concerns into collective action, and yet their involvement in the debate was nervously seen as a potentially cumulative effort. British women reacted individually, but their separate responses produced a climate of hostility among many male and female commentators. Establishment British men feared that women writers sought to be accepted as equal *citoyennes* in the sphere of diverse opinions. Personal attacks in print culture were the order of the day. The gloves were off towards transgressive British women as they were for disruptive men, like Richard Price, Thomas Paine and William Godwin.

The storming of the Bastille on 14 July 1789 produced Rational Dissenter Richard Price's expressions of jubilation at its occurrence, and famously prompted Edmund Burke to denounce both the principles of the French Revolution and their results, curiously, in part, through the prism of gender. Burke mourned Marie Antoinette as the tragic symbol of bygone feudal chivalry. Mary Wollstonecraft weighed in almost immediately with her *Vindication of the Rights of Men* (1790), which defended Price and pointedly rejected Burke's arguments. Catharine Macaulay responded to Burke as well, in equally adamant tones and opposing terms. Macaulay was a self-trained, self-proclaimed independent commentator on the vicissitudes of history through the lens of the British past, particularly the regicide of Charles I and the 'rediscovery of the idea of liberty'[2] in the so-called 'Glorious' Revolution that followed in 1688. In her *Observations on the Reflections of the Rt. Honourable Edmund Burke* (1790), Macaulay used her republican principles as an analytic tool to expose Burke's polemic as emotional, sentimental and pessimistic, with no appreciation of the heart of the new republic, 'the will of the people'. Macaulay's sober, even-handed reaction was one of the many responses to Burke's incendiary publication, and by his own admission, one that he took seriously.

The independently minded Macaulay in her last and proto-feminist work, *Letters on Education* (1790), applied the principle of liberty to gender issues, setting in play vexed questions about sex and power, perhaps in response to the scurrilous things said about her when she married a much younger man and gave herself a magnificent party for her forty-sixth birthday. Using a variation on the Socratic dialogue between teacher and student, both female in the *Letters*, Macaulay linked republican ideals with the inadequacies of female education and argued for the beneficial promise that the same moral and intellectual training for girls and boys held for future republican citizens of both sexes. She insisted, as Wollstonecraft and Mary Hays did later, that lack of a solid education rendered women incapable of sound judgements, powerless, dependent on and hostile to men, manipulative and disruptive. 'By the intrigues of women, and their rage for personal power and importance, the whole world has been filled with violence and injury' (Macaulay, *Letters*, p. 213). Macaulay devoted Letter XXIV to the pivotal question of how to educate girls and 'give such an idea of chastity, as shall arm their reason and their sentiments on the side of this useful virtue' (p. 218). The female teacher-narrator determined to 'breed my pupils up to act a rational part in the world, and not to fill up a niche in the seraglio of a sultan'. Thus the need to train girls to use their reason:

> I shall inform them of the great utility of chastity and continence; that the one preserves the body in health and vigor, and the other, the purity and independence of the mind, without which it is impossible to possess virtue or happiness. I shall intimate, that the great difference now beheld in the external consequences which follow the deviations from chastity in the two sexes, did in all probability arise from women having been considered as the mere property of men; and, on this account had no right to dispose of their own persons.
>
> (p. 220)

Macaulay traced the gendered definition of chastity to the notion that women are property. Like education, Macaulay insisted, 'the principles of true religion and morality' (p. 220) must function equally as guides for both sexes. To assign chastity exclusively to women was to enslave them. Macaulay's groundbreaking analysis proclaimed morality gender-neutral and therefore universal.[3] Macaulay championed gender equality predicated on the same education for girls as for boys. 'There is but one rule of right for the conduct of all rational beings; consequently that true virtue in one sex must be equally so in the other' (p. 201).

Macaulay criticized the corollary assumption that the loss of chastity is fatal to a woman's reputation. In Letter XXIII, *Coquettry* (*sic*), she argued, 'The first fault against chastity in woman has a radical power to deprave the character. But no such frail beings come out of the hands of Nature. The human mind is built of nobler materials than to be so easily corrupted' (Macaulay, *Letters*, p. 212). The particular errors imputed to Eve and her daughters were not innate to God's creation but rather imposed by man. Chastity was not gender-specific.

Mary Wollstonecraft was galvanized by Macaulay's radical principles. In the *Vindication of the Rights of Woman* (1792) Wollstonecraft declared that chastity was not a sexual virtue, and that the fall from grace, the rejection from society, was too harsh a penalty for female infractions. In chapter 8 Wollstonecraft argued, '[The] regard for reputation [arises from] the grand source of female depravity, the impossibility of regaining respectability by a return to virtue, though men preserve theirs during the indulgence of vice' (*MW Works*, vol. v, p. 203).

Later, Jane Austen commented on the disparities in social sanctions on male and female indiscretions with reference to the consequences of the adultery committed by Maria Bertram Rushton and Henry Crawford in

Mansfield Park: 'That punishment, the public punishment of disgrace, should in a just measure attend *his* share of the offence is, we know, not one of the barriers which society gives to virtue. In this world, the penalty is less equal than could be wished.'[4]

Another area of intense debate was the civil status of dissenters, and this provided Anna Laetitia Barbauld, the celebrated poet and commentator, an opportunity to express her views. In 1790 Barbauld published *An Address to the Opposers of the Repeal of the Corporation and Test Acts*, in which she rejected 'toleration' as no longer necessary; 'What you call toleration, we call the exercise of a natural and unalienable right.'[5] Barbauld made the connection between religious and political freedom, moral and just public action:

> England, nursed at the breast of liberty, and breathing the purest spirit of enlightened philosophy, views a sister nation with affected scorn and real jealousy . . . Let public reformation prepare the way for private. May the abolition of domestic tyranny introduce the modest train of household virtues, and purer incense be burned upon the hallowed altar of conjugal fidelity . . . May you never lose sight of the great principle you have held forth, the natural equality of men.[6]

Barbauld never developed further the gendered implication of her metaphor, but she implicitly posed an obvious question, what of the natural equality of women? The inclusion of 'domestic tyranny' in Barbauld's visionary invocation signalled her acknowledgement that in addition to the national and theological demands for reform that were part of the Revolution debate she was well aware that there were strong concerns on the part of feminists.

Barbauld did not parse 'the natural equality of men' for its relevance to women; that work was done by Mary Hays, Rational Dissenter, religious controversialist, experimental novelist and feminist biographer. Hays discerned that the rights of men could and must be applied to women. She represented the extreme left among the women at war, a disturbing presence, sometimes shrill, who insisted on being heard in the republic of letters. Yet more than any other among her female contemporaries, her voice joined the issues of religious and political dissent to concerns of gender. Hays discerned the pro-woman sympathies among her male associates; in print she was one of the late Enlightenment thinkers to explore the possibility that Rational Dissent, to date solidly male, had the potential to become something more inclusive and therefore more radical, that its theological inquiries gestured towards a new kind of human equality, feminism.

In her Wollstonecraftian *Letters and Essays, Moral, and Miscellaneous* (1793), Hays included a piece written during the terrible days of the Terror in post-revolutionary France. In 'Letter II: Thoughts on Civil Liberty', Hays exposed the social menace as women reacted to the Revolution debate:

> As women have no claims to expect either pension or place, they are less in the vortex of influence; they are also more unsophisticated by education, having neither system, test, or [sic] subscription imposed upon them; and some subjects require only to be examined with an impartial and unprejudiced eye, to ensure conviction... The emancipated mind is impatient of imposition, nor can it, in a retrogade [sic] course, unlearn what it has learned, or unknow what it has known.[7]

Here, then, was a clear and present danger for conventional society. According to Hays, untutored women could look with great clarity at the political scene and make their own judgements, irrespective of the impediments that divided men – loyalty oaths, party ties, or others' persuasions – for what partisan man would judge it necessary to convince a woman of the need to support his opinions in parliamentary voting, except perhaps for elite women who made a difference in high-wire electoral politics? Hays's phrase, 'the emancipated mind', suggests that every woman who put pen to paper and contributed to the Revolution debate believed she possessed a legitimate opinion and the right to voice it. Hays alluded to Rational Dissenter Joseph Priestley's conviction that in the divinely appointed progress of human understanding, knowledge would spread almost without the intention of readers, students and the people generally to include the ineluctable, irresistible expansion of women's knowledge. The very dissonance of the choir of female voices continued to demonstrate that they were present, if not absolutely united by their shared gender, yet still observing the female condition in the larger conflicts, reflecting and commenting.

Reaction to *Letters and Essays* among male reviewers was swift. The gentleman who wrote for the conservative periodical *The English Review* described Hays, more in anger than sorrow, as 'the *baldest* disciple of Mrs Wollstonecraft'. He continued, 'Miss Mary Hays conceives but her conceptions are an indigested heap and the whole of this paper is an abortion.' 'Female philosophers', he advised, 'while pretending to superior powers carry with them (such is the goodness of providence) a mental imbecility which *damns* them to fame.'[8]

Conservative responses to Hays's publications grew more vituperative through the decade. They announced a new campaign of gender warfare in opposition to the proposals of gender radicals, in which sex, politics and the potential for revolution that might extend to domestic life collided with even greater consequences. The British Establishment view was that the liberty women presumed when they aired their views in public threatened to become almost as noxious as sexual activity by unmarried women. Conservative Reverend Richard Polwhele expressed this fear in its most hysterical terms when in 1798 he proposed a new category of gender identity for the 'unsex'd females', 'a female band despising NATURE'S law'.[9]

Chastity persisted as the great moral directional for all women, no matter how learned or intellectual or of which political or religious persuasion. Women's published reflections on the subject had already begun to undermine the reflexive Christian habit of laying all the blame for seduction on the weak nature of 'woman' as a daughter of Eve. The controversy over the political implications of chastity announced by Macaulay was extended by Amelia Alderson (later Opie), the daughter of a respected physician, herself attractive, lively, well read, reared and active within the sophisticated Norwich Unitarian community centred on the Octagon Church. The Norwich circle greeted the French Revolution enthusiastically. In her first novel, *The Dangers of Coquetry* (1790), Alderson dramatized the effects of social training on a talented young woman who was transformed into a much admired flirt and, in the way the Anglican Macaulay predicted, was ultimately betrayed by the false values and irresponsible behaviour she acquired.[10] Alderson later published a second novel, *The Father and Daughter* (1801), in which she rejected the loss of chastity as the ultimate determinant in the life of a woman. Agnes Fitzhenry, the heroine, succumbs to the temptations of the 'libertine' Clifford: he is called to duty with his regiment and soon after, Agnes discovers that 'she should in all probability be a mother before she became a wife'. She rolls 'herself on the floor' to induce a miscarriage but without success. In time, she gives birth to a healthy son and attempts to redeem herself. Agnes's closest female friend refutes polite society's opinion that the unchaste woman must be a social outcast: 'I know many instances ... of women restored by perseverance in a life of expiatory amendment ... Keeping her eye steadily fixed on the end she has in view, [the fallen but repentant woman] will [not] seek the smiles of the world, till, instead of receiving them as a favour, she can demand them as a right.'[11] Like Wollstonecraft, Alderson built on Macaulay's foundational hypothesis: chastity was not innately gendered female, it was constructed so by historical misogyny. Like Wollstonecraft, Alderson insisted that women have the same human right as men to be allowed and forgiven sexual transgression and incorporated again in God's grace and therefore society's.

Helen Maria Williams witnessed the Revolution. In *Julia, a Novel* (1790) and *Letters Written in France in the Summer of 1790* (1790), Williams offered a new brand of female dissident proto-journalism using a range of genres to communicate the complexity of issues and early events of the Revolution. Charlotte Smith, radical, published *Desmond: A Novel* (1792), in which she responded in opposition to Burke's *Reflections* and in support of Helen Maria Williams's pro-Revolution *Letters*. The poet William Cowper later suggested that Smith may have been in the pay of the radicals when she wrote *Desmond*.[12]

When Louis XVI was executed in January 1793, followed by the execution of Marie Antoinette and the declaration of war between Britain and France, patriotism was closely linked to gender conformity. Women writers brought their battles back to the domestic realm, where they continued the critique of gender prejudice. That year Mary Ann Hanway published a novel, *Ellinor; or, The World as It Is* (1793), in which she responded to the new drive for autonomy among British women writers. Despite her Anglicanism and conservative politics, Hanway endorsed the view that women are ill equipped by their mediocre early education to fulfil themselves as God intended. 'Did we make greater exertions, and call into action those powers entrusted to us by the Creator of the Universe, we should find that he has distributed his gifts nearly equal between the sexes.' Hanway went so far as to assert that 'There are very few arts or sciences that women are not capable of acquiring, were they educated with the same advantages as men',[13] a position that only Mary Hays in *Appeal to the Men of Great Britain in Behalf of Women* (1798), published anonymously, also advanced.

By 1795 Prime Minister William Pitt's 'cold war' against political radicals and their publications had intensified. Invasion fears and near invasion by the French off the coast of Ireland created a heightened climate of fear and suspicion. Women writers began focusing more on issues of education and less on explicitly political discourse. They recognized the expedience of genre, as an outward expression of gender conformity, and published their views in fictional epistolary exchanges that dealt with women's public roles and the implications of these in their sexual dilemmas. Maria Edgeworth, daughter of Irish inventor and educationist Richard Edgeworth, drew on a distressing experience from her own idiosyncratic upbringing in *Letters for Literary Ladies* (1795). In this, her first publication, two gentlemen exchange letters: they are modelled on Richard Edgeworth and his great friend, Thomas Day, novelist and adherent of Rousseau's pronouncements in *Emile* (1762) that women are meant to be the passive foils and comfort of men. The first gentleman extends his congratulations to the second on the birth of his daughter but expresses his concern that the Richard Edgeworth character is 'a champion for the rights of woman and insist[ed] on the equality of the sexes' which might translate into educational equity for girls. He cautions the new father against fanciful enthusiasms that could turn his offspring into a prodigy with aspirations for prominence and power beyond what is appropriate for her sex. The father rejects his friend's description of himself – he also denies that

> knowledge must be hurtful to the [female] sex, because it will be the means of their acquiring power. It seems to me impossible that women can acquire the species of direct power which you dread: the manners of society must totally change before women can mingle with men in the busy and public scenes of life. They must become Amazons before they can effect this change; they must cease to be women before they can desire it.[14]

Rather, he insists, 'Women have not the privilege of choice as we have; but they have the power to determine.'[15] Maria Edgeworth argued for women's right to education on the basis of their equal intellectual potential and their aspirations to express views in the republic of letters. The piece concludes with the father's assertion, 'It is absolutely out of our power to drive the fair sex back to their former state of darkness; – the art of printing has totally changed their situation; their eyes are opened, – the classic page is unrolled, they *will* read.'[16]

The possibility of women's sexual, as well as intellectual, freedom was proposed by Eliza Fenwick, wife of Godwin's associate John Fenwick and friend to Wollstonecraft and Hays, who extended the reach of female autonomy in her novel *Secresy; or, The Ruin on the Rock* (1795). Fenwick contemplated the effects of 'marriage' without parental approval or religious rites. Using the device of conversation between two female friends, Fenwick tells the story of an isolated young woman who proposes a consensual 'marriage' to her illicit lover that is sealed only by sexual intercourse. She becomes pregnant, gives birth to a stillborn child, and dies. Her friend provides a running commentary on characters and events that is political critique, more elevated than gossip. She meditates on a woman's education, in the Lockean sense of the full experience of a life, explicitly connected to a woman's ability to navigate the shoals of her sexuality:

> With such an education as [your guardian] has given you, unless you had been a mere block without ideas, it was impossible you should not become a romantic enthusiast... I well know, my friend, that you did not mean to separate duty and pleasure. Motives the most chaste and holy guided you. No forms or ceremonies could add an atom to your purity, or make your's [sic] in the sight of heaven more a marriage.[17]

In 1796 Mary Hays published *Memoirs of Emma Courtney*, a fiction based on her correspondence with Godwin and William Frend, Unitarian mathematician and the object of her real-life passion. Through letters, Hays tells a dramatic story in the context of a blazing critique of political, economic and gender realities. She turns the tables in pursuit of love: her heroine is the aggressor while the hero flees and withholds sex and romance. Hays proposes a revised balance of power in heterosexual relations by exposing a real woman's meditations on sex and aggression. In the most notorious statement in the book, Hays's apostasy as a respectable woman is mischievously broadcast as she blurts out Frend's name as a homophone: '*My friend*,' Emma cries, '*I would give myself to you* – the gift is not worthless.'[18] Hays's novel was greeted with invective from readers of both sexes and all persuasions.

Emma Courtney marked the halfway point of the women's war: what followed for the women debaters was worse than what came before. In the year after Hays's novel was published and widely read, Wollstonecraft died of the after-effects of childbirth, Pitt's campaign against radicals intensified and so did the differences of opinion between women contributors to the Revolution debate, but not on the great questions of sex, sexuality and intellectual competence. Ironically, as women came under new pressure to choose sides, the consensus between them on women's issues grew clearer.

Talented, ambitious and energetic, Hannah More was a figure of authority and controversy throughout her life.[19] More's published works revealed her ambivalence about women's public presence. She anonymously published *Essays on Various Subjects, Principally Designed for Young Ladies* (1777), probably triggered by republican Catharine Macaulay's ostentatious celebration of her forty-sixth birthday. More quoted the Athenian general Pericles that woman's 'greatest commendation [is] not to be talked of one way or the other'.[20] In 1799 More published her influential *Strictures on the Modern System of Female Education*, which went into a seventh edition within seven months. More argued against the radical implications of the feminism of Macaulay, Wollstonecraft and Hays. Yet she shared with them more assumptions than she conceded, as astute readers recognized. Mary Berry, a self-educated minor bluestocking, bitter about her lack of formal training, wrote to a friend after reading *Strictures* that she found it 'amazing, or rather... not amazing, but impossible... [that Hannah More and Mary Wollstonecraft] agree on all the great points of female education'. Berry predicted that 'H. More will... be very angry when she hears this, though I would lay a wager that she never read... [Wollstonecraft].'[21]

In *Strictures* More argued that as women have 'equal [intellectual] parts' as men, like men, they should be deliberately trained for their appropriate 'profession' to exert their influence as 'daughters, wives, mothers, and mistresses of families'. More attacked novels tainted by foreign influences with socially destabilizing messages. She compared women's novel reading to a 'complicated drug' capable of arousing erotic fantasies and the neglect of female Christian duties. Ladies who take the lead in society, More instructed, must 'act as the guardians of public taste as well as public virtue' to stem revolutionary tides washing across the Channel from France and Germany into elite boudoirs.[22]

More responded directly to Hays's Unitarian revision of the conduct book for women, *Letters and Essays, Moral, and Miscellaneous*. In chapter VII of *Strictures*, 'On female study, and initiation into knowledge', More refuted specifics of Hays's recommendations for the female reader in her own chapter VII, 'On reading Romances, &c.' More emphasized her differences from Macaulay, Wollstonecraft and Hays: intellectual women according to her plan were primarily Christian reformers, subscribing to the view that 'education be a school to fit us for life, and life be a school to fit us for eternity'.[23] Here was the great divide between More and her feminist Enlightenment peers: she wanted women disciplined for earthly, individual atonement; they envisioned female education for active republican citizenship and self-expression. Yet *Strictures* was as much a defence of More's reputation as an assault on the ideas of others. More meant to reassert her role as defender of Establishment religious and political values, probably because she had come under fire from Anglican churchmen when she organized a mini empire of Sunday Schools for the poor. In this war of words, More was identified with Jacobin and dissenting subversion and accused of sabotaging the Church of England.

Scottish novelist Elizabeth Hamilton staked a middle ground between the conservatism of Hannah More and the radical positions of Macaulay, Wollstonecraft, Hays and their associates. Unlike More, Hamilton expressed admiration for Wollstonecraft, whom she described as a 'very sensible authoress [who] has sometimes permitted her zeal to hurry her into expressions which have raised a prejudice against the whole' and considered the *Rights of Woman* 'an ingenious publication'.[24] Hamilton chose different tactics to express her brand of feminism in the women's war, deploying genre to display female competence in hitherto male-dominated forms like satire. Hamilton argued for the need for female economic independence, but she insisted on the pitfalls of sexual emancipation for her readers.

Hamilton published *Letters on the Elementary Principles of Education* (1801), in which she condemned the intellectual pretensions and unseemly public ambitions of Wollstonecraft, Hays and their female allies. Hamilton argued that 'By far the greater part of those who have hitherto taken upon them to stand forth as champions for sexual equality, have done it upon grounds that to me appear indefensible, if not absurd.' Nevertheless, Hamilton's position on women's mental competence was more nuanced than her critique might suggest. She argued against 'Contempt for the Female Character' and resisted 'sexual prejudice'. She agreed with Hays and Wollstonecraft about the dire condition of women's education. Although Hamilton pointedly attacked Hays, she endorsed Wollstonecraft's critique of Rousseau in the *Vindication of the Rights of Woman*. Hamilton, too, promoted the social benefits of training women 'for self-sufficiency and usefulness'; she advocated employing single women.[25] Hamilton stood her own ground: she did not look to improvements in female education to make revolutionary changes in gender relations or society in general. She was intent on equipping women better to fulfil their Christian roles.

At the turn into the nineteenth century, conservatives were in power and the most radical voices of both men and women were muted, but not stilled. Consumer demand for biographies exploded. Life-writing emerged as a more socially acceptable form of female history. Mary Hays, still recovering from the public assaults on her by detractors, turned to a major undertaking in which she advocated the contributions to human progress made by Macaulay, Roland and Wollstonecraft, and their importance for all women, *Female Biography: or Memoirs of Illustrious and Celebrated Women of All Ages and Countries* (1803).

Hays wrote the first death notice of Wollstonecraft in September 1797. In 1800 she published anonymously 'Memoirs of Mary Wollstonecraft' in the short-lived *Annual Necrology for 1797–8*. Her sombre meditation on Wollstonecraft's life and works testified to the feminist lineage from Catharine Macaulay's *Letters on Education* to *Vindication of the Rights of Woman*. Hays implied that the unheralded connection between the ideas of these two distinguished women thinkers provided yet another example of the invisibility of women's intellectual history. The absence of women was then explained as the result, rather than the cause, of their lack of achievements. Without a parallel history linking female endeavours to each other, each female thinker and her texts were perceived as idiosyncratic, without context and unconnected to any other. In the absence of a recognized lineage of women's thought, every woman believed that she was alone and must begin anew. Hays prophesied that Wollstonecraft's pioneering life was not lived in vain. 'The spirit of reform is silently pursuing its course', she promised, 'Who can mark its limits?'[26]

The memoir of Wollstonecraft was probably meant to be the first item in Hays's *Female Biography*, which contained portraits of 300 women, a daring experiment in history writing, and Hays knew it. In six volumes Hays constructed a new story of the past which paralleled existing ones. Her memoir of Macaulay addressed the fraught question of Macaulay's public career: 'A female historian, by its singularity', Hays wrote, 'could not fail to excite attention: she seemed to have stepped out of the province of her sex; curiosity was sharpened, and malevolence provoked.' Macaulay's brilliance was undeniable, so her critics turned their attention to her appearance. Hays spoke for Macaulay and for herself in describing the slurs the female historian incurred: 'She is deformed (said her adversaries, wholly unacquainted with her person), she is unfortunately ugly, she despairs of distinction and admiration as a woman, she seeks, therefore, to encroach on the province of man.'[27]

Hays resisted the oppressive climate of opinion to be the first to include Manon Roland in a compilation about women, and also dared to insert large excerpts from Roland's revelatory *An Appeal to Impartial Posterity*. She promoted Roland as heroine and Girondin martyr of the French Revolution, explaining that whatever her readers' political views, they would benefit from the fierce womanly honesty and courage displayed in Roland's story, an argument she had also used in the memoirs of Wollstonecraft. Hays sought to arouse enthusiasm for women's achievements, irrespective of conventional prejudices towards a political party or religious persuasion, endorsing figures that did not conform to traditional moral codes.

British women writers who participated in the Revolution debate displayed courage that had great and lasting consequences. Their staying power during the volatile 1790s and the Napoleonic Wars laid the foundations for their successors, such as Anna Jameson, Barbara Bodichon, Elizabeth Barrett Browning, Harriet Martineau, Jane Carlyle, George Eliot and Mary Somerville, to come forward as public female intellectuals. In the third quarter of the nineteenth century, British women were first admitted to British universities and the Married Women's Property Acts were passed by Parliament (1870, 1882), giving wives legal identity and rights. In this regard, the Revolution debate had marked a historic turning point for British women writers.

NOTES

1 Darline Gay Levy, Harriet Branson Applewhite and Mary Durham Johnson, eds., *Women in Revolutionary Paris 1789–1795* (Urbana: University of Illinois Press, 1979), p. 5.
2 Karen O'Brien, 'Catharine Macaulay's Histories of England: A Female Perspective on the History of Liberty', in Barbara Taylor and Sarah Knott, eds., *Women, Gender and Enlightenment* (Houndsmill: Palgrave Macmillan, 2005), pp. 523–37; p. 526.

3 Sarah Hutton, 'Liberty, Equality and God: The Religious Roots of Catherine Macaulay's Feminism', in Taylor and Knott, eds., *Women, Gender and Enlightenment*, pp. 538–50; p. 542.

4 Jane Austen, *Mansfield Park*, ed. June Sturrock (Peterborough, ON: Broadview Press, 2001), pp. 463–4.

5 Anna Letitia Barbauld, *An Address to the Opposers of the Repeal of the Corporation and Test Acts* (London: J. Johnson, 1790), p. 13.

6 *Ibid.*, pp. 35, 38, 39.

7 Mary Hays, *Letters and Essays, Moral, and Miscellaneous*, ed. Gina Luria (New York: Garland Publishing, 1974), pp. 11–12, 16.

8 *Letters and Essays* was reviewed in the *English Review*, 2nd series 22 (October 1793), 253–7, but this passage is quoted from a letter to Hays from J. E. Evans, [1793?] Pforzheimer, MS. MH. 2202. Quoted by kind permission of the Carl H. Pforzheimer Collection of Shelley and His Circle, The New York Public Library, Astor, Lenox and Tilden Foundations.

9 Richard Polwhele, *The Unsex'd Females: A Poem* (New York: Garland Publishing, 1974), p. 6.

10 Shelley King and John B. Pierce, 'Introduction', *The Father and Daughter with Dangers of Coquetry*, by Amelia Opie, ed. King and Pierce (Peterborough, ON: Broadview Press, 2003), pp. 47–8.

11 Amelia Opie, *The Father and Daughter*, pp. 139–40.

12 Antje Blank and Janet Todd, 'Introduction', *Desmond*, by Charlotte Smith, ed. Blank and Todd (Peterborough, ON: Broadview Press, 2001), p. 22.

13 Mary Ann Hanway, *Ellinor, or the world as it is*, ed. Gina Luria (New York: Garland Publishing, 1974), p. 302.

14 Maria Edgeworth, *Letters for Literary Ladies. To which is added, an essay on the noble science of self-justification* (London: J. Johnson, 1795), p. 52.

15 *Ibid.*, p. 73.

16 Maria Edgeworth, *Letters for Literary Ladies. To which is added, an essay on the noble science of self-justification*, 2nd edn (London: J. Johnson, 1799), p. 102.

17 Eliza Fenwick, *Secresy; or, The Ruin on the Rock*, ed. Isobel Grundy (Peterborough, ON: Broadview Press, 1994), pp. 140–1.

18 Mary Hays, *Memoirs of Emma Courtney*, 2 vols. (London: G. G. and J. Robinson, 1796), vol. II, p. 68.

19 Anne Stott, *Hannah More: The First Victorian* (Oxford: Oxford University Press, 2004), p. 318.

20 Hannah More, *Essays on Various Subjects, Principally Designed for Young Ladies* (London: J. Wilkie, 1777), title page.

21 Quoted in Charles Howard Ford, *Hannah More: A Critical Biography* (New York: Peter Lang, 1996), p. 16.

22 Hannah More, *Strictures on the Modern System of Female Education* (New York: Garland Publishing, 1974), p. 98.

23 *Ibid.*

24 Claire Grogan, *The Feminist Politics of Elizabeth Hamilton (1758–1816)*, forthcoming.

25 Elizabeth Hamilton, *Letters on the Elementary Principles of Education*, 3rd edn, 2 vols. (Bath: R. Cruttwell, 1803), vol. I, p. 252.

26 Mary Hays, 'Memoirs of Mary Wollstonecraft', in *Annual Necrology for 1797–8; Including, also, Various Items of Neglected Biography* (London: R. Phillips, 1800), p. 459.

27 Mary Hays, 'Catharine Macaulay Graham', in *Female Biography*, 6 vols. (London: R. Phillips, 1803), vol. V, p. 292.

11

M. O. GRENBY

Novels of opinion

On 13 April 1792, Anna Larpent, an avid reader whose diary happily survives, called the debate on the French Revolution 'a controversy that I cannot in its full heat form a Judgement on', adding 'it is impossible in these prejudiced moments to determine who is right and wrong'. To help her form her judgement she had been reading political pamphlets, including Thomas Paine's *Rights of Man* (1791–2) and James Mackintosh's *Vindiciae Gallicae* (1791). By August, though, it was through the lens of 'a prettily wrought novel' that she was viewing what she called the 'french troubles in consequence of the Revolution'. The novel was *Desmond*, by Charlotte Smith, which had appeared a few weeks earlier in June. Although 'an odd work', 'hurried' and 'somewhat forced', Larpent praised Smith for defending the Revolution 'with the enthusiasm of a woman and a poetess'. In the end, however, Smith's 'fine imagination, & command of Language' did not convert Larpent to her cause and she pronounced the author to be 'a wild leveller'.[1] Perhaps we might have predicted such a response from the affluent and urbane Larpent, daughter of the ambassador at Constantinople and wife of the Lord Chamberlain's inspector of plays, but what is remarkable is that she was gaining her political information, and shaping her political views, at least in part from fiction. In this she was not alone. During the 1790s and early 1800s dozens of 'novels of opinion' issued from British presses – so many indeed, that cultural historians are still rediscovering further examples. Even if, today, few of them are regarded as major literary achievements, they were, for certain sections of the population, probably as influential in moulding socio-political attitudes in late eighteenth-century Britain as any other form of cultural production discussed in this book.

It has been standard scholarly practice to divide these novels of opinion into two groups: 'Jacobin' and 'anti-Jacobin'. Although this distinction does have some legitimacy, it also has its problems. First of all, the novel was only one of the forms of fiction affected by the French Revolution crisis. Fiction was published in tracts and pamphlets, perhaps most famously as part of

Hannah More's Cheap Repository scheme. Fiction written for children was also drawn into the war of ideas. A careful search of the archives reveals, in fact, all manner of ephemeral and sometimes jejune works of fiction published during the 1790s and 1800s as vehicles for the rapid transportation of political ideas. It is by no means clear, for example, how we should classify the *Trial and Execution of the Grand Mufti* (1795), an eight-page attack on the anti-revolutionary Bishop of Rochester written in the form of an Oriental tale. Or what should we make of the anonymous *Modern Gulliver's Travels* (1796) or Mary Anne Burges's *The Progress of the Pilgrim Good-Intent, in Jacobinical Times* (1800), lengthy continuations of Swift and Bunyan designed as interventions in the Revolution controversy? What is certain is that, as the publisher and anti-Jacobin novelist George Walker put it in 1799, complaining of the radicals' literary activities, 'no channel is deemed improper by them, which can introduce their sentiments'. The radicals made exactly the same complaint. 'No vehicle was too mean, no language too coarse and insulting, by which to convey the venom of my adversaries', protested William Godwin, adding that 'not even a petty novel for boarding-school misses now ventures to aspire to favour, unless it contains some expressions of dislike or abhorrence to the new philosophy'.[2] Both Walker and Godwin, if a little paranoid, were correct. The Revolution controversy was conducted in fiction as much as in the pages of the political tracts and pamphlets that have traditionally been understood to constitute the 'war of ideas'.

However, it might be more accurate to say that the war of ideas was being waged in novels *before* Richard Price, Edmund Burke, Thomas Paine fired their famous salvoes. Gary Kelly's pioneering 1976 study *The English Jacobin Novel* discussed four writers – Robert Bage, Elizabeth Inchbald, Thomas Holcroft and William Godwin. All were expressing liberal views prior to the fall of the Bastille, and, rather than any actual shift in the political tendency of their fiction, it was the events of the 1790s that made them seem more radical. Bage's four novels of the 1780s, for example, are imbued with some of the key values that would characterize the 'Jacobin' novels of the 1790s: a hostility towards established authority, particularly inherited status and power; a contempt for the perceived foolishness or corruption of the upper classes; an idealistic confidence in rationality, religious toleration, egalitarianism and 'middle-class' values; and a belief in the power of local action to effect general social reform. These remained the central themes of Bage's two post-Revolutionary novels, *Man As He Is* (1792) and *Hermsprong; or, Man As He Is Not* (1796).

Hermsprong – one of the most successful Jacobin novels – is essentially a parable of Britain's corruption and renewal, though drawn out to three volumes and – like a number of other novels of opinion – loosely modelled on the plot of Samuel Richardson's *Clarissa* (1747–8). The hero, Hermsprong, has been raised by Native Americans, which makes him the very embodiment of Jean-Jacques Roussseau's 'noble savage'. When he arrives in Britain he is appalled by all the frivolities and faults he finds. Among the many people he rescues from various predicaments – each prefiguring his more general redemption of British society – is Caroline Campinet. Like Richardson's Clarissa, she is being forced by her dictatorial father, Lord Grondale, into marriage, in this case with the repellent Sir Philip Chestrum. Both men represent the corruption of temporal power, while their associate, the Reverend Blick, personifies the decay of spiritual authority. By confronting them and publicly exhibiting their faults Hermsprong forces them to realize the moral and political bankruptcy of the system they uphold, and that upholds them. Naturally – for the best Jacobin novels succeed in fusing the personal and the political, and work within the established conventions of the novel – Hermsprong is then revealed to be the rightful heir to Grondale's estate, and marries Caroline, restoring the proper order on a local and, by extension, national level. That Bage knew perfectly well that the context in which he was writing had changed, making his reformist sentiments seem more radical than they would have appeared in the 1780s, is evidenced by his inclusion in *Hermsprong* of a riot scene. Far from fomenting the disturbance, Hermsprong pacifies the discontented workers, telling them that equality of property must always be utterly impossible, and reprimanding them for insulting the King, which must, he said, almost as if quoting from a loyalist pamphlet, 'weaken the *concord* that ought to subsist betwixt him and all his *subjects*, and overthrow all *civil* order'.[3] By 1796, after the execution of Louis XVI, the Terror and the outbreak of war, Bage was evidently concerned to show that he was no advocate of revolution.

Many Jacobin novels share similar motifs, themes, structures and aims with *Hermsprong*. Elizabeth Inchbald's *Nature and Art* (1796) also includes a protagonist who has been educated outside corrupt British society, on an African island, and who returns to expose the callousness, bigotry, injustice and hypocrisy of the British legal, ecclesiastical and social systems. The hero of Thomas Holcroft's *Adventures of Hugh Trevor* (1794–7) is another picaresque seeker after truth who exposes society's degeneration, in this case the stranglehold the upper classes have over all aspects of social and economic life. In *The Adventures of Caleb Williams* (1794) William Godwin similarly sought to expound the calamitous state of what the novel's full title called 'Things As They Are'. It too revolves around the interaction between the decadent holders of hereditary power and a younger, humbler hero – although this being surely the most sophisticated of the novels of opinion, the battle-lines are never quite so clearly drawn. Caleb is Godwin's agent of enquiry, driven to investigate the secret of Ferdinando Falkland, his urbane and apparently estimable patron. Caleb's discovery that Falkland has avenged an insult from the boorish and domineering Barnabus Tyrrel by murdering him in secret causes Falkland to turn Caleb out and to use his agents and influence relentlessly to pursue him. At last, Caleb turns to confront him. In the ending Godwin originally planned Falkland successfully concludes his persecution, and Caleb dies with only his memoirs – the novel we have been reading – posthumously to vindicate him. The conclusion with which Godwin replaced this seems more hopeful, with Falkland abruptly confessing his guilt before dying, repentant. Yet Caleb's remorse at causing Falkland's death, and our realization that he has, in effect, simply become another agent of persecution, makes this published ending rather more pessimistic. Without a general reform of society even the most estimable individual cannot avoid corruption.

Caleb Williams needs to be read both as a fictional continuation of Godwin's *Enquiry concerning Political Justice* (1793), in which he had argued for wholesale socio-political reform, and as a riposte to Burke's *Reflections on the Revolution in France* (1790). Falkland represents the aristocracy as Burke thought it should be: generous, liberal, enlightened. But he is undone by one, distinctly Burkean fault: an obsession with chivalry and hence reputation, which causes his murder of Tyrrel and persecution of Caleb. Thus Godwin tried to demonstrate the hollowness of Burke's political philosophy. Caleb, though, is almost equally flawed. Unlike paragons such as Hermsprong or Hugh Trevor, Caleb's search for enlightenment leads only to ruin and self-reproach. Godwin condemns sudden acts of violent uprising, as perpetrated by both Falkland and Caleb. A gradual approach to reform is more calculated to succeed. But *Caleb Williams* also offers a critique of the radical conviction, advanced by most of Godwin's allies, that the surest way to overthrow the *ancien régime* was to bring its workings to light. Until true 'political justice' has been achieved, *Caleb Williams* insists, any attempt at exposure, reform or revolution will be futile.

Godwin's bleakness contrasts markedly with the optimism of just one or two years earlier. Holcroft's *Anna St Ives* (1792), another reworking of *Clarissa*, proposed an individual solution to general social problems. The virtuous heroine is threatened with marriage to the dissolute and bullying Sir Coke Clifton, but loves Frank Henley, the humbler son of her father's bailiff. The first radical twist on the established formula derives from Anna and Frank's shared commitment to enlightened philosophy. They calmly debate whom Anna should marry, disregarding their own passion to decide Clifton the better candidate. After all, once inevitably reformed by Anna, he will be able to use his elevated social position for the general benefit of society. The second twist comes when, after Clifton has imprisoned Frank and attempted to rape Anna, he *does* become a convert to their reformist views. No cynicism clouds the confidence with which Frank looks forward to what we now read as a socialist paradise: 'that state of society when personal property no longer shall exist ... and when all shall labour for the good of all!' Indeed, in response to the objections of an only initially dubious Clifton, Frank takes his triumphant iconoclasm in an ever more radical direction, arguing against marriage and monogamy. There is nothing more despotic, he says, than the regulations that 'bind not only body to body but soul to soul, to all futurity'. Female virginity, currently thought a crime to lose, 'will again be guilt to keep'. No one will be able to say '*This is my child*', he argues, for all progeny will be 'children of the state'.[4]

Questions of marriage, sex and childcare would be picked up by the majority of Jacobin novelists, especially women, though seldom were they advanced with such confident utopianism. Mary Wollstonecraft's *Maria; or, The Wrongs of Woman* (1798), for instance, published in an incomplete form after the author's death, presents husbands as despots and marriage as a form of slavery. But Maria finds that she cannot escape her husband's tyranny by changing allegiance to a new partner, and that sexual desire, far from being liberating, seems only to forge more chains. If there is any hope for Maria, and for women in general, in this novel it comes from the establishment of the cross-class, cross-generational but female-only community sketched out in one of the fragmentary endings that Wollstonecraft was apparently considering. She was not the only novelist to present the problems of patriarchy. Smith's *Desmond* showed its heroine, Geraldine, shackled by marriage, and bought and sold from one man to another as if she was a commodity. The fact that even Desmond fathers a child with another, married woman, while Geraldine, whom he loves, remains chaste, unveils the double standards governing male and female propriety. It was a remonstrance made more emphatically in Mary Hays's *Memoirs of Emma Courtney* (1796), perhaps the novel most completely dedicated to explaining the economic and social disadvantages under which women were forced to exist. While Smith's Geraldine remains passive, Emma Courtney seeks to take control of her own destiny by actively pursuing the man she loves. The result, though, is tragedy. After the optimism of *Anna St Ives* and (to an extent) *Desmond*, *Emma Courtney*, like *Caleb Williams* and *Maria*, articulates the pessimism of the second half of the decade.

Smith was deeply interested in politics and strongly opinionated, yet, being perennially short of money and in many ways the consummate professional author, she was always anxious that her work should coincide with public opinion. This tension makes her novels particularly interesting for anyone studying the British response to the Revolution. *Celestina* (1791), her third novel, had been as scathing about the venality of the aristocracy as anything by Bage or Holcroft, and its final volume, set in France, had openly celebrated the Revolution. *Desmond* was even more enthusiastic. Much of the novel is set in a contented, prosperous and fertile post-Revolutionary France, and the characters' letters home insist that 'nothing is more unlike the real state of this country, than the accounts which have been given of it in England'. Attacking Burke and his allies directly, Smith has her hero insist that 'the sanguinary and ferocious democracy, the scenes of anarchy and confusion, which we have had so pathetically described and lamented, have no existence but in the malignant fabrications of those who have been paid for their misrepresentations'.[5] Indeed, in Smith's novel, the greatest threat to France's continued well-being comes from dispossessed French aristocrats who combine a reactionary desire to overturn the Revolution with all the personal iniquities of the gothic villain.

In her next novel, *The Old Manor House* (1793), Smith retreated into a historical setting. Locating the action during the War of American Independence allowed her to continue exploring authority's corruption but to avoid engaging directly with rapidly unfolding events in France. She returned to them in 1794, *The Banished Man* picking up chronologically exactly where *Desmond* had left off, just after the September Massacres of 1792, but with Revolutionary France now presented as savage and shattered. In *The Banished Man*, the men and women who, overthrowing tyrannical fathers, had offered such hope for a better future in *Celestina* and *Desmond*, have been forced into exile. The fight is now between reactionary aristocrats, who aim to re-impose the *ancien régime*, and equally self-serving revolutionaries, who have abandoned the egalitarian principles of the Revolution's early stages. Hopes for a new, better France have failed, and with them have vanished Smith's dreams of a reformed Britain. Indeed, Smith contrives a happy ending only by transporting her French, English and Polish heroes and heroines to Italy, where they establish a community untouched by *ancien régime* corruption and revolutionary violence alike. For some critics, such as Adriana Craciun, this should be understood as part of a cosmopolitan, feminist project to imagine a new kind of community that could supersede family, nation and other antiquated loyalties. Yet *The Banished Man* can seem like a tactical retreat. Smith used its preface to explain why it had been perfectly reasonable to support the Revolution in its early stages, but to distance herself from what had followed.

Besides the unfolding events in France (and the marriage of her favourite daughter to an émigré French aristocrat in 1793), the increasing muteness of Smith's reformism probably had much to do with her awareness of its unsaleability from about 1793 on. Whether on principle, or because they no longer saw a market for it, from the mid-1790s publishers declined to print radical fiction. They were no doubt influenced by the changed critical climate, for reviewers were attacking any work of fiction in which they detected the taint of Jacobinism, both in well-regarded journals like the *Monthly* and *Critical Reviews* and in some of the more partisan publications that had sprung up precisely for this purpose, such as the *British Critic* (from 1793) and *Anti-Jacobin Review* (from 1798), or in Sarah Trimmer's review journal for children's books, the *Guardian of Education* (1802–6). In fact, in the loyalist press, Smith's early Girondism was enough to stain her reputation in perpetuity. In James Gillray's famous print, 'The New Morality', which appeared in the *Anti-Jacobin* in 1798, her novel, *The Young Philosopher* (1798), was shown tumbling out of a 'Cornucopia of Ignorance' along with works by Godwin, Wollstonecraft, Thelwall and many other celebrated radicals.

The pressure exerted by publishers, reviewers and a new breed of zealously loyalist, freelance critic exerted a censorship on fiction that ensured that 1796 was the last year in which a substantial number of Jacobin novels appeared. Although one or two appeared later – notably Wollstonecraft's *Maria* and Hays's *Victim of Prejudice* (1799) – the novel that best articulates what had happened to the radical cause in the second half of the decade is Godwin's *St Leon* (1799). A gothicized extended fable, it tells of a sixteenth-century nobleman who finds the secrets of eternal youth and limitless wealth but is prevented from being of benefit to humanity by the prejudices of an ungrateful populace. The mob riots against him. He withdraws into sullen and impotent isolation. Godwin seems to have meant his readers to understand St Leon partly as Burke, whom Godwin thought had wasted his gifts, and partly as Joseph Priestley, forced to flee Britain when the Birmingham crowd attacked his house and laboratory in 1791. The novel was somewhat autobiographical too. But, more generally, the persecuted and disillusioned Reginald de St Leon is the embodiment of failed radical hopes. The Revolution had promised a better world but had only unleashed the people's baser instincts and delivered a more divided, cruel and vicious society.

As radicalism slumped, the conservative novel's popularity – with publishers, reviewers and, apparently, readers – swelled. In excess of fifty anti-Jacobin novels were published by about 1804: more by far than had manifested a radical commitment. The majority of these were not published until the second half of the 1790s, but a few were earlier – preceding the most celebrated of the Jacobin novels. Edward Sayer, for example, followed his pamphlet *Observations on Doctor Price's Revolution Sermon* (1790) with the novel *Lindor and Adelaïde, a Moral Tale* (1791), in which, as the novel's subtitle put it, were '*exhibited the Effects of the Late French Revolution on the Peasantry of France*'. Compared with later anti-Jacobin novels, these early attempts to fuse propaganda and fiction can seem primitive. About a third of Sayer's novel is taken up by laboured expositions of Burkean political philosophy. At one point, a minor character gives a disquisition on the nature of French and British government that, at eighty-six pages, is far longer than Sayer's earlier pamphlet.

On the other hand, these early examples do exhibit many of the topoi that would come to characterize the anti-Jacobin novel. The most obvious is the damning depiction of the Revolution, as pioneered in *Lindor and Adelaïde*. This line of attack seems particularly to have appealed to authors who had been supporters of the Revolution in its early stages, but who later wished to explain and excuse their former enthusiasm. Smith, with her *Banished Man*, was one; others included the celebrated actor, poet and feminist Mary Robinson and the physician, travel writer and sometime French republican John Moore. Robinson's *The Natural Daughter* (1799) and Moore's *Mordaunt* (1800) were both set during the Terror and featured Marat and Robespierre as central characters, fully assimilated into the narratives.

Perhaps the most impressive in terms of its integration of plot and politics was Helen Craik's *Adelaide de Narbonne* (1800). Both Marat and his assassin Charlotte Corday feature in prominent roles, the former metamorphosed by Craik from the austere Revolutionary leader into a remorseless Lothario who forces legislation though the Revolutionary Assembly only to expedite his lust. The novel's heroine, Adelaide, a quiet but determined royalist, is his prey. Marat killed her first husband and in order to resist his advances Adelaide was forced to wed her loathsome, Jacobinical second husband. Adelaide distracts herself from her wretchedness by organizing a sanctuary for fleeing royalists in a series of caverns deep within the Rock of Narbonne. Playing with gothic convention, Craik explains that the Rock has for generations been used to shelter the victims of France's political vicissitudes, the local inhabitants keeping away because they regard it as haunted. Adelaïde's son is also the leader of the local band of counter-Revolutionaries. When Marat arrives in the vicinity determined to suppress the counter-Revolution, Charlotte Corday, having come to realize the iniquity of the Revolution, and wrongly informed that Marat has killed Adelaide and her son, assassinates him. When Craik has Charlotte cry 'Madame de Narbonne' as she plunges the dagger into Marat's breast, several ends are being served: first, the various strands of the novel are being dextrously woven together; second, the repudiation of premature support for the Revolution – so common in

Britain – is being dramatically enacted; and third, the Jacobins are being covered in even greater opprobrium, becoming not only political villains but also the persecutors of a beautiful and innocent heroine.

Other anti-Jacobin novelists preferred to depict revolution at a geographical or historical remove. Their chief motivation remained the same: to show that, however legitimate the complaint against the old order, revolution must always be destructive. Matthew Lewis's sensational gothic novel *The Monk* (1796) provides a characteristic example. Set loosely in medieval Madrid, it dwells in lurid detail on the abuses of the church, but when the mob rises to vent its fury, the consequences are only the deaths of many innocent nuns and indeed of the rioters themselves, for, with evident symbolism, they bring the roof of a convent down on their own heads. Various other novels, some written for children, made a similar point about West Indian slave rebellions. For instance, in Elizabeth Helme's *Farmer of Inglewood Forest* (1796) and Maria Edgeworth's story 'The Grateful Negro' (in *Popular Tales*, 1804), the injustice of slavery is acknowledged, or at least its cruel enforcement, but the revolts, when they happen, are shown to be equally brutal and disastrously counter-productive. Many anti-Jacobin novels went further, determined to demonstrate that rebellion was always fomented by scoundrels concerned only with their own selfish interests. Walker's *The Vagabond* (1799) was set partly during the 1780 Gordon Riots. The riots had been fuelled by anti-Catholicism, but in Walker's novel its leaders are merely rabble-rousers who happily seize on any cause from which they may profit politically, financially or sexually. Several novels published in the wake of the 1798 Irish Rebellion, such as Charles Lucas's *The Infernal Quixote* and Mrs Bullock's *Dorothea; or, a Ray of the New Light* (both 1801), similarly expose the selfish motives of villains who, when their seditious schemes are frustrated in England, move to Ireland, where they hope to profit from the rebellion that they help to organize. The decision to represent insurgency in Ireland so soon after the Rebellion had been narrowly defeated was intended to remind British readers of the danger, for what could happen there might easily cross to the mainland. Yet simultaneously this exposé of the true nature of rebels and revolutionaries was designed to be comforting. Presenting radicalism merely as the mask for self-interest denied it the status of a legitimate political cause. Moreover, revolution was not inevitable, the novels argued, but could be prevented by individual and state vigilance and by judicious reform that would stifle the discontent which the agitators required.

Indeed, by the second half of the 1790s, most loyalist fiction had become less apprehensive about revolution and more concerned to ridicule radical ideas and heap invective on the individuals associated with them. This led to some fine satirical novels, written by a miscellaneous collection of authors. Some were ideologues, such as the biographer of Burke and committed conservative journalist, Robert Bisset, who published *Douglas; or, The Highlander* at the 'Anti-Jacobin Press' in 1800. Others seem less fanatical, their novels apparently elaborate *jeux d'esprit*, such as *The Democrat: Interspersed with Anecdotes of Well Known Characters* (1795) by the Poet Laureate Henry James Pye, *Vaurien: or, Sketches of the Times* (1797) by Isaac D'Israeli and *St Godwin* (1800) by Edward Dubois. A number of women writers – including Elizabeth Hamilton (*Translations of the Letters of a Hindoo Rajah*, 1796) and Sophia King (*Waldorf; or, The Dangers of Philosophy*, 1798) – chose to make their first serious ventures into publication with anti-Jacobin novels. This might seem surprising, but by producing novels thick with the most orthodox of political, social and religious sentiments, women were able to gain a voice in an age when their intervention in public affairs was routinely condemned.

Above all, the conservative reconfiguration of Jacobinism as a moral and essentially domestic issue – a process to which novelists, both radical and conservative, had contributed – brought it within the 'proper' ambit of women writers. In the conservative imagination it was not that large political and public issues were being *reduced* to their private and individual consequences, but rather that Jacobinism was now being understood as a poison that would affect individuals. As a result it was not political revolution that became the focus of attack but a nebulous 'new philosophy', an amalgam of the ideas of Paine, Rousseau, Godwin, Wollstonecraft and others, generally misrepresented. The most common tactic was to avoid debate by personifying philosophical ideas, not expounding them. For example, Elizabeth Hamilton's second novel, *Memoirs of Modern Philosophers* (1800), is full of caricatured figures who have taken up radical social ideas either through their own folly and miseducation, or, less innocently, because of the rewards they hope to reap from them. In the first category are Bridgetina Botherim, a pastiche of Mary Hays, whose *Memoirs of Emma Courtney* had defended women's intellectual and sexual autonomy, and Julia, less headstrong but made vulnerable to the new philosophy by her atheistic upbringing and devotion to novels. In the second category is Vallaton, who seduces Julia with a combination of travestied Godwinianism and the artful construction of himself as a novelistic hero – orphaned in childhood, notionally the usurped heir to an estate and rejected by Julia's father because of his ostensibly lowly birth. In short, he presents himself as another Hermsprong.

Both Bridgetina and Julia are rendered easy prey to the new philosophy because of their devotion to novel-reading. Although attacking novel-reading within a novel was paradoxical, this was a common theme in anti-Jacobin fiction. Indulging too enthusiastically in novels was presented as another form of quixoticism, exactly comparable with an engagement with new philosophy. Both set up an artificial code of behaviour which, when transposed to real life, always proved fallacious, and was generally productive of the most grievous results. In *Memoirs of Modern Philosophers*, new philosophy spreads like a contagion, from rogues like Vallaton to fools like Bridgetina, and from them to those, like Julia, who were unable to understand that their abstract schemes can never work in reality. While Vallaton is eventually forced to flee, the comical Bridgetina lives to acknowledge her errors but the tragic Julia dies. This chain of transmission from the villainous to the quixotic to the credulous and vulnerable is an emblem of the wider conservative concern that through fiction, political ideas would percolate down to new audiences – the lower classes, women and the young – who would be unable to discriminate between theory and practice. This was why, in spite of their uneasiness about the polarization of novels, anti-Jacobins were so concerned to bring the 'war of ideas' to fiction. It was in novels, they felt, that the war would be won or lost.

Having looked at several Jacobin and anti-Jacobin novels, a number of questions present themselves. One regards what function both sets of novels were supposed to perform. These may have been novels of *opinion*, but were they novels of *ideas*? Or should we understand them merely as propaganda, or lampoons? On the radical side, some productions were little more than skits. The anonymous *Excursion of Osman* (1792), for instance, was a painfully blatant, pseudo-Oriental allegory in which the hero travels through 'Slavonia' (elucidated in a prefacing key as Europe) meeting such figures as 'Benvolus' (Paine) and 'The Spectre' (Burke). The contrast with a novel like *Caleb Williams* is palpable. The latter was a truly philosophical novel, Godwin having adopted the form only because it was most suitable to communicate 'political principles . . . to persons, whom books of philosophy and science are never likely to reach'.[6] Studies by, among others, Pamela Clemit and Nancy E. Johnson, have confirmed that the radicals were producing novels that genuinely, and almost unprecedentedly, did seek to explain and advance political and philosophical ideas, and to explore their effects in fictional case studies. They were not agit-prop. Godwin, Holcroft, Hays, Wollstonecraft and others sought to show their readers how flawed the status quo was, but not to inspire them to sudden political action. The French could be congratulated on their Revolution, but, for Britain, even the most radical Jacobin novelists tended to endorse only gradual and nonviolent reform which would emanate from individual enlightenment. If there were exceptions – radical novels that could be labelled propagandistic – they were works that focused on specific and limited causes, such as John Thelwall's *Daughter of Adoption* (1801), which argued forcefully against 'the arbitrary distinctions of races and of colours' and 'bending the necks of a large proportion of the human race under the iron yoke of slavery'.[7]

Anti-Jacobin fiction has usually been seen as less philosophical and more propagandistic. Certainly many were snide satires, lampooning individuals and seizing on a few radical arguments that could easily be ridiculed. The same pseudo-Godwinian ideas are travestied again and again, and radical philosophy is distilled down to an attack on piety, property, personal responsibility and, above all, chastity and marriage. Yet novels campaigning for 'liberal' causes were not written exclusively by radicals. Propaganda against the slave trade was a routine feature of children's fiction, even that written by loyalist authors, and George Walker, author of the fiercely anti-Jacobin *Vagabond*, could attack another racial stereotype in *Theodore Cyphon; or The Benevolent Jew* (1796). Moreover, some anti-Jacobin novels were substantial intellectual achievements. Alongside its account of the anti-hero's new philosophical rakishness, its depiction of the Irish Rebellion and its comic exposé of a coven of 'Illuminati', Lucas's *Infernal Quixote* includes a vast and elaborate classification of British radicalism into its various genera that takes up almost the whole of one of the novel's four volumes. Lucas's taxonomy was facetious, but he was engaging directly with radical ideas and exhibiting considerable erudition, for he illustrated his assault with references to recent literary controversies and scientific developments, as well as to classical mythology, the Bible and the writings of Godwin, Hume, Voltaire and others. Recent scholarship has also drawn attention to the sustained and reasoned social and political critiques presented in the novels of some female anti-Jacobins, such as Craik and Hamilton. It was certainly possible, in other words, to be conservative *and* serious. Kevin Gilmartin has made this point most fully, arguing that the counter-revolutionary was a coherent political position, not only an anxious reflex reaction to events and ideas, and that conservative novelists were making interventions in a debate on ethics, rights and duties that were as intellectual and significant as those appearing in pamphlets, sermons, reviews and treatises.

This raises the question of whether we should be so confident in differentiating between Jacobin and anti-Jacobin fiction. The case can be made that they belong together – as novels of ideas, or as a fiction of reform, aiming to point out the faults of British society and suggest possibilities of improvement that, for Jacobins and anti-Jacobins alike, would make violent upheaval unnecessary. In short, was there really much of a difference between the social satire of the 'Jacobin' Bage and the 'anti-Jacobin' Hamilton, say? Equally, should we really see Smith's shift from *Desmond* to *The Banished Man* as a recantation? In support of this indivisibility argument several novels might be cited which have been claimed by critics as both radical and conservative, perhaps the best of which is *Adeline Mowbray* (1804) by Amelia Opie, friend of Godwin and Wollstonecraft (whose complicated lives may have inspired the novel). In conventional anti-Jacobin style, the novel begins by introducing a heroine who has received a dangerously new philosophical education from her mother. Accordingly, when Adeline's lecherous stepfather begins to harass her, she runs away with the philosopher Glenmurray, boldly rejecting marriage because it contravenes their idealistic principles. Since they are scorned by society, the ailing Glenmurray recommends that, when he dies, Adeline marry his cousin. She tries to avoid this by living independently as a schoolteacher, but when her 'shameful' past becomes known she is cast out and forced into the hateful marriage. Finally, she dies, repentant, asking that her child should be taught to be 'slow to call the experience of ages contemptible prejudices'.[8] Here, then, is a conventional anti-Jacobin ending to match the beginning. But, more subversively, the novel has clearly shown Adeline happy outside marriage and miserable within it. Moreover, she spends much of the novel as another Caleb: a pariah, always pursued by defaming accounts of her brave attempt to live by principle and reason. *Adeline Mowbray* demands to be read as a critique of the narrow-mindedness and misogyny that have made its heroine an outcast. We might even read its ostentatiously orthodox conclusion as a ruse – a deliberate attempt to dress up the author's radical sentiments in a form that readers would find acceptable, and thus to fend off precisely the kind of hostility that Opie presents as the regrettable result of Adeline's freethinking.

It can seem also that contemporaries did not see a clear distinction between Jacobin and anti-Jacobin novels. William Lane published such apparently oppositional books as *Hermsprong* and *Adelaide de Narbonne* from his Minerva Press, while, shortly after *Caleb Williams* and *Desmond*, the reformist firm of Robinson's produced the anti-radical *Dorothea* and *Memoirs of Modern Philosophers*. Some readers happily consumed both, too. The Sheffield teenager Joseph Hunter habitually borrowed radical books from libraries, including novels by Wollstonecraft and Inchbald, but also borrowed the anti-Jacobin novel *The Minstrel; or, Anecdotes of Distinguished Personages in the Fifteenth Century* (1793), which he thought 'one of the prettiest novels I have ever read'.[9]

Yet just because readers chose to read both does not mean that they did not see a difference. Like many other commentators, Anna Laetitia Barbauld, writing in 1810, drew a distinction between novels 'devoted to recommend, or to mark with reprobation, those systems of philosophy or politics which have raised so much ferment of late years'.[10] In the politically fraught 1790s, reviewers certainly pointed out the differences. There is also evidence that libraries not only identified Jacobin novels amongst their stock, but expelled them.[11] Above all, both radical and conservative novelists seem to have seen themselves as contributors to one side or the other. Hamilton associated *Memoirs of Modern Philosophers* with 'some other recent publications, which, like it, have avowedly been written in opposition to the opinions generally known by the name of the *New Philosophy*'; Jane West named Hamilton's novels, among others, as bearing 'a resemblance to her own'.[12]

It is this open avowal and approval of the politicization, and factionalism, of fiction, that makes the 1790s and early 1800s a crucial period in the development of the novel. These novels of opinion are interesting and significant as interventions in the Revolution debate, showing us how otherwise often silent sections of society responded to the political issues of the day. But they are also important for the literary precedent they set. Fiction in Britain was not treading water during the French Revolution crisis, as has sometimes been said, simply ensuring that the novels of Walter Scott and Jane Austen would be, as William Hazlitt put it, 'a relief to the mind, rarefied as it has been with modern philosophy'.[13] Rather, the novels of ideas produced during this period – openly ideological novels that, for the first time, were designed for women, the young and the lower and middle classes – paved the way for the fiction of political and moral engagement that would flourish in the nineteenth century.

NOTES

1 Quoted in John Brewer, 'Reconstructing the Reader: Prescriptions, Texts and Strategies in Anna Larpent's Reading', in James Raven, Helen Small and Naomi Tadmor, eds., *The Practice and Representation of Reading in England* (Cambridge: Cambridge University Press, 1996), pp. 226–45; pp. 232 and 237.

2 George Walker, *The Vagabond, a Novel*, 2 vols. (3rd edn, London: G. Walker, 1799), vol. I, p. vi; William Godwin, *Thoughts Occasioned By The Perusal Of Dr. Parr's Spital Sermon*, in *Political and Philosophical Writings of William Godwin*, gen. ed. Mark Philp (London: Pickering & Chatto, 1993), vol. II, pp. 163–213; p. 177.

3 Robert Bage, *Hermsprong; or, Man As He Is Not*, 3 vols. (1796; London: William Lane, 1799), vol. III, p. 198.

4 Thomas Holcroft, *Anna St. Ives*, 7 vols. (London: Shepperson and Reynolds, 1792), vol. V, pp. 32–40.

5 Charlotte Smith, *Desmond*, 3 vols. (London: G. G. J. and J. Robinson, 1792), vol. I, p. 105.

6 William Godwin, 'Preface' ('withdrawn in the original edition, in compliance with the alarms of booksellers'), *The Collected Novels and Memoirs of William Godwin*, gen. ed. Mark Philp (London: Pickering & Chatto, 1992), vol. III, ed. Pamela Clemit, p. 279.

7 'John Beaufort' (pseud. for John Thelwall), *The Daughter of Adoption; A Tale of Modern Times*, 4 vols. (London: R. Phillips, 1801), vol. I, pp. 268–9.

8 Amelia Opie, *Adeline Mowbray, or the Mother and Daughter: A Tale*, 3 vols. (London: Longman, Hurst, Rees & Orme, 1805), vol. III, p. 270.

9 'Journal of Joseph Hunter', 29 April 1798. BL Add. MSS. 24, 879, f.9v.

10 Anna Laetitia Barbauld, 'On the Origin and Progress of Novel-writing', in *Anna Letitia Barbauld: Selected Poetry and Prose*, ed. William McCarthy and Elizabeth Kraft (Peterborough, ON: Broadview, 2002), pp. 377–417; p. 415.

11 H. J. Jackson, *Marginalia: Readers Writing in Books* (New Haven, CT: Yale University Press, 2001), p. 78.

12 Elizabeth Hamilton, *Memoirs of Modern Philosophers*, 2 vols. (London: G. G. and J. Robinson, 1800), vol. I, p. xiii; Jane West, *A Tale of the Times*, 3 vols. (London: Longman and Rees, 1799), vol. I, p. iii.

13 William Hazlitt, *The Spirit of the Age*: 'Sir Walter Scott', in *The Complete Works of William Hazlitt*, ed. P. P. Howe, 21 vols. (London, 1930–4), vol. XI, p. 65.

12

GILLIAN RUSSELL

Revolutionary drama

The French Revolution transformed British theatre and dramatic writing, making the 1790s a pivotal decade in the nation's theatre history. The theatre of 1789 was still recognizably that of David Garrick, the pre-eminent actor-manager and dramatist who dominated the Georgian era: by 1800, however, a tectonic shift had occurred. That the Revolution had this effect was not only due to the magnitude of events in France and their impact in Britain: it was also because the Revolution challenged and defined the ideas and practices of theatricality that were integral to eighteenth-century society.

The maintenance of authority, based on the pillars of the monarchy, the church, the law and Parliament, was heavily reliant on the 'show' of power: George III, for example, would display himself to the people by means of processions, attendance at church and at other public occasions such as military and naval reviews, while the authority of the law was communicated by means of the solemn procession of judges through towns at assize time or by the more macabre theatre of the public execution. At the other end of the social spectrum, the lower orders often responded to the performances of the elite with their own theatrical forms of behaviour such as ritualized rioting or the burning of effigies. At the centre of this theatricalized political culture was the theatre itself. Play-going functioned not merely as a form of leisure activity but as a means of participating in the body politic. The auditorium of the typical Georgian theatre consisted of the pit at the ground level, identified with the professional middle classes, the boxes at the side which were the domain of the elite, and the gallery at the upper level, the home of the lower orders. This spatial hierarchy represented both the ideal of the visibility of the classes to each other and the necessity of distinction between them. The experience of play-going was therefore capable of interacting in complex ways with the manifold 'show' that constituted Georgian society as a whole. The theatre was a social laboratory in which what it meant to be a man and woman in this society could be daily affirmed, tested and potentially re-imagined.

The French Revolution represented a profound challenge to the cultural politics of the Georgian theatre because of the way it reconfigured the relationship between rulers and ruled, dismantling the 'natural' authority of the elite and thereby questioning the very idea of who was entitled to perform for whom in the theatre of the political nation. The elite no longer held centre stage, as the only meaningful show was the newly proclaimed sovereignty of the people, a theatre which did not need the traditional division of box, pit and gallery as its mirror but was theoretically boundless. The challenge posed by the French Revolution to the theatricality of late Georgian political culture was also accentuated by the fact that it was communicated and debated in Britain primarily by means of print culture – i.e. through the channels of the newspaper and the periodical press and the outpouring of books and pamphlets as a consequence, in particular, of Edmund Burke's *Reflections on the Revolution in France* (1790). The Revolution occurred at a time when print and the written rather than the spoken word were eclipsing traditional theatrical modes of political communication – modes such as public oratory or the aura conveyed by the person of the monarch – which relied on the power of embodiment and material space.

William Hazlitt was among the first to recognize this change when he claimed in the *Life of Napoleon* (1828–30) that the French Revolution 'might be described as a remote but inevitable result of the invention of the art of printing' (*WH Works*, vol. XIII, p. 38). The Revolution, Hazlitt claimed in the *London Magazine* in 1820, had 'rivetted all eyes, and distracted all hearts', compelling Britain to become a 'nation of politicians and newsmongers', too obsessed with the larger drama of the rise and fall of nations to be interested in the woes of fictitious characters on the stage of a theatre (*WH Works*, vol. XVIII, p. 304). 'Literature and civilization' had 'abstracted man from himself so far, that his existence is no longer *dramatic*; and the press has been the ruin of the stage, unless we are greatly deceived' (p. 305). This chapter will explore Hazlitt's claim in relation to some key dramatic texts of the 1790s. Theatre and drama were transformed in this period and a comprehensive account of this response has yet to be written. What follows suggests some of the ways in which the magnitude of the crisis of the 1790s was manifested in the theatre and dramatic writing, beginning with the most notable 'Revolutionary drama' of the decade, the argument enacted between Burke and Thomas Paine in the pages of the *Reflections* and *Rights of Man* (1791–2).

'I cannot consider Mr Burke's book in scarcely any other light than a dramatic performance', declared Paine in *Rights of Man*, '. . . Mr Burke should recollect that he is writing History, and not *Plays*' (Paine, *RM*, pp. 110, 100). Paine was not the first to identify theatricality as central to both the substance of the *Reflections* and the flamboyance of its literary style, but he was the first to engage directly and comprehensively with Burke's dramatic theory of politics. Theatre and theatricality function in the *Reflections* in complex ways, most notably in Burke's argument that the natural response to the events in France should be analogous to witnessing a tragedy in the theatre. Attacking the dissenting minister Richard Price for his triumph over the fall of the French monarchy in his sermon to the Revolution Society in November 1789, Burke argues that such events should instead be perceived as shocks to the moral order of truly tragic proportions. To be moved and shaken by the performances of Sarah Siddons, the leading tragic actress of the period, and yet exult over the fate of Louis XVI and Marie Antoinette, as Price had done, is a sign of the latter's moral deficiency, a failure which in Burke's eyes exposes the danger of Price's political principles:

> in the theatre, the first intuitive glance, without any elaborate process of rea-
> soning, would shew, that this method of political computation [i.e. Price's
> response to the Revolution] would justify every extent of crime...Justifying
> perfidy and murder for public benefit, public benefit would soon become the
> pretext, and perfidy and murder the end; until rapacity, malice, revenge, and
> fear more dreadful than revenge, could satiate their insatiable appetites. Such
> must be the consequences of losing in the splendour of these triumphs of the
> rights of men, all natural sense of wrong and right.
> (*EB Writings*, vol. VIII, pp. 132, 133)

This passage illustrates Burke's indebtedness to public oratory and the grandiloquence of tragic drama, particularly Shakespeare. Paine responded to Burke's construction of the Revolution as tragedy by attacking his opponent as an elitist who was incapable of appreciating the genuine suffering of ordinary people:

> He is not affected by the reality of distress touching his heart, but by the showy
> resemblance of it striking his imagination. He pities the plumage, but forgets
> the dying bird...His hero or his heroine must be a tragedy-victim expiring in
> show, and not the real prisoner of misery, sliding into death in the silence of a
> dungeon. (Paine, *RM*, p. 102)

Instead Paine argued that the institution of monarchy more justifiably deserved to be regarded as pantomime or burlesque, a sophisticated manip-ulation of the artifices of illusion designed to divert and bamboozle but with no intrinsic moral, aesthetic or political value. Whereas Burke uses theatri-cality to enhance the mystique of monarchy, Paine mobilizes its effects to achieve the opposite, pulling away the 'curtain' of the show of power to expose its artificiality and essential ludicrousness (p. 234). Some commentators have interpreted *Rights of Man* as being anti-theatrical, but this is far from being the case. Both antagonists in this 'Revolutionary drama' show themselves to be immersed in theatre and theatricality and the effectiveness of their argument is dependent on their readers' familiarity not only with the theatricality in the abstract but also with the specificity of the contemporary theatre.

A notable example of this is Burke's characterization of the Revolution as a 'monstrous tragi-comic scene' and of the members of the National Assembly as conducting a farce before the French people:

> they act like the comedians of a fair before a riotous audience; they act amidst the tumultuous cries of a mixed mob of ferocious men, and of women lost to shame, who, according to their insolent fancies, direct, control, applaud, explode them . . . As they have inverted order in all things, the gallery is in the place of the house. (*EB Writings*, vol. VIII, pp. 60, 119)

The Revolution, according to Burke, is a grotesque adulteration of genres, class and sexual proprieties. He makes an implicit contrast between the generic purity and dignity of the British constitution, as symbolized by Siddons, tragedy and the hierarchy of box, pit and gallery, and the chaos and perversion of the Revolution, signified by the ascendancy of low genres and the takeover of the royal theatre by the licentious and disorderly theatre of the fair (evoking the carnivalesque of London's major summer fair, Bartholomew Fair). Most important, though, is the violation of the hierarchy signified by the distinctions between box, pit and gallery. In Burke's nightmarish vision, the lower orders in the gallery of the French polity are not merely demanding to be heard – they have taken 'the place of the house'. In other words, they are no longer the audience of and for power but are capable of constituting power in their own right – the 'theatre royal' was now a theatre of the people.

In contrast, Paine's mobilization of low genres such as pantomime as a metaphor for monarchy implicitly legitimates these genres as ways of viewing the world. Moreover, *Rights of Man* counters Burke's image of the Revolution as a theatre in which the lower orders in the gallery have taken over by proposing an alternative kind of theatre altogether – the 'representative system' of government which 'like the nation itself . . . possesses a perpetual stamina, as well of body as of mind, and presents itself on the open theatre of the world in a fair and manly manner' (Paine, *RM*, p. 235). In this 'manly' theatre of Revolution (in contrast to the feminized tragic theatre of Burke in which Siddons is the most noble exemplar), what has been secret can be revealed and what has been silent – 'real' misery – can be voiced for the first time. Rather than the gallery taking the place of the house, the house itself had figuratively been abandoned because the sovereignty of the people did not need to find its place within the old order. This change has implications for the distinction which Paine makes between 'history' and 'plays': rather than being anti-theatrical, 'history' is figured as analogous to the 'open theatre of the world', signifying a need for a revolution in representation itself, a more mobile and transparent form of communication that was capable of advancing the rights of man. Writing, like the theatre itself, could no longer be confined to established genres or institutions.

The long-term significance of the *Reflections* and *Rights of Man* lay in the way that they revealed the power of the printed word to effect historical change. While both texts evoke and indeed debate the power of the spoken word, as in Burke's attack on Price's sermon, and reading aloud was one of the main ways in which *Rights of Man* (especially part two) was disseminated, their main impact was in making print the fulcrum of the national conversation about the Revolution. The fact that events in France, particularly the Terror, seemed to realize what Burke predicted – a 'fear more dreadful than revenge' – only enhanced the impact of the *Reflections*. The possibility that Burke had not only responded to historical events but, in a sense, imagined them into being, was to have a profound influence on first-generation Romantic writers such as Wordsworth and Coleridge.

How dramatists, performers and theatre managers responded to events in France and the ensuing Revolution controversy in Britain was shaped by conditions of censorship and regulation that pre-dated 1789. Since 1737, all dramatic texts had been subject to scrutiny prior to performance, a system of censorship reinforced by the regulation of theatres that determined where plays, and what kind of play, could be staged. The performance of the 'legitimate' drama of writers such as Shakespeare was limited to theatres that were licensed by Parliament, or, in the case of the two major London theatres, Covent Garden and Drury Lane, had patents or special authority from the monarch. The so-called 'minor' theatres of London such as Sadler's Wells were prohibited by law from performing the legitimate drama and specialized instead in 'low' forms such as pantomime, a cultural distinction that Burke and Paine exploited in their representation of the Revolution as theatre. Because of an accident of timing, the minor theatres were the first to represent events in Paris: Covent Garden and Drury Lane were closed during the summer months so playhouses such as Sadler's Wells, the Royalty Theatre in the East End, and the Circuses of Philip Hughes and Philip Astley took the lead in catering to public interest in events in Paris by re-enacting the fall of the Bastille.

John Dent's *The Triumph of Liberty: or, The Fall of the Bastille* was produced at Hughes's Royal Circus on August 5 1789, less than three weeks after the event had taken place in Paris. Philip Astley competed with Hughes by offering his own 'extraordinary entertainment' two weeks later, entitled *Paris in an Uproar*: 'grounded on authentic Facts', its chief attraction was a scale model of the city of Paris 'covering the whole Theatre'.[1] This was a new kind of illegitimate drama, very different from other traditional 'low' genres such as pantomime. Deprived by law of their right to perform legitimate literary drama, these minor establishments were creating a form of theatre that communicated the topical immediacy of what was happening in France, and in particular, the fluidity and energy of the mobilized Revolutionary crowd. This was theatre as news, anticipating not only the expansiveness of Paine's 'open theatre of the world' but also Hazlitt's sense of the cultural shift caused by the Revolution – a move in focus away from the drama of the individual to the drama of 'history' and its mediations.

By November 1789, however, the Censor for Plays, John Larpent, was beginning to monitor more closely any references in the theatre to events in France. In that month he excised references to the rights of man from a ballad opera staged at Covent Garden theatre, John St John's *The Island of St Marguerite*. Rather than rendering the theatre 'safe' from the Revolution, however, the effect of censorship was to intensify the political atmosphere, making writers ingenious in their attempts to elude Larpent and sensitizing audiences to potential political meanings in texts. A notable example of the latter occurred in October 1795 when the radical lecturer John Thelwall and a group of supporters hijacked a performance of the Restoration tragedy *Venice Preserv'd* (1682) by Thomas Otway, a play about conspiracy and rebellion: when one of the characters declared 'Curs'd be your senate, curs'd your constitution', Thelwall and his friends enthusiastically applauded the lines in an attempt to apply them to the conditions of late 1795. As a result *Venice Preserv'd* was removed from the repertory and not performed again until the 1830s.

Throughout Britain the theatre became a battleground between loyalists and radicals as factions within audiences clashed over the singing of 'God save the King' or the Revolutionary anthem 'Ça ira'. Such tension was particularly acute in garrison and naval towns as Britain became more militarized after 1793: military and naval officers used the theatre to demonstrate their loyalty and flush out local sympathizers of the Revolution. An example of such behaviour is a riot at the Portsmouth theatre in February 1795, occasioned by the performance of Elizabeth Inchbald's comedy *Every One Has His Fault* (1793): a group of naval officers rushed into the theatre with a 'hideous yell', causing the performance to be quickly terminated.[2] Inchbald's play highlights the different circumstances which writers, theatre managers and audiences had to confront in the 1790s.

Every One Has His Fault concerns the efforts of a good-natured man, Mr Harmony, to resolve the marital difficulties of a group of friends and bring about the reconciliation between Lord Norland and his daughter, rejected by her father after she marries an impecunious military officer, Mr Irwin, for love. At the beginning of the play the Irwins have been forced to return to London because of their poverty, after years of service in America. In January 1793 Britain was within a few weeks of going to war with Revolutionary France and the plight of Irwin, driven by desperation to the brink of suicide, raises important though implicit questions about the costs of war and the obligations of the elite to those who fight in its name. The most controversial aspect of the play, however, was felt to be Mr Harmony's reference to the 'scarcity of provisions' as the reason why the poor were driven to crime, alluding to food shortages in late 1792–3. This phrase, repeated a number of times, and deemed permissible by the censor, was seized upon by the pro-government newspaper, the *True Briton*, which claimed that 'such allusions' were 'highly objectionable', revealing the 'cloven foot' of Inchbald the '*Democrat*'. Significantly the *True Briton* also linked the questionable 'tendency' of *Every One Has His Fault* to a generic indeterminacy: 'we are at a loss what to term this new species of composition; 'tis neither Comedy, nor Tragi-Comedy, but something anomalous in which the two are jumbled together'.[3]

The military officers who rioted against *Every One Has His Fault* are likely to have been responding to this branding of the play and its author as democratic in their 'tendency'. It is possible that the 'provisions are so scarce' line was a clever ruse on Inchbald's part, designed to distract the attention of the censor and the loyalist press while at the same time priming audiences and readers to be alert to more subtle allusions, such as the representation of the military or the condition of women in marriage, an important dimension of the Revolution debate. The prologue of the play linked it explicitly with Mary Wollstonecraft's *Vindication of the Rights of Woman* (1792), the arguments of which Inchbald dramatizes when Lord Norland criticizes his ward Miss Wooburn's unwillingness to marry his choice of husband for her by declaring: 'You are reversing the order of society; men, only, have the right of choice in marriage.'[4] Elsewhere, the play raises some important issues about the compatibility of justice and mercy as well as questioning the qualifications of the elite to exercise such virtues. At one point Mr Harmony, the play's embodiment of the ideals of philanthropy and benevolence, challenges Lord Norland's insistence on the necessity of punishing transgression: 'let me tell you, my Lord, that amidst all your authority, your state, your grandeur, I often pity you.'⁵ This comment adapts Paine's famous claim that Burke was inclined to 'pity the plumage' and forget the 'dying bird' of 'real' suffering (Paine, *RM*, p. 102): it suggests that not only were the ruling orders incapable of feeling for the poor but that in the failure of this social duty they were themselves pitiable.

Inchbald's comedies, like those of Thomas Holcroft, exemplify the rapid evolution of the genre as it responded to the conditions of the 1790s, but even *Every One Has His Fault* did not extend its focus beyond the sphere of genteel life. Within a few years playwrights such as George Colman the Younger and Thomas Morton were producing comedies which were more socially inclusive and indeed questioning of the social hierarchy. Colman's *The Heir at Law* (1797), for example, concerns a lower middling-order family, the Dowlases, who became elevated to the peerage on the death of a distant cousin, Lord Duberly. Daniel Dowlas is a Gosport merchant trading in 'coals, cloth, herrings, linen ... bacon, and brick-dust', while his wife is a specialist washerwoman, a 'clear-starcher', details which Inchbald would later describe as creating 'true pictures of common life' (*British Theatre*, vol. XXI, pp. 7, 76, 4). The fact that the Dowlases owe their elevation to a newspaper advertisement placed by the Duberly lawyer indicates Colman's emphasis on print and commerce as the main engines of change in British society, and on social identity as transferable and a performance, rather than fixed and natural. The former clear-starcher adapts to life as Lady Duberly with ease and recruits a scholar, Dr Pangloss, to give her husband a veneer of respectability, while their son, Dick Dowlas, relishes the opportunity to play the part of the upstart London dandy, 'the beau brewer, from the Borough' (p. 46).

A contrast to these pseudo-aristocrats is a range of types from sentimental comedy, including the genteel but impoverished heroine Caroline Dormer. She employs as an act of benevolence Cicely Homespun, who, with her brother Zekiel, has gone to London after the death of their parents leaves them destitute and their landlord turns them out. Caroline Dormer is mourning the loss of her fiancé Henry Morland, the son and heir of Lord Duberly, presumed lost at sea. Morland has in fact survived and returns to London in the company of his friend Stedfast to claim his place as the rightful heir. Like *Every One Has His Fault*, *The Heir at Law* includes a number of lines which would have had particular resonance in the 1790s: Caroline Dormer declares her faith in 'nature! – spite of the inequalities which birth or education have placed between thy children'; Stedfast tells Henry Morland that 'rich or poor, great or small, we all form one chain', while Zekiel Homespun is adamant that 'the law of the land' makes 'no difference 'twixt a peer and a ploughman' (*British Theatre*, vol. XXI, pp. 26, 40, 56). Colman, unlike Inchbald, was no 'democrat', and would later become a rigid censor of the drama when he succeeded Larpent. The lines quoted above are cleverly susceptible to both radical and loyalist readings. Zekiel's confidence in the impartiality of the legal system, for example, can be seen as loyalist propaganda directed at the restive lower orders in the gallery, as making an implicit claim that this is how the law should be, or as ironically exposing such a position to the charge of naïvety (contemporary novels such as Godwin's *Caleb Williams* (1794) had drawn attention to how much the law was biased against the poor).

Colman therefore exploits the conditions of censorship to enhance the ambivalence of *The Heir at Law* and conceal his own 'tendency', while at the same time making the point that porous social identities and mobility have profoundly destabilized the social order. While Lord Norland has a powerful presence in *Every One Has His Fault*, aristocracy in *The Heir at Law* is notable for its figurative death or absence. Its return in the form of Henry Morland's miraculous escape from drowning 'like a young salmon, out of the water' (*British Theatre*, vol. XXI, p. 86) is not so much a validation of the 'natural' social order, as a fantasy resolution to the crisis of the 1790s that discloses and revels in the increasing irrelevance of the Burkean mystification of rank. A popular play well into the nineteenth century, *The Heir at Law* exemplifies how thoroughly engaged British drama was with the debates and circumstances of the 1790s: while in no way classifiable as a 'Jacobin' drama, Colman's comedy registers the profundity of the impact of the Revolution, its exploration of irrevocable social change, anticipating the literature of the Regency and, ultimately, Dickens.

While dramatists such as Inchbald and Colman worked within the limits of censorship, other writers in the 1790s evaded such conditions and indeed the theatre altogether by producing plays for reading rather than performance. The most notable example of this is the only play of the decade, apart from the illegitimate spectacles of the summer of 1789, to deal directly with events in France – *The Fall of Robespierre*, a collaboration between the young Samuel Taylor Coleridge and Robert Southey. Published in late September 1794, just a few weeks after the execution of Robespierre on 28 July 1794 had been reported in the British press, the play, like the spectacles at the minor theatres, attempted to capture the white-heat immediacy of events in France. Its status as a kind of docudrama is reflected in the play's subtitle: 'An Historic Drama': this was a play about history as it was happening. *The Fall of Robespierre* is a three-act chamber piece, quite literally so in that a significant amount of the action is located within the chamber of the French National Convention. It dramatizes the fissiparous energy of French politics as the Thermidorian faction led by Barrere, Tallien and Legendre struggle for control of the Revolution against the triumvirate led by Robespierre. Alone at the beginning of the play, Barrere declares his 'fear' of the 'Tyrant's *soul*' –

> Sudden in action, fertile in resource,
> And rising awful 'mid impending ruins;
> In splendor gloomy, as the midnight meteor,
> That fearless thwarts the elemental war.[6]

Critics such as Nicholas Roe have noted echoes of Milton's Satan in the representation of Robespierre, arguing that in the mirror of his flawed, 'baneful' majesty, Coleridge and Wordsworth saw an 'alarming, distorted version' of their own initial commitment to the ideals of the French Revolution and the failure or perversion of those ideals.[7] In that sense, the Robespierre of Coleridge and Southey's play is the model of a type that would recur and indeed be constitutive of what was later termed as 'Romantic drama' – the hero whose genius has turned in upon itself, apparent in the character of Rivers in Wordsworth's *The Borderers* (1797), Joanna Baillie's *De Monfort* (1798–1800), Robert Maturin's *Bertram* (1816) and Byron's *Manfred* (1816–17).

The Fall of Robespierre is even more significant than this because it showed why such individual dramas and the very idea of the tragic hero could no longer adequately represent the magnitude of social and personal experience in the wake of the Revolution. The play is a 'historic drama', not a tragedy: Robespierre's fall is ultimately subsumed by the momentum of the Revolution itself, Barrere at the end of the play declaring that:

> Sublime amid the storm shall France arise,
> And like the rock amid surrounding waves
> Repel the rushing ocean...
> ...She shall blast
> The despot's pride, and liberate the world![8]

This evocation of the Revolution as an unfolding, potentially never-ending process, as writing itself into being, is in line with the revolution in representation implied by Paine's 'open theatre of the world'. The emphasis in *The Fall of Robespierre* on the French Revolution as happening in the real time of writers, readers and the historical actors in Paris exemplifies Paineite 'history' as opposed to Burkean 'plays'. Coleridge and Southey had embraced the opportunities of print culture in the early 1790s to create their own 'dramatic performance' which also asserted their candidacy as actors in their own right in the public sphere of British politics and literary culture. They, like Burke and Paine, could make things happen through writing. Rather than being anti-theatrical, as such plays have been interpreted, *The Fall of Robespierre* shows how integral drama and theatre were to representations of the Revolution. It could not be imagined without them.

The revolution in genre signified by *The Fall of Robespierre* became a matter of increasing concern in the 1790s. We have already seen the *True Briton's* dismissal of *Every One Has His Fault* as generically 'anomalous', not easily identifiable as either comedy or tragi-comedy. Genre mattered because, as Burke had reminded his readers, it was central to the ideas and practices of legitimacy underpinning both culture and politics: to destabilize generic hierarchy in the theatre in the wake of the Revolution was to threaten, as Lord Norland's ward had done, the 'order of society'.

A factor in this confusion of genres was changes to the structures of the theatres themselves. Covent Garden and Drury Lane underwent major reconstructions in 1792 and 1794 respectively, increasing both the capacity of their auditoriums and the size of their stages. Significantly, the renovations to Covent Garden entailed an attempt to reduce the capacity of the one-shilling gallery, the area associated with the lower orders, a move which led to disturbances in the theatre. The large stages of the new Covent Garden and Drury Lane were more conducive to the kind of spectacular effects associated with the innovative re-enactments developed by the minor theatres after 1789. Particularly after war was declared in 1793, Covent Garden and Drury Lane reinforced their status as national theatres by staging large-scale pageants and spectacles commemorating naval and military victories, productions which were designed to enhance the prestige of the monarch and the armed forces, as well as countering anti-war and radical dissent. Shakespeare was mobilized for the cause in adaptations such as the actor-manager John Philip Kemble's *Henry V* (1789), while new plays were staged such as George Watson-Taylor's historical drama *England Preserved* (1795). This loyalist theatre, while defending church and King, nonetheless exacerbated the dissolution of dramatic genres as well as eroding the distinction between legitimate and illegitimate theatres and practices. Productions such as Andrew Franklin's *A Trip to the Nore*, which commemorated George III's attendance at a Portsmouth naval review in 1797 from the perspective of the patriotic crowds rushing to see the King, represented a loyalist version of Paine's 'open theatre of the world'. They signified a recognition that the 'people' needed to be taken into account, if only to make sure that the people were on the right side.

The most important theatrical and literary forms to emerge from the meltdown of dramatic genres in the wake of the Revolution, with long-term implications for modern culture, were gothic drama and melodrama. Gothic drama, that is, plays dealing with wild, improbable events, set in exotic locations often in the past, and with supernatural themes, predates 1789, but the genre took off in the 1790s due to a combination of factors. These factors included the success of the gothic novels of Ann Radcliffe, the expansion of the major theatres enabling more spectacular scenic effects and, most significantly, the prevalence of the gothic as a key trope of the Revolution debate. Mary Wollstonecraft, for example, had claimed in *A Vindication of the Rights of Woman* that Burke's defence of the ruling order was based on 'gothic notions of beauty', a mistaken respect for what was crumbling into decay, like an old castle, which possibly concealed darker secrets and perversions behind its ivy-clad walls, such as Paine's 'real prisoner of misery' (*MW Works*, vol. v, p. 10; Paine, *RM*, p. 102). Matthew 'Monk' Lewis's gothic drama, *The Castle Spectre*, was a sensational success in 1797: while not explicitly political, it nonetheless contributed to an idea of the British aristocracy as sinister, its power and traditions representing a decadent, tottering edifice. By pathologizing power in this way, gothic drama was also able to mediate what it meant in psychic terms for British society to come to terms with the impact of the Revolution. It explores the terror, as well as the excitement, entailed in questioning the validity of the ruling order.

Gothic drama was also capable of 'spooking' the Paineite ideal of transparency, that is, it queried the value of pulling away the curtain of the theatre of power in order to see it as it 'really' is. Be careful what you wish for, gothic drama seems to be saying, advice which underpins Burke's argument that tearing the drapery away from the mystique of monarchy produces a dangerous uniformity that negates all value. Melodrama, another emergent genre of the 1790s, is similarly ambivalent. The first play to be explicitly defined as a melodrama was Thomas Holcroft's *A Tale of Mystery* (1802), an adaptation of the French playwright Guilbert de Pixérécourt's *Coelina*. One of the leading dramatists of the period, Holcroft was well known for his radical affiliations – he was one of the group, including Horne Tooke and Thomas Hardy, indicted for high treason in 1794, which blighted his subsequent career in the theatre. In the advertisement to the published edition of his comedy *Knave or Not?* (1798), Holcroft protested the 'unrelenting opposition' which he had experienced, forcing him to leave England for Germany in 1799.[9] The plays which he brought back to London, *A Tale of Mystery* and the earlier *Deaf and Dumb* (1801) are significantly different from his social realist comedies of the early 1790s in their emphasis, in particular, on characters who are unable to speak. Muteness in both plays is indicative of the capacity of this new genre to articulate the powerlessness of those without a voice, such as the silence of Paine's 'real prisoner of misery'. As Jane Moody notes, it also emblematizes the condition of censorship and counter-revolution which Holcroft had experienced, the silencing of his 'voice'.[10] But, as in the case of gothic drama, such tropes were double-edged: resorting to a language of corporeal gesture or pantomime, to mouths that open but do not speak, confronts the ideal of transparent, open communication between individuals and societies with the inadequacy of words and the failure of communication. One effect of the French Revolution on British drama, therefore, was to polarize it between the emphasis on the dramatic performances of print, as exemplified by the texts of Burke and Paine and *The Fall of Robespierre*, and a theatre dominated by the visual languages of spectacle, the body, and a poetics of silence.

Another emergent genre of the late 1790s, sharing many of the features of melodrama, was what was known as the 'German drama', principally identified with the plays of August von Kotzebue. A Kotzebue craze swept British theatre and the reading public, as many translations of his plays were produced, and stage adaptations, including Richard Brinsley Sheridan's version of his play about the Spanish conquest of Peru, *Pizarro* (1799), were phenomenally successful. Kotzebue's plays were notable for their generic indeterminacy, exacerbating the trend towards the apparent dissolution of the genres of tragedy and comedy. They often rendered as comedy what were customarily themes for tragedy, such as adultery, by absolving transgressions or reconstituting broken families. *The Stranger* (1798), for example, included one of Sarah Siddons's most famous roles of the 1790s, 'Mrs Haller', the assumed name of a countess who leaves her husband for another man and then, realizing her error, returns to care for her children in the disguise of a governess. The play ends with a tableau in which the estranged husband and penitent wife embrace each other as their children gather around them in melodramatic dumb show. *The Stranger* was highly controversial, not least for how it seemed to be condoning adultery in the context of a general moral panic about adultery and divorce in the 1790s, often blamed on the contagious principles of the Revolution. It was also regarded as travestying the tragic dignity of Sarah Siddons, some commentators expressing horror at the very idea of contemplating her in the role of a rehabilitated adulteress. In *The Fall of Robespierre* the feminized domestic sphere in the form of the home of Tallien, where his loyal wife sings a song of peace, forms a refuge amidst the maelstrom of male-dominated politics. The importance of the German drama lay in the way that it made such a distinction untenable, collapsing the public, political realm into the domestic, and vice versa. It was at this point, according to Coleridge, writing in 1816, that British drama became truly 'Jacobinical', the failure to punish the transgression of women being the ultimate sign of the 'confusion and subversion of the natural order of things'.[11]

Siddons also features in another hybrid drama, Joanna Baillie's gothic thriller, *De Monfort*. Originally published in Baillie's *Series of Plays on the Passions* (1798), *De Monfort* was adapted in 1800 as a vehicle for Siddons and her brother John Philip Kemble, who used the resources of the large Drury Lane stage to surround the play's study of jealousy and paranoia with gothic gloom and magnificence. Siddons played Jane De Monfort, the sister of the eponymous hero who is afflicted by a deforming jealousy of his childhood rival Rezenvelt. De Monfort regards Rezenvelt as a parvenu, someone of low social origins whose rise to a position of eminence affronts the proper 'order of things'. Identified by some literary critics as indicating an anti-theatrical turn to the individual and interiority, and a rejection of the social and the theatre, *De Monfort* is in fact a profoundly political play, embedded in its times. Through the characters of De Monfort and his sister Jane, Baillie explores the collective breakdown of a social class, i.e. the aristocracy. De Monfort's eventual murder of Rezenvelt is both an individual and a social response: it is the extreme reaction of a social order to the prospect of its usurpation. Jane De Monfort stands for the dignity and glory of that aristocratic tradition – she is 'gigantic' in stature, moving in 'high, habitual state', her robes like 'unfurled banners' (*British Theatre*, vol. XXIV, p. 25). Baillie's emphasis on her nobility exploits both Siddons's regal persona and implicitly her role in the Revolution debate as the epitome of the beauty of nobility which Burke knew the Revolution would destroy. However, as the 'virgin mother of an orphan race', Jane De Monfort is the last of her kind, left alone when her brother simply cannot live after killing Rezenvelt (p. 32). *De Monfort* mourns the loss of 'pride' as well as suggesting that the old order could no longer sustain it: together the De Monforts represent a caste that has consumed itself. Sarah Siddons in her noble roles, as de facto Marie Antoinette for Burke, and as the orphan aristocrat Jane De Monfort, frames the Revolutionary drama of the 1790s, signifying the magnitude of the events of 1789 for British society as well as the irrevocability of the change they caused.

NOTES

1 *Public Advertiser*, 17 August 1789, p. 1.
2 *Hampshire Chronicle*, 16 February 1795.
3 *True Briton*, 30 January 1793, p. 2.
4 Jeffrey N. Cox and Michael Gamer, eds., *The Broadview Anthology of Romantic Drama* (Peterborough, ON: Broadview, 2003), 57.
5 *Ibid.*, p. 64.
6 Samuel Taylor Coleridge, *Poetical Works* III, *Plays: Part 1*, ed. J. C. C. Mays (Princeton: Princeton University Press, 2001), p. 13.

7 Nicholas Roe, *Wordsworth and Coleridge: The Radical Years* (Oxford: Clarendon Press, 1988), p. 210.
8 Coleridge, *Poetical Works* III, p. 44.
9 Thomas Holcroft, *Knave or Not?* (London: G. G. and J. Robinson, 1798), p. iii.
10 Jane Moody, *Illegitimate Theatre in London, 1770–1840* (Cambridge: Cambridge University Press, 2000), p. 90.
11 Samuel Taylor Coleridge, *Biographia Literaria* II, ed. James Engell and W. Jackson Bate (London: Routledge and Kegan Paul, 1983), p. 221.

13

SIMON BAINBRIDGE

Politics and poetry

Poetry and the spirit of the age

In his essay 'Mr Wordsworth' in *The Spirit of the Age* (1825), the radical essayist William Hazlitt offers a polemical, tendentious and highly influential account of the relationship between the French Revolution and the work of one of the era's most important poets. Opening with a flourish, Hazlitt makes the historicist argument that 'Mr Wordsworth's genius is a pure emanation of the Spirit of the Age', proceeding to present the poet as a verse terrorist (in the 1790s sense of the word):

> [His poetry] is one of the innovations of the time. It partakes of, and is carried along with, the revolutionary movement of our age: the political changes of the day were the model on which he formed and conducted his poetical experiments. His Muse (it cannot be denied, and without this we cannot explain its character at all) is a levelling one. It proceeds on a principle of equality, and strives to reduce all things to the same standard.
>
> (*WH Works*, vol. XI, p. 87)

Wordsworth, Hazlitt suggests, marches poetry to the guillotine with a Robespierrean ruthlessness, striving to rid it of its literary heritage and its generic hierarchies:

> His popular, inartificial style gets rid (at a blow) of all the trappings of verse, of all the high places of poetry... The purple pall, the nodding plume of tragedy are exploded as mere pantomime and trick, to return to the simplicity of truth and nature. Kings, queens, priests, nobles, the altar and the throne, the distinctions of rank, birth, wealth, power, 'the judge's robe, the marshal's truncheon, the ceremony that to great ones 'longs,' are not to be found here. The author tramples on the pride of art with greater pride. The Ode and Epode, the Strophe and the Antistrophe, he laughs to scorn. The harp of Homer, the trump of Pindar and of Alcæus are still. The decencies of costume, the decorations of vanity are stripped off without mercy as barbarous, idle, and Gothic.
>
> (p. 87)

As Hazlitt illustrates, the politics of poetry is not only a matter of content but of genre, form, language and tradition. Hazlitt locates Wordsworth's poetry within the Revolution controversy of the 1790s and by so doing makes it a part of that debate. By echoing Edmund Burke's famous lament in *Reflections on the Revolution in France* that 'all the decent drapery of life is to be rudely torn off' (*EB Writings*, vol. VIII, p. 128), he brilliantly clinches his argument that Wordsworth's poetry can only really be understood within the context of the French Revolution and the pamphlet war it sparked in Britain.

Hazlitt clearly relishes characterizing Wordsworth's poetry as 'levelling', particularly given what he saw as the increasingly conservative trajectory of Wordsworth's allegiances following his period of revolutionary sympathies in the 1790s. Hazlitt frequently extended his argument to the wider movement of the Lake School of poetry (which also included Robert Southey and Samuel Taylor Coleridge), commenting that it 'had its origin in the French revolution, or rather in those sentiments and opinions which produced that revolution' (*WH Works*, vol. V, p. 161). But Hazlitt's account is only the most extreme of several influential arguments that see the period's poetry (and literature more generally) as shaped, at least in part, by French Revolutionary events and the controversy they produced in Britain. Writing from the other end of the political spectrum to Hazlitt, Francis Jeffrey, the conservative literary critic and co-founder of the *Edinburgh Review*, identified the 'agitations of the French revolution, and the discussions as well as the hopes and terrors to which it gave occasion' as a major factor in what he described as 'the revolution in our literature'.[1] For both Hazlitt and Jeffrey, events in France provided a structure as well as a cause for a 'revolution' in literature, though the trajectory of many writers away from support of the French cause during the 1790s has prompted many critics to reassess the literature of the 1790s as counter-revolutionary, both in politics and form. (Wordsworth's and Coleridge's collection *Lyrical Ballads* with its use of the 'language really spoken by men'[2] and its 'low' subject matter remains a favourite site for these critical debates.) The link between revolutionary events and the era's poetry was given its most forceful modern statement by M. H. Abrams in an essay of 1963 entitled 'English Romanticism: The Spirit of the Age'. As the title of this essay suggests, Abrams is concerned with a canonical Romanticism, but there is a more general relevance to his argument that 'the Romantic period was eminently an age obsessed with the fact of violent and inclusive change, and Romantic poetry cannot be understood, historically, without awareness of the degree to which this preoccupation affected its substance and form'.[3]

For poets, as for others living at the time, there was no doubt that the French Revolution was the era's crucial event and a key literary subject. In 1816, the year after the British victory over the French signalled the final defeat of any lingering hopes for those who still clung to the Revolutionary cause, Percy Shelley described the French Revolution as 'the master theme of the epoch in which we live' (*PBS Letters*, vol. I, p. 504). During the 1790s all the main poetic forms were used to respond to the Revolution, from tragedy, epic and romance, through odes, elegies, hymns and sonnets, to ballads, songs, satires and squibs. For ambitious poets, the Revolution offered a major challenge. Shelley suggested the topic to his friend Lord Byron as suitable for an epic poem worthy of his fellow poet's power, though later identified it as a subject he himself might tackle. (He can be seen to be wrestling with the legacy of the Revolution and the questions it raised in all his major works, particularly *Queen Mab*, *Laon and Cythna*, and *Prometheus Unbound*.) Two decades earlier, Coleridge had similarly written to his friend and fellow poet Wordsworth identifying the Revolution as the theme for the era's definitive poem, writing in September 1799 that 'I wish you would write a poem, in blank verse, addressed to those, who, in consequence of the complete failure of the French Revolution, have thrown up all hopes of the amelioration of mankind...It would do great good' (*STC Letters*, vol. I, p. 527). These ambitious poems remained unwritten (though Coleridge's urgings clearly informed Wordsworth's examination of the Revolution's impact in *The Prelude* and *The Excursion*), but poems on events in France had started to appear very quickly.

As early as August 1789, for example, only a month after the fall of the Bastille, Anna Seward published the following 'Sonnet to France on her present Exertions' in the *Gentleman's Magazine*:

> Thou, that where Freedom's sacred fountains play,
>> Which sprung effulgent, though with crimson stains,
>> On transatlantic shores and widening plains,
>> Hast, in their living waters, washed away
> Those cankering spots, shed by tyrannic sway
>> On thy long drooping lilies; English veins
>> Swell with the tide of exultation gay
>> To see thee spurn thy deeply-galling chains.
> Few of Britannia's free-born sons forbear
>> To bless thy cause; cold is the heart that breathes
>> No wish fraternal. France, we bid thee share
> The blessings twining with our civic wreaths,
>> While Victory's trophies, permanent as fair,
>> Crown the bright sword that Liberty unsheathes.[4]

The greater part of Seward's sonnet expresses standard and fairly widespread early reactions to events in France: the Freedom that had originated during the Revolution in America ('transatlantic shores') has now spread to France, a development welcomed in the constitutional monarchy of Britain where it is viewed as a movement away from the tyranny of absolute monarchy and towards the mixed form of government that Britain itself has enjoyed since the 'Glorious Revolution' of 1688. The sonnet illustrates how easily fashionable poetic modes and forms could absorb the events of the Revolution at this early stage; the poem is very much a sonnet of sensibility which celebrates the sympathetic response of the body ('veins', 'heart') of the British nation, and Seward uses the sonnet's sestet to provide something of an explanatory gloss on the octet's extended natural metaphors. More controversially, the sonnet's closing lines suggest that the progress of freedom may involve bloodshed, as Liberty unsheaths her sword, and it is probably because of this seemingly positive anticipation of the later violent stages of the Revolution that Anna Seward never republished the sonnet. Indeed, Seward would be strongly influenced by Burke's *Reflections* and would go on to chastise other writers and poets for their continuing support of the Revolution, particularly after the execution of Louis XVI, describing France to Helen Maria Williams in 1793 as a 'land of carnage' operating an 'equalizing system which . . . lifts every man's hand against his brother'[5] and denouncing Robert Southey as a 'beardless Paricide' inspired by a 'treach'rous Muse' in a 1797 poem 'After Reading Southey's "Joan of Arc"' (Bennett, pp. 198–9).

In its publication history, Seward's sonnet is representative of much verse written on the Revolution; given the rapidity of developments across the Channel, the shifting nature of British responses to them and the increasing dangers that came with publication (a Royal Proclamation Against Seditious Writings and Publications was made in May 1792), poems were often published only once, were heavily revised when republished or were never published at all. The first book of William Blake's proposed seven-book poem *The French Revolution* was printed as a proof in 1791 but seems never to have been published, perhaps as a result of his publisher's fear of prosecution or the author's own uncertainty about the project. Some writers, such as Amelia Opie, were much more supportive of the Revolutionary cause in their private letters than in their public verse. The most sustained poetic account of an individual's response to the events in France, William Wordsworth's *The Prelude*, was not published until after the poet's death in 1850, though Wordsworth did publish the famous passage commencing 'Oh! Pleasant exercise of hope and joy!' under the title 'French Revolution, As It Appeared to Enthusiasts at Its Commencement' in Coleridge's periodical *The Friend* in 1809, reprinting it in his *Poems* of 1815, and presented a version of his own history, combined with that of a number of others, in the figure of the solitary in *The Excursion* (1814).

The politics of poetry in the 1790s

By 1794, one anonymous poet was complaining, albeit with a degree of hyperbole, that modern poetry was dominated by Revolutionary subject matter. In a poem entitled 'The Spinning Wheel' published in the *Gentleman's Magazine*, this poet asks if 'In this dread season, when the rage of War / And din of Anarchy confound the world, / When madding Nations scorn the scepter'd sway / Of ancient Rulers':

> ...can a single voice
> Be heard, that neither sounds the martial trump,
> Nor swells the frantic mob's tumultuous strife,
> Nor mourns thy fate, poor Louis! but descends
> From Europe's dangers...?[6]

These lines characterize the ideological intent of two major strands of 1790s poetry, patriotic bellicose verse (Britain and France had been at war since 1793) and pro-revolutionary, pro-Gallic pieces, here represented as pieces of popular agitation. In its use of the personifications 'Anarchy' and 'War', 'The Spinning Wheel' is also representative of a wide range of texts which present world affairs and political developments as acted out by giant forms (Freedom, Tyranny, Liberty, War, Peace, Discord, Slaughter, Valour, Glory, Gallia, Albion, Britannia) or symbolized by natural forces (storms, whirlwinds, volcanic explosions, daybreak). The allusion to 'poor' Louis XVI's 'fate' also invokes one of the major poetic topics of these years, the treatment of the French royal family (the subject of poems by Mary Robinson and Charlotte Smith, amongst others), and illustrates a mode widely used in response to the Revolution and the subsequent war, sensibility (as in Seward's sonnet above). The eighteenth-century cult of sensibility provided a key mode for understanding and representing events in France, and its ethic of feeling for those who suffer underpins works such as Charlotte Smith's *The Emigrants*, with its series of portrayals of the victims of political events, and Wordsworth's *The Prelude*, in which the poet's encounter with 'a hunger-bitten girl' becomes the crucial moment in his conversion to the Revolutionary cause (*Prelude* (1805), IX. 512–34).

Poetry was very much part of the Revolution controversy of the 1790s and poets sought to play a role in the decade's political debates (much popular verse on the Revolution is collected in two excellent anthologies, Betty Bennett's *British War Poetry in the Age of Romanticism, 1793–1815* and Michael Scrivener's *Poetry and Reform: Periodical Verse from the English Democratic Press, 1792–1824*). Poems on the Revolution were published in a range of different print media, as broadsides or pamphlets, in newspapers and magazines, as well as in collections of verse. Variant versions of poems were produced for these different forms and with different readerships in mind. For example, the relatively elevated 'An Ode on the Restoration of Freedom to France', published in the *Gentleman's and London Magazine* in January 1793, was also published as a radical broadsheet ballad 'Millions be Free: A New Song. Tune – "To Anacreon in Heaven"'. While the 'Ode' concludes each stanza by proclaiming that the French Decree 'tears off their chains, and bids millions be free', the broadside promises its readership that the Decree 'Tears off *our* chains, and Bids MILLIONS BE FREE', a considerably more radical statement in its desire to extend to Britain the Decree of November 1792 offering 'fraternity and assistance to all peoples who seek to recover their liberty'.[7] As the ballad version of 'Millions be Free' illustrates, much 1790s poetry shared the ambition of many participants in the pamphlet war of involving a much wider readership (and audience) in political activity than had previously been the case, mixing oral and print traditions. Many poems on the Revolution were designed to be experienced communally, recited or sung in theatres, taverns or at political meetings. Indeed, poetry was often perceived to be a more powerful medium than prose because its metre, rhyme and frequent association with popular tunes made it more appealing to a less educated readership and encouraged collective performance, uniting the performers within the ideological gestures of the song. A letter by a 'friend to Church & State' written to John Reeves, the Secretary of the Association for the Preservation of Liberty and Property against Republicans and Levellers, gives a good illustration of ideological aims and methods of distribution:

> It occured [*sic*] to me, that any thing written in voice [verse?] & especially to an Old English tune…made a more fixed Impression on the Minds of the Younger and Lower Class of People, than any written in Prose, which was often forgotten as soon as Read…By printing copies of the inclosed, as Common Ballads, and putting them in the hands of individuals; or by twenties into the hands of Ballad Singers who might sing them for the sake of selling them. I own I shall not be displeased to hear Re-echoed by Every Little Boy in the Streets during the Christ.ᵐᵃˢ Holidays. –
>
> > Long may Old England, Possess Good Cheer and Jollity
> > Liberty, and Property, and No Equality.
> > > (Palmer, pp. 16–17)

As this proposed scheme suggests, patriotic or anti-Gallican verse frequently recycled traditional songs, facilitating a communal performance of anti-Revolutionary sentiments. For example, in March 1793, the *Gentleman's*

Magazine published a poem entitled 'Church and King', which offered new words to be sung to the tune of 'Rule Britannia', beginning as follows:

> While o'er the bleeding corpse of France
>   Wild Anarchy exulting stands,
> And female fiends around her dance,
>   With fatal *Lamp-cords* in their hands,
> *Chorus.* – We Britons still united sing,
> Old England's Glory, – Church and King.
>
> (Bennett, p. 71)

Pro-French and anti-war groupings similarly sought to use verse as a weapon in the pamphlet war. Publications linked to the London Corresponding Society, Daniel Eaton's *Politics for the People* and Thomas Spence's *Pig's Meat*, included poems and songs, while the words of hymns sung at meetings were published in sympathetic newspapers or journals; for example, in March 1794 the *Cambridge Intelligencer* published the 'Hymn, Sung at a Meeting of the Friends of Peace and Reform in Sheffield, held on the late Fast Day', a version of the Hymn 'O God of Hosts' which concludes by calling on God to:

> Burst every Dungeon, every Chain;
> Give injur'd Slaves their Rights again;
> Let TRUTH prevail, let Discord cease;
> Speak – and the World shall smile in PEACE!
>
> (Bennett, p. 112)

Pro-Revolutionary writers also produced new versions of traditional songs, as in a street ballad parody of the national anthem beginning 'God save – "The Rights of Man!"' of November 1792 (Palmer, p. 258). While the Revolution controversy is often thought of as a print war, then, it was also a song contest with a strong oral element, as the conclusion to a frequently reprinted piece emphasizes:

> . . . [we] mean to live happy, while frantic you sing
>   Your fav'rite *Ca ira*,
>   And hymn *Marseillois*,
> For the true Briton's song shall be 'God save the King'.
>
> (Bennett, p. 213)

This popular poetry on the Revolution was very closely engaged with the prose writing of the pamphlet war, frequently referring to key works or phrases in the controversy. Paine himself was a regular target for attack in patriotic verse ('*Sing Tanta-ra-ra-ra Rogue* PAIN'; 'GOD *save* GEORGE *our*

KING, / *Let us for ever sing – down with Tom Paine*' (Palmer, p. 258)). Burke's *Reflections* was a major source of imagery and language. While a poem like 'Stanzas, supposed to be written whilst the late QUEEN of FRANCE was sleeping, by her attendant in the TEMPLE' (Bennett, pp. 87–9) approvingly drew on Burke's famous description of Marie Antoinette, numerous verses ironically invoked his infamous term 'Swinish Multitude', as in the street ballad of 1795 entitled 'Wholsome Advice to the Swinish Multitude':

> You lower class of human race, you working part I mean,
> How dare you so audacious be to read the works of Pain,
> The Rights of Man – that cursed book – which such confusion brings,
> You'd better learn the art of war, and fight for George our King.
> *But you must delve in politics, how dare you thus intrude,*
> *Full well you do deserve the name of swinish multitude.*
> There's the laborer and mechanic too, the cobler in his stall,
> Forsooth must read the Rights of Man, and Common Sense and all!
> For shame, I desire ye wretched crew don't be such meddling fools,
> But be contented in your sphere, and mind King Charles's rules.
>
> (Palmer, pp. 257–8)

Here, the ironic parodying of Burkean attitudes facilitates a celebration of 'lower' or 'working' class participation in the print culture of the Revolution debate.

The poems discussed above are clearly designed as intervention within the debate on the Revolution or as opportunities to perform, display and confirm particular ideological positions within it. But during the decade of the 1790s, there was a much more general sense that poetry (and literature) was inherently political. The conservative satirist, T. J. Mathias, stated that 'LITERATURE, *well or ill conducted*, IS THE GREAT ENGINE *by which*, I am fully persuaded, ALL CIVILIZED STATES *must ultimately be supported or overthrown*',[8] while Samuel Taylor Coleridge wrote in 1800 that he was planning 'an Essay on the Elements of Poetry / it would in reality be a *disguised* System of Morals & Politics' (*STC Letters*, vol. 1, p. 632), anticipating Hazlitt's paralleling of poetry and politics in 'Mr Wordsworth'.

One powerful indication of the politicization of poetry in the decade following the fall of the Bastille was the launch in 1797 of *The Anti-Jacobin*, a weekly newspaper established by future Prime Minister George Canning to combat Jacobinism in all its forms, including literary ones. In the first issue, Canning provided an 'Introduction' to the poetry section of the paper in which he argued that the dominant poetry of the period was 'that of the *Jacobins*' and outlined the key characteristics of the '*Jacobin* poet':

> The poet in all ages has despised riches and grandeur.
>
> The *Jacobin* Poet improves this sentiment into a hatred of the rich and the great.
>
> The Poet of other times has been an enthusiast in the love of his native soil.
>
> The *Jacobin* Poet rejects all restriction in his feelings. *His* love is enlarged and expanded so as to comprehend all human kind. The love of all human kind is without doubt a noble passion: it can hardly be necessary to mention, that its operation extends to *Freemen*, and them only, all over the world.[9]

Canning had Robert Southey particularly in mind in this description, and early editions of *The Anti-Jacobin* carried a number of parodies of Southey's verse, most famously '(Imitation.) Sapphics. The Friend of Humanity and the Knife-Grinder', which mimics Southey's humanitarian poetry, linking it to Paine's *Rights of Man*. What made Southey particularly challenging to conservative writers was his use of classical forms, to which he drew attention in his titles, as in the case of his two anti-war poems 'The Widow: Sapphics' and 'The Soldier's Wife: Dactylics', from his *Poems* (1797). This controversial use of elevated and classical forms for radical subject matter was most evident in the work for which Southey was best known in the late 1790s, *Joan of Arc: An Epic Poem*, the opening lines of which reveal how Southey invokes epic tradition, form and language (with an allusion to Virgil's *Aeneid*) only to invert traditional epic values:

> War's varied horrors, and the train of ills
> That follow on Ambition's blood-stain'd path
> And fill the world with woe; of France preserv'd
> By maiden hand, what time her chiefs subdued,
> Or slept in death, or lingered life in chains,
> I sing: nor wilt thou FREEDOM scorn the song.[10]

As an anti-war epic poem controversially celebrating 'Freedom' and a historic French victory over Britain at a time when the two countries were again at war, *Joan of Arc* provided a focus for discussions of the relationship between politics and poetry. For fellow '*Jacobin* Poet' Coleridge (frequently grouped with Southey as a leader of the 'New School of Poetry', as in Gillray's caricature 'The New Morality', which portrays them alongside Charles James Fox, John Thelwall, Thomas Paine, Joseph Priestley, William Godwin and Mary Wollstonecraft), Southey's epic was 'a poem which exhibits fresh proof that great poetical talents and high sentiments of liberty do reciprocally produce and assist each other'.[11] Anna Seward, however, drew attention to what she saw as the incompatibility of the 'base purpose' of Southey's 'Epic Song' with the power of the 'Poesy . . . [which] / Wraps in reluctant ecstacy the soul / Where Poesy is felt' (Bennett, p. 199). While Seward's poetic response to *Joan of Arc* is itself politically motivated, it is also indicative of the developing idea that poetry should exist separately from politics, a separation that can be seen as in part a legacy of poetry's involvement in the Revolution debate.

The poetry of politics in the 1790s

The previous section has sought to illustrate the extent to which poetry was politicized in the 1790s, not only in its explicit content but also in relation to issues of form and genre. But to many contemporary observers the events of the Revolution (especially in its early stages) appeared to be like poetry, as Wordsworth emphasizes in his famous retrospective account of his feelings while in France in 1792:

> O pleasant exercise of hope and joy,
> For great were the auxiliars which then stood
> Upon our side, we who were strong in love.
> Bliss was it in that dawn to be alive,
> But to be young was very heaven! O times,
> In which the meagre, stale, forbidding ways
> Of custom, law, and statute took at once
> The attraction of a country in romance –
> When Reason seemed the most to assert her rights
> When most intent on making of herself
> A prime enchanter to assist the work
> Which then was going forwards in her name.
> *(Prelude* (1805), x. 689–700)

Politics here becomes poetry, taking on the 'attraction of a country in romance', a reference to the elevated literary genre of chivalrous quest and the supernatural that was frequently used to represent events in France (chivalry is a key value in Burke's *Reflections on the Revolution in France*, while in a poem of 1794 Coleridge presented himself as a heroic knight battling oppression: 'Red from the Tyrant's wound I shook the lance, / And strode in joy the reeking plains of France!' (*STC Poetical Works*, p. 65)). Here and in the rest of this passage, Wordsworth presents the events of this stage of the Revolution as enacting what previously had only been imagined, an idea later articulated by Southey, who commented that 'Few persons but those who have lived in it can conceive or comprehend what the memory of the French Revolution was, nor what a visionary world seemed to open upon those who were just entering it. Old things seemed passing away, and nothing was dreamt of but the regeneration of the human race.'[12]

Wordsworth's natural metaphors here and in the rest of the passage above present Revolutionary France in 1792 as experiencing a new start ('dawn', 'budding rose'), but his phrase 'very heaven' invokes an apocalyptic or millennial register found more explicitly in Southey's reference to 'the regeneration of the human race' and elsewhere in *The Prelude*, as when the poet describes the period of his first visit to France in 1790 as 'a time when Europe was rejoiced, / France standing on the top of golden hours, /And human nature seeming born again' (*Prelude* (1805), VI. 352–4). It was in such millennial terms that many poets responded to events in France in the early years of the decade, understanding these events through biblical prophecy and particularly the Book of Revelation as the second coming of Christ, bringing about the end of the old world and the creation of a new one of peace and plenty in which mankind is redeemed, a time when 'Earth shall once again / Be Paradise', to quote Southey's *Joan of Arc*.[13] Samuel Taylor Coleridge's summary of the 'Argument' of his millennial poem 'Religious Musings' shows how theological and political thinking were intertwined in such works and illustrates how historical events could be understood as part of this pre-ordained narrative: 'Introduction. Person of Christ. His prayer on the Cross. The process of his Doctrines on the mind of the Individual. Character of the Elect. Superstition. Digression to the present War. Origin and Uses of Government and Property. The present State of Society. The French Revolution. Millenium. Universal Redemption. Conclusion' (*STC Poetical Works*, p. 108). Popular poetry too made use of millennial register: 'The Triumph of Freedom' published in *The Cambridge Intelligencer* (1794), begins with the line 'The Trumpet of Liberty sounds through the World' (Bennett, p. 128).

The popular millenarianism of the 1790s is powerfully felt in the prophetic poetry of William Blake, who has been seen as representative of the decade's radicalism, combining the religious 'enthusiasm' of Richard Brothers with the Enlightenment rationalism of Tom Paine. Blake's poem *The French Revolution* includes a prophecy of 'the dawn of our peaceful morning' when 'the happy earth sing in its course, / The mild peaceable nations be opened to heaven, and men walk with their fathers in bliss' (Blake, *Poems*, pp. 138, 139). In this poem, Blake gives his most explicit treatment of specific events in France (covering the period 19 June to 15 July 1789), incorporating them into the symbolic millennial structure of the dawn of a new day. Following *The French Revolution*, Blake's treatment of contemporary events becomes increasingly symbolic and obscure but retains a tremendous sense of apocalyptic power and revolutionary energy. In 'The Song of Liberty' (1792–3) that Blake appended to his illuminated book *The Marriage of Heaven and Hell*, he traces the spread of Revolution from America to France, alluding to the destruction of the Bastille and a hoped-for end to Papal power:

1. The Eternal Female groaned; it was heard over all the earth.
2. Albion's coast is sick, silent; the American meadows faint.
3. Shadows of prophecy shiver along by the lakes and the rivers, and mutter across the ocean. France, rend down thy dungeon!
4. Golden Spain, burst the barriers of old Rome!
5. Cast thy keys, O Rome! into the deep – down falling, even to eternity down falling,
6. And weep.
7. In her trembling hands she took the new-born terror, howling.
8. On those infinite mountains of light, now barred out by the Atlantic sea, the new-born fire stood before the starry king... (Blake, *Poems*, p. 122)

Moving through a series of apocalyptic exclamations ('The fire, the fire, is falling!'), the 'Song' achieves a millennial conclusion:

the son of fire in his eastern cloud, while the morning plumes her golden breast,
20. Spurning the clouds written with curses, stamps the stony law to dust, loosing the eternal horses from the dens of night, crying:
Empire is no more! And now the lion & wolf shall cease.   (pp. 123–4)

According to a number of influential critical accounts, it was the failure of the millennial hopes for the Revolution that produced the poetry we now think of as 'Romantic', celebrating the self, the imagination and the natural world rather than engaging with politics (though other critics have questioned and made more complex such accounts). It is somewhat ironic that while M. H. Abrams asserted the significance of the Revolution for an understanding of the writing of Wordsworth, Blake and Coleridge in 'The Spirit of the Age', he did so by arguing that it was the gradual disillusionment with the French cause that led these writers to discover their true vocations as poets of the imagination. By the end of the 1790s, Abrams proposes, the disastrous events in France prompted the poets who lived through the decade to turn away from what Wordsworth terms 'the very world which is the world / Of all of us' (*Prelude* (1805), x. 725–6) and seek utopia through the imagination and an internalization of political plans. 'Hope', he argues, is 'shifted from the history of mankind to the mind of the single individual, from militant external action to an imaginative act.'[14] Coleridge's major poetic publications can be seen to offer one such history of disillusionment. In 'Religious Musings' (which he dated 1794), Coleridge presented the French Revolution in apocalyptic terms as a 'storm', 'whirlwind' and 'earthquake' that would lead to the millennium. His personification of 'the Giant Frenzy / Uprooting empires with his whirlwind arm' (*STC Poetical Works*, p. 121) can be compared with Blake's figure of Orc as a representation of Revolutionary energy. But by March 1798, Coleridge had 'snapped [his] squeaking baby-trumpet of Sedition' (*STC Letters*, vol. I, p. 397), to use his own anti-millennial and anti-Jacobin phrase. Following the French invasion of Switzerland in March 1798, Coleridge reviewed his response to events in 'France: An Ode', describing what he terms 'the Poet's Recantation'. In the 'Argument' that he appended to an 1802 version of the poem, Coleridge gave a summary of his redefined understanding of Freedom and Liberty, ideals he had previously associated with the Revolution:

> An address to Liberty, in which the Poet expresses his conviction that those feelings and that grand *ideal* of Freedom which the mind attains by its contemplation of its individual nature, and of the sublime surrounding objects... do not belong to men, as a society, nor can possibly be either gratified or realised, under any form of human government; but belong to the individual man, so far as he is pure, and inflamed with the love and adoration of God in Nature.
> (*STC Poetical Works*, p. 244)

It is through interaction with the natural world, rather than through politics, that Coleridge finds the Liberty that France has failed to realize.

The poet who gives the fullest account of his engagement with the French Revolution, and on whom the Revolution arguably had the most powerful shaping influence, is William Wordsworth. In his early version of his epic poetic autobiography, *The Prelude*, Wordsworth made very little reference to events in France. It is only in the closing movement of the 1799 version of the poem that Wordsworth suddenly alludes to the historical context in which he is writing:

> ... if in these times of fear,
> This melancholy waste of hopes o'erthrown,
> If, 'mid indifference and apathy
> And wicked exultation, when good men
> On every side fall off we know not how
> To selfishness, disguised in gentle names
> Of peace and quiet and domestic love –
> Yet mingled, not unwillingly, with sneers

On visionary minds – if, in this time
Of dereliction and dismay, I yet
Despair not of our nature, but retain
A more than Roman confidence, a faith
That fails not, in all my sorrow my support,
The blessing of my life, the gift is yours
Ye mountains, thine O Nature.

(Prelude (1799), II. 478–92)

Like Coleridge in 'France: An Ode', Wordsworth concludes his self-examination with a celebration of the relationship between the individual and the natural world, but this passage illustrates the extent to which the crisis of poetic vocation Wordsworth confronts in *The Prelude* is a historical crisis, the aftermath of the Revolution. This crisis becomes the central subject of the poem as Wordsworth expands it to become the 1805 version, describing in Books VI, IX and X his visits to France in 1790 and 1791–2 and his reaction to events while in Britain. The Miltonic structure of Wordsworth's epic of self-development underlines the centrality of the French Revolution to the poet's discovery of his vocation. In *Paradise Lost*, Adam's fall occurs in Book IX. By describing his own enthusiasm for the Revolution in the equivalent book of *The Prelude*, Wordsworth presents it as his own fall, with redemption coming through his realization of the power of the Imagination, the role of nature, and the value of the friends that the poem directly addresses, his sister Dorothy and particularly Coleridge.

The figure of Wordsworth brings us back to the issue with which this chapter started, and the question of the relationship between poetry and politics in the 1790s. As we have seen, while poetry plays a significant role in the Revolution debate, influential models of Romanticism focused on the writings of Wordsworth and Coleridge (and to a lesser extent Blake) have argued that the decade witnesses an increasing distancing of poetry from politics. Certainly some of these poets' retrospective accounts of their writing sought to detach the political world of 'realities' from the poetic world of 'fancy': these are Coleridge's terms in his 1817 'Apologetic Preface to "Fire, Famine and Slaughter"' in which he offers a defence of his savage anti-Pitt 'war eclogue' of 1798 by arguing that poetry operates in an entirely different sphere from politics, a separation of the imaginative from the social that he would develop in texts such as *Lectures on Literature*, *Biographia Literaria* and the *Statesman's Manual*. And it is in the context of such attempts to rid poetry of its Revolutionary affiliations that Hazlitt's essay 'Mr Wordsworth' is so striking, relocating the poet within the debates of the 1790s. While Hazlitt seeks to repoliticize Wordsworth, another writer of the post-Waterloo period sought to take on his mantle as a political poet. In his early sonnet 'To Wordsworth', Percy Shelley described the sense of betrayal he felt at Wordsworth's increasing conservatism, writing that:

> In honoured poverty thy voice did weave
> Songs consecrate to truth and liberty, –
> Deserting these, thou leavest me to grieve,
> Thus having been, that thou shouldst cease to be.[15]

While Wordsworth has deserted 'truth and liberty', Shelley's dedication to their cause underpins his own poetic project, one in which he continues to engage with 'the master theme of the epoch in which we live'. His famous declaration that 'Poets are the unacknowledged legislators of the World'[16] shows his desire to reforge the links between poetry and politics that were such a defining feature of the writing of the 1790s.

NOTES

1 Francis Jeffrey, *Contributions to the Edinburgh Review*, 4 vols. (London: Longman, Brown, Green and Longmans, 1844), vol. I, p. 167.
2 William Wordsworth, *The Major Works*, ed. Stephen Gill (Oxford: Oxford University Press, 1984), p. 602.
3 M. H. Abrams, 'English Romanticism: The Spirit of the Age', in *The Correspondent Breeze: Essays on English Romanticism* (New York and London: W.W. Norton & Co., 1984), pp. 44–75; p. 46.
4 Duncan Wu, ed., *Romantic Women Poets: An Anthology* (Oxford: Blackwell, 1997), pp. 6–7.
5 Quoted *ibid.*, p. 230.
6 'The Spinning Wheel', *Gentleman's Magazine*, 64 pt. 1 (April 1794), 362.
7 Betty T. Bennett, ed., *British War Poetry in the Age of Romanticism: 1793–1815* (New York and London: Garland, 1976), p. 69; Bodleian Library, *allegro* Catalogue of Ballads, Harding B 22 (173); Geoffrey Best, *War and Society in Revolutionary Europe, 1770–1870* (Stroud, Gloucestershire: Sutton Publishing, 1998), p. 82.
8 T. J. Mathias, *The Pursuits of Literature: A Satirical Poem in Dialogue. With Notes. Part the Fourth and Last*, 2nd edn (London, 1797), p. i.
9 Simon Bainbridge, ed., *Romanticism: A Sourcebook* (Basingstoke: Palgrave, 2008), p. 223.
10 Robert Southey, *Joan of Arc: An Epic Poem* (Bristol and London: Joseph Cottle, Cadell and Davies, and G.G. and J. Robinson, 1796), I. 1–6.
11 Samuel Taylor Coleridge, *The Watchman*, ed. Lewis Patton, vol. II of *The Collected Works of Samuel Taylor Coleridge* (London and Princeton: Routledge and Kegan Paul and Princeton University Press, 1970), p. 44.

12 *The Correspondence of Robert Southey with Caroline Bowles*, ed. E. Dowden (Dublin: Hodges, Figgis and Co., 1881), p. 52.
13 Southey, *Joan of Arc*, IX. 867–8.
14 Abrams, 'The Spirit of the Age', p. 66.
15 Percy Shelley, *Shelley's Poetry and Prose*, ed. Donald H. Reiman and Neil Fraistat (New York and London: W. W. Norton & Co., 2002), p. 92.
16 *Ibid.*, p. 535.

GUIDE TO FURTHER READING

Editions of primary texts

Barrell, John, and Jon Mee, eds. *Trials for Treason and Sedition 1792–1794*. 8 vols. London: Pickering and Chatto, 2006–7.

Bennett, Betty T., ed. *British War Poetry in the Age of Romanticism, 1793–1815*. New York and London: Garland, 1976.

Blake, William. *The Complete Poems*. 2nd edn. W. H. Stevenson ed. London and New York: Longman, 1989.

Burke, Edmund. *A Philosophical Enquiry into the Origin of our Ideas of the Sublime and the Beautiful*. J. T. Boulton ed. London: Routledge and Kegan Paul, 1958.

The Correspondence of Edmund Burke. Thomas Copeland gen. ed. 10 vols. Cambridge: Cambridge University Press, 1958–78.

The Writings and Speeches of Edmund Burke. Paul Langford gen. ed. 9 vols. to date. Oxford: Clarendon Press, 1981–.

Butler, Marilyn, ed. *Burke, Paine, Godwin and the Revolution Controversy*. Cambridge: Cambridge University Press, 1984.

Byron, George Gordon, Lord. *Selected Poems*. Susan J. Wolfson and Peter J. Manning ed. Harmondsworth: Penguin, 1996.

Claeys, Gregory, ed. *Political Writings of the 1790s*. 8 vols. London: Pickering and Chatto, 1995.

Cobban, Alfred, ed. *The Debate on the French Revolution 1789–1800*. 2nd edn. London: Adam and Charles Black, 1960.

Coleridge, Samuel Taylor. *Poetical Works*. Ernest Hartley Coleridge ed. London: Oxford University Press, 1969.

Davis, Michael T., ed. *London Corresponding Society, 1792–1799*. 6 vols. London: Pickering and Chatto, 2002.

Godwin, William. *Collected Novels and Memoirs of William Godwin*. Mark Philp gen. ed. 8 vols. London: Pickering and Chatto, 1992.

Political and Philosophical Writings of William Godwin. Mark Philp gen. ed. 7 vols. London: Pickering and Chatto, 1993.

Hampsher-Monk, Iain, ed. *The Impact of the French Revolution: Texts from Britain in the 1790s*. Cambridge: Cambridge University Press, 2005.

Hazlitt, William. *The Complete Works of William Hazlitt*. P. P. Howe, ed. 21 vols. London: J. M. Dent, 1930–4.

Paine, Thomas. *The Life and Major Writings of Thomas Paine*. Philip S. Foner ed. 2 vols. Secaucus, NJ: Citadel Press, 1948.
 Rights of Man, Common Sense and Other Political Writings. Mark Philp ed. Oxford: Oxford University Press, 1995.
Robertson, William. *History of the Reign of the Emperor Charles V, with a View of the Progress of Society in Europe*, in *The Works of William Robertson D.D.* Dugald Stewart ed. 12 vols. London: Cadell and Davies, 1812: vols. IV–VI.
Scrivener, Michael, ed. *Poetry and Reform: Periodical Verse from the English Democratic Press, 1792–1824*. Detroit: Wayne State University Press, 1992.
Shelley, Percy Bysshe. *Shelley's Poetry and Prose*. Donald H. Reiman and Neil Fraistat ed. New York and London: W. W. Norton & Co., 2002.
Smith, Adam. *An Inquiry into the Nature and Causes of the Wealth of Nations*. R. H. Campbell, A. S. Skinner and W. B. Todd ed. 2 vols. Oxford: Clarendon Press, 1976.
Spence, Thomas. *The Political Works of Thomas Spence*. H. T. Dickinson ed. Newcastle Upon Tyne: Avero Publications, 1982.
Thale, Mary, ed. *Selections from the Papers of the London Corresponding Society 1792–1799*. Cambridge: Cambridge University Press, 1983.
Verhoeven, W. M., gen. ed. *Anti-Jacobin Novels*. 10 vols. London: Pickering and Chatto, 2005.
Wollstonecraft, Mary. *The Works of Mary Wollstonecraft*. Marilyn Butler and Janet Todd ed. 7 vols. London: Pickering and Chatto, 1989.
 The Letters of Mary Wollstonecraft. Janet Todd ed. London: Allen Lane, 2003.
Wordsworth, William. *The Prelude 1799, 1805, 1850*. Jonathan Wordsworth, M. H. Abrams and Stephen Gill ed. New York and London: W. W. Norton and Co., 1979.
 The Major Works. Stephen Gill ed. Oxford: Oxford University Press, 1984.
Wu, Duncan, ed. *Romantic Women Poets: An Anthology*. Oxford: Blackwell, 1997.

Secondary reading

The political context

Barrell, John. *Imagining the King's Death: Figurative Treason, Fantasies of Regicide 1793–1796*. Oxford: Oxford University Press, 2000.
Christie, Ian R. *Stress and Stability in Late Eighteenth-Century Britain*. Oxford: Clarendon Press, 1984.
Claeys, Gregory. *The French Revolution in Britain: The Origins of Modern Politics*. Basingstoke: Palgrave Macmillan, 2007.
Cookson, J. E. *The Friends of Peace: Anti-War Liberalism in England, 1793–1815*. Cambridge: Cambridge University Press, 1982.
 The Armed Nation 1793–1815. Oxford: Clarendon Press, 1997.
Dickinson, H. T. *British Radicalism and the French Revolution, 1789–1815*. Oxford: Blackwell, 1985.
Dickinson, H. T., ed. *Britain and the French Revolution, 1789–1815*. Basingstoke: Macmillan, 1989.
Dozier, Robert R. *For King, Constitution and Country: The English Loyalists and the French Revolution*. Lexington: University Press of Kentucky, 1983.

Duffy, Michael. 'William Pitt and the Origins of the Loyalist Association Movement of 1792', *Historical Journal* 39 (1996): 943–62.

Emsley, Clive. 'An Aspect of Pitt's "Terror": Prosecutions for Sedition During the 1790s', *Social History* 6 (1981): 155–84.

'Repression, "Terror" and the Rule of Law in England during the Decade of the French Revolution', *English Historical Review* 100 (1985): 801–25.

Evans, Chris. *Debating the Revolution: Britain in the 1790s*. London: I. B. Tauris, 2006.

Goodwin, Albert. *The Friends of Liberty: The English Democratic Movement in the Age of the French Revolution*. London: Hutchinson, 1979.

Harris, Bob. *The Scottish People and the French Revolution*. London: Pickering and Chatto, 2008.

Jones, Colin, ed. *Britain and Revolutionary France: Conflict, Subversion and Propaganda*. Exeter: Exeter University Press, 1983.

Macleod, Emma Vincent. *A War of Ideas: British Attitudes to the Wars Against Revolutionary France, 1792–1802*. Aldershot: Ashgate, 1998.

Mori, Jennifer. *William Pitt and the French Revolution, 1785–1795*. Edinburgh: Keele University Press, 1997.

Morris, Marilyn. *The British Monarchy and the French Revolution*. New Haven: Yale University Press, 1998.

O'Gorman, Frank. *The Whig Party and the French Revolution*. London: Macmillan, 1967.

Philp, Mark, ed. *The French Revolution and British Popular Politics*. Cambridge: Cambridge University Press, 1991.

Thompson, Edward. *The Making of the English Working Class*. Rev. edn. London: Penguin, 1991.

Wells, Roger. *Insurrection: The British Experience 1795–1803*. Gloucester: Alan Sutton, 1983.

Burke, *Reflections on the Revolution in France*

Boulton, James. *The Language of Politics in the Age of Wilkes and Burke*. London: Routledge and Kegan Paul, 1963.

Cobban, Alfred. *Edmund Burke and the Revolt against the Eighteenth Century: A Study of the Political and Social Thinking of Burke, Wordsworth, Coleridge, and Southey*. London: George Allen and Unwin, 1929.

Gilmour, Ian. *Riot, Risings and Revolution: Governance and Violence in Eighteenth-Century England*. London: Hutchinson, 1992.

Janes, Regina. 'Edmund Burke's Flying Leap from India to France', *History of European Ideas* 7 (1986): 509–27.

Lock, F. P. *Edmund Burke*, Volume II: 1784–1797. Oxford: Clarendon Press, 2006.

O'Brien, Conor Cruise. 'Introduction', *Reflections on the Revolution in France*. By Edmund Burke. Harmondsworth: Penguin, 1970.

Pocock, J. G. A. 'Burke and the Ancient Constitution: A Problem in the History of Ideas', in *Politics, Language and Time: Essays on Political Thought and History*. London: Methuen, 1972: 202–32.

Wood, Neal. 'The Aesthetic Dimension of Burke's Political Thought', *Journal of British Studies* 4 (1964): 41–64.

Paine, *Rights of Man*

Aldridge, A. O. *Man of Reason: The Life of Thomas Paine*. London: Cresset Press, 1960.

Claeys, Gregory. *Thomas Paine: Social and Political Thought*. London: Unwin Hyman, 1989.

Doyle, William. 'Thomas Paine and the *Girondins*', in *Officers, Nobles and Revolutionaries: Essays on Eighteenth-Century France*. London: Hambledon, 1995: 209–20.

Innes, Joanna. 'The State and the Poor: Eighteenth-Century England in European Perspective', in *Rethinking Leviathan: The Eighteenth-Century State in Britain and Germany*. John Brewer and Eckhart Hellmuth ed. Oxford: Oxford University Press, 1999: 225–80.

Kalyvas, Andreas, and Ira Katznelson. *Liberal Beginnings: Making a Republic for the Moderns*. Cambridge: Cambridge University Press, 2009.

Kates, Gary. 'From Liberalism to Radicalism: Tom Paine's Rights of Man', *Journal of the History of Ideas* 50:4 (1989): 569–87.

Kaye, Harvey J. *Thomas Paine and the Promise of America*. New York: Hill and Wang, 2005.

Parssinen, T. M. 'Association, Convention and Anti-Parliament in British Radical Politics, 1771–1848', *English Historical Review* 88 (1973): 504–33.

Philp, Mark. 'The Fragmented Ideology of Reform', in *The French Revolution and British Popular Politics*. Mark Philp ed. Cambridge: Cambridge University Press, 1991: 50–77.

Pocock, J. G. A. *Virtue, Commerce and History: Essays on Political Thought and History, Chiefly in the Eighteenth Century*. Cambridge: Cambridge University Press, 1985.

Stedman-Jones, Gareth. *An End to Poverty*. London: Profile Books, 2004.

Whatmore, Richard. '"A gigantic manliness": Thomas Paine's Republicanism in the 1790s', in *Economy, Polity and Society: British Intellectual History, 1750–1950*. Stefan Collini, Richard Whatmore and Brian Young ed. Cambridge: Cambridge University Press, 2000: 135–57.

Burke and Paine: contrasts

Barrell, John, ed. *'Exhibition Extraordinary!!': Radical Broadsides of the mid 1790s*. Nottingham: Trent Editions, 2001.

Bindman, David. *The Shadow of the Guillotine: Britain and the French Revolution*. London: British Museum Publications, 1989.

Blakemore, Steven. *Burke and the Fall of Language: The French Revolution as Linguistic Event*. Hanover, NH: University Press of New England, 1988.

Intertextual War: Edmund Burke and the French Revolution in the Writings of Mary Wollstonecraft, Thomas Paine, and James Mackintosh. Madison, WI: Fairleigh Dickinson University Press, 1997.

Boulton, James T. *The Language of Politics in the Age of Wilkes and Burke*. London: Routledge and Kegan Paul, 1963.

Claeys, Gregory. *Thomas Paine: Social and Political Thought*. London: Unwin Hyman, 1989.

De Bruyn, Frans. *The Literary Genres of Edmund Burke: The Political Uses of Literary Form*. Oxford: Clarendon Press, 1996.

Donald, Diana. *The Age of Caricature: Satirical Prints in the Reign of George III*. New Haven: Yale University Press, 1996.

Duff, David. *Romanticism and the Uses of Genre*. Oxford: Oxford University Press, 2009.

Fennessey, R. R. *Burke, Paine and the Rights of Man: A Difference of Political Opinion*. The Hague: Martinus Nijhoff, 1963.

Furniss, Tom. *Edmund Burke's Aesthetic Ideology: Language, Gender and Political Economy in Revolution*. Cambridge: Cambridge University Press, 1993.

Hill, Draper, ed. *Fashionable Contrasts: Caricatures by James Gillray*. London: Phaidon, 1966.

Hodson, Jane. *Language and Revolution in Burke, Wollstonecraft, Paine, and Godwin*. Aldershot: Ashgate, 2007.

Lock, F. P. *Burke's Reflections on the Revolution in France*. London: Allen and Unwin, 1985.

Paulson, Ronald. *Representations of Revolution (1789–1820)*. New Haven: Yale University Press, 1983.

Robinson, Nicholas K. *Edmund Burke: A Life in Caricature*. New Haven: Yale University Press, 1996.

Smith, Olivia. *The Politics of Language 1791–1819*. Oxford: Clarendon Press, 1984.

Whale, John, ed. *Edmund Burke's Reflections on the Revolution in France: New Interdisciplinary Essays*. Manchester: Manchester University Press, 2000.

Wollstonecraft, *Vindications* and *Historical and Moral View of the French Revolution*

Barker-Benfield, G. J. 'Mary Wollstonecraft, Eighteenth-Century Commonwealthswoman', *Journal of the History of Ideas* 50 (1989): 95–115.

The Culture of Sensibility: Sex and Society in Eighteenth-Century Britain. Chicago: University of Chicago Press, 1992.

Claeys, Gregory. 'The French Revolution Debate and British Political Thought', *History of Political Thought* 11:1 (1990): 59–80.

Moran, Mary Catherine. '"The Commerce of the Sexes": Gender and the Social Sphere in Scottish Enlightenment Accounts of Civil Society', in *Paradoxes of Civil Society: New Perspectives on Modern German and British History*. Frank Trentmann ed. New York and Oxford: Berghahn, 2000: 61–84.

O'Neill, Daniel. *The Burke–Wollstonecraft Debate: Savagery, Civilization and Democracy*. University Park: Pennsylvania State University Press, 2007.

Pendleton, Gayle Trusdel. 'Towards a Bibliography of the *Reflections* and *Rights of Man* Controversy', *Bulletin of Research in the Humanities* 85 (1982): 65–103.

Rendall, Jane. '"The grand causes which combine to carry mankind forward": Wollstonecraft, History and Revolution', *Women's Writing* 4:2 (1997): 155–72.

Sapiro, Virginia. *A Vindication of Political Virtue: The Political Theory of Mary Wollstonecraft*. Chicago: University of Chicago Press, 1992.

Taylor, Barbara. *Mary Wollstonecraft and the Feminist Imagination*. Cambridge: Cambridge University Press, 2003.

Todd, Janet. *Mary Wollstonecraft: A Revolutionary Life*. London: Weidenfeld and Nicolson, 2000.

Tomalin, Claire. *The Life and Death of Mary Wollstonecraft*. Harmondsworth: Penguin, 1992.

Godwin, *Political Justice*

Claeys, Gregory. 'The Concept of "Political Justice" in Godwin's *Political Justice*: A Reconsideration', *Political Theory* 11 (1983): 565–84.
  'William Godwin's Critique of Democracy and Republicanism and Its Sources', *History of European Ideas* 7 (1986): 253–69.
Clark, John P. *The Philosophical Anarchism of William Godwin*. Princeton, NJ: Princeton University Press, 1977.
Clemit, Pamela. 'Self-Analysis as Social Critique: The Autobiographical Writings of Godwin and Rousseau', *Romanticism* 11 (2005): 161–80.
  'Readers Respond to Godwin: Romantic Republicanism in Letters', *European Romantic Review* 20 (2009): 701–9.
Fitzpatrick, Martin. 'Heretical Religion and Radical Political Ideas in Late Eighteenth-century England', in *The Transformation of Political Culture: England and Germany in the Late Eighteenth Century*. Eckhart Hellmuth ed. Oxford: Clarendon Press, 1990: 339–72.
Fleisher, David. *William Godwin: A Study in Liberalism*. London: George Allen and Unwin, 1951.
Marshall, Peter H. *William Godwin*. New Haven and London: Yale University Press, 1984.
Monro, D. H. *Godwin's Moral Philosophy: An Interpretation of William Godwin*. London: Oxford University Press, 1953.
Philp, Mark. *Godwin's Political Justice*. London: Duckworth, 1986.
  'Thompson, Godwin, and the French Revolution', *History Workshop Journal* 39 (1995): 89–101.
St Clair, William. *The Godwins and the Shelleys: The Biography of a Family*. London: Faber, 1989.
Scrivener, Michael H. 'Godwin's Philosophy: A Revaluation', *Journal of the History of Ideas* 39 (1978): 615–26.

Wollstonecraft and Godwin: dialogues

Barker-Benfield, G. J. *The Culture of Sensibility: Sex and Society in Eighteenth-Century Britain*. Chicago: University of Chicago Press, 1992.
Blakemore, Steven. *Crisis in Representation: Thomas Paine, Mary Wollstonecraft, Helen Maria Williams, and the Rewriting of the French Revolution*. Madison, WI and Teaneck, NJ: Fairleigh Dickinson University Press, 1997.
Butler, Marilyn. *Jane Austen and the War of Ideas*. Oxford: Clarendon Press, 1975.
Clemit, Pamela. *The Godwinian Novel*. Oxford: Clarendon Press, 1993.
Conger, Syndy McMillen. *Mary Wollstonecraft and the Language of Sensibility*. Madison, WI and Teaneck, NJ: Fairleigh Dickinson University Press, 1994.
Deane, Seamus. *The French Revolution and Enlightenment in England 1789–1832*. Cambridge, MA: Harvard University Press, 1988.
Johnson, Claudia, ed. *The Cambridge Companion to Mary Wollstonecraft*. Cambridge: Cambridge University Press, 2002.
Jones, C. B. *Radical Sensibility*. London: Routledge, 1993.
Kelly, Gary. *The English Jacobin Novel 1780–1805*. Oxford: Clarendon Press, 1976.

London, April. *Women and Property in the Eighteenth-Century English Novel.* Cambridge: Cambridge University Press, 1999.

Markley, A. A. *Conversion and Reform in the British Novel in the 1790s: A Revolution of Opinions.* New York: Palgrave Macmillan, 2009.

Marshall, Peter H. *William Godwin.* New Haven and London: Yale University Press, 1984.

Sapiro, Virginia, *A Vindication of Political Virtue: The Political Theory of Mary Wollstonecraft.* Chicago: University of Chicago Press, 1992.

Staves, Susan. *Married Women's Separate Property in England, 1660–1800.* Cambridge, MA: Harvard University Press, 1990.

Taylor, Barbara. *Mary Wollstonecraft and the Feminist Imagination.* Cambridge: Cambridge University Press, 2003.

Todd, Janet. *Mary Wollstonecraft: A Revolutionary Life.* New York: Columbia University Press, 2000.

Watson, Nicola J. *Revolution and the Form of the British Novel 1790–1825: Intercepted Letters, Interrupted Seductions.* Oxford: Clarendon Press, 1994.

Whale, John. *Imagination Under Pressure, 1789–1832.* Cambridge: Cambridge University Press, 2000.

Popular radical culture

Andrew, Donna T. 'Popular Culture and Public Debate: London 1780', *Historical Journal* 39 (1996): 405–23.

Barrell, John. *The Spirit of Despotism: Invasions of Privacy in the 1790s.* Oxford: Oxford University Press, 2006.

Bugg, John. 'Close Confinement: John Thelwall and the Romantic Prison', *European Romantic Review* 20 (2009): 37–56.

Davis, Michael T. '"That Odious Class of Men Called Democrats": Daniel Isaac Eaton and the Romantics 1794–1795', *History* 84 (1999): 74–92.
  'The Mob Club?: The London Corresponding Society and the Politics of Civility in the 1790s', in *Unrespectable Radicals?: Popular Politics in the Age of Reform.* Michael T. Davis and Paul A. Pickering ed. Aldershot: Ashgate, 2008: 21–40.

Emsley, Clive. 'An Aspect of Pitt's "Terror": Prosecutions for Sedition during the 1790s', *Social History* 6 (May 1981): 155–84.

Epstein, James A. *Radical Expression: Political Language, Ritual, and Symbol in England, 1790–1850.* New York and Oxford: Oxford University Press, 1994.

Epstein, James A., and David Karr. 'Playing at Revolution: British "Jacobin" Performance', *Journal of Modern History* 79 (2007): 495–530.

Gough, Hugh, and David Dickson, eds. *Ireland and the French Revolution.* Dublin: Irish Academic Press, 1990.

Green, Georgina. 'John Thelwall's Radical Vision of Democracy', in *John Thelwall: Radical Romantic and Acquitted Felon.* Steven Poole ed. London: Pickering and Chatto, 2009: 71–82.

Harris, Bob. *The Scottish People and the French Revolution.* London: Pickering and Chatto, 2008.

Keen, Paul. *The Crisis of Literature in the 1790s: Print Culture and the Public Sphere.* Cambridge: Cambridge University Press, 1999.

McCalman, Iain. *Radical Underworld: Prophets, Revolutionaries and Pornographers in London, 1795–1840.* Cambridge: Cambridge University Press, 1988.

Mee, Jon. 'The Strange Career of Richard "Citizen" Lee: Poetry, Popular Radicalism and Enthusiasm in the 1790s', in *Radicalism in British Literary Culture, 1650–1830: From Revolution to Revolution*. Timothy Morton and Nigel Smith ed. Cambridge: Cambridge University Press, 2002: 151–66.

'Libertines and Radicals in the 1790s: The Strange Case of Charles Pigott I', in *Libertine Enlightenment: Sex, Liberty and Licence in the Eighteenth Century*. Peter Cryle and Lisa O'Donnell ed. London: Palgrave, 2003: 185–203.

'"A Bold and Freespoken Man": The Strange Career of Charles Pigott', in *'Cultures of Whiggism': New Essays on English Literature and Culture in the Long Eighteenth Century*. David Womersley ed. Newark, NJ: University of Delaware Press, 2005: 330–50.

'The Magician No Conjuror: Robert Merry and the Political Alchemy of the 1790s', in *Unrespectable Radicals?: Popular Politics in the Age of Reform*. Michael T. Davis and Paul A. Pickering ed. Aldershot: Ashgate, 2008: 41–55.

'"The Dungeon and the Cell": The Prison Verse of Coleridge and Thelwall', in *John Thelwall: Radical Romantic and Acquitted Felon*. Steven Poole ed. London: Pickering and Chatto, 2009: 107–16.

Philp, Mark. 'The Fragmented Ideology of Reform', in *The French Revolution and British Popular Politics*. Mark Philp ed. Cambridge: Cambridge University Press, 1991: 50–77.

Poole, Steve. 'Pitt's Terror Reconsidered: Jacobinism and the Law in Two South-Western Counties, 1791–1803', *Southern History* 17 (1995): 65–87.

Rogers, Nicholas. 'Pigott's Private Eye: Radicalism and Sexual Scandal in Eighteenth-Century England', *Journal of the Canadian Historical Association* 4 (1993): 247–63.

Thale, Mary. 'The Robin Hood Society: Debating in Eighteenth-Century London', *London Journal* 22 (1997): 33–50.

Worrall, David. *Radical Culture: Discourse, Resistance and Surveillance 1790–1820*. New York and London: Harvester Wheatsheaf, 1992.

Counter-revolutionary culture

Butler, Marilyn. *Romantics, Rebels, and Reactionaries: English Literature and its Background, 1760–1830*. Oxford: Oxford University Press, 1981.

Colley, Linda. *Britons: Forging the Nation 1707–1837*. New Haven: Yale University Press, 1992.

Duffy, Michael. 'William Pitt and the Origins of the Loyalist Association Movement of 1792', *Historical Journal* 39 (1996): 943–62.

Dyer, Gary. *British Satire and the Politics of Style, 1789–1832*. Cambridge: Cambridge University Press, 1997.

Gilmartin, Kevin. *Writing Against Revolution: Literary Conservatism in Britain, 1790–1832*. Cambridge: Cambridge University Press, 2007.

Hole, Robert. *Pulpits, Politics and Public Order in England, 1760–1832*. Cambridge: Cambridge University Press, 1989.

Innes, Joanna. 'Politics and Morals: The Reformation of Manners in Later Eighteenth-Century England', in *The Transformation of Political Culture: England and Germany in the Late Eighteenth Century*. Eckhart Hellmuth ed. Oxford: Oxford University Press, 1990: 57–118.

Johnson, Claudia. *Jane Austen: Women, Politics, and the Novel*. Chicago: University of Chicago Press, 1988.

Pedersen, Susan. 'Hannah More Meets Simple Simon: Tracts, Chapbooks, and Popular Culture in Late Eighteenth-Century England', *Journal of British Studies* 25 (1986): 84–113.

Philp, Mark. 'Vulgar Conservatism, 1792–3', *English Historical Review* 110 (1995): 42–69.

Sack, James J. *From Jacobite to Conservative: Reaction and Orthodoxy in Britain, c. 1760–1832*. Cambridge: Cambridge University Press, 1993.

Williams, Raymond. *Culture and Society, 1780–1950*. New York: Columbia University Press, 1983.

Women's voices

Blank, Antje, and Janet Todd, eds. 'Introduction', *Desmond*. By Charlotte Smith. Peterborough, ON: Broadview Press, 2001.

Chalus, Elaine. *Elite Women in English Political Life c. 1754–1790*. Oxford: Oxford University Press, 2005.

Ford, C. H. *Hannah More: A Critical Biography*. New York: Peter Lang, 1996.

Grogan, C. *The Feminist Politics of Elizabeth Hamilton (1758–1816)*. Farnham: Ashgate Publishing, forthcoming.

Hutton, Sarah. 'Liberty, Equality and God: The Religious Roots of Catherine Macaulay's Feminism', in *Women, Gender and Enlightenment*. Barbara Taylor and Sarah Knott ed. Houndsmill: Palgrave Macmillan, 2005: 538–50.

King, Shelley and John B. Pierce, eds. 'Introduction', *The Father and Daughter with Dangers of Coquetry*. By Amelia Opie. Peterborough, ON: Broadview Press, 2003.

Levy, Darline Gay, Harriet Branson Applewhite and Mary Durham Johnson, eds. *Women in Revolutionary Paris, 1789–1795*. Urbana: University of Illinois Press, 1979.

O'Brien, Karen. 'Catharine Macaulay's Histories of England: A Female Perspective on the History of Liberty', in *Women, Gender and Enlightenment*. Barbara Taylor and Sarah Knott ed. Houndsmill: Palgrave Macmillan, 2005: 523–37.

Page, Anthony. '"A Great Politicianess": Ann Jebb, Rational Dissent and Politics in Late Eighteenth-century Britain', *Women's History Review* 17 (2008): 743–65.

Schellenberg, Betty A. *The Professionalization of Women Writers in Eighteenth-Century Britain*. Cambridge: Cambridge University Press, 2005.

Stott, Anne. *Hannah More: The First Victorian*. Oxford: Oxford University Press, 2003.

Walker, Gina Luria. *Mary Hays (1759–1843): The Growth of a Woman's Mind*. Farnham: Ashgate Publishing, 2006.

Walker, Gina Luria, ed. *The Idea of Being Free: A Mary Hays Reader*. Peterborough, ON: Broadview Press, 2006.

Novels of opinion

Butler, Marilyn. *Jane Austen and the War of Ideas*. Oxford: Clarendon Press, 1975.

Clemit, Pamela. *The Godwinian Novel: The Rational Fictions of Godwin, Brockden Brown, Mary Shelley*. Oxford: Clarendon Press, 1993.

Craciun, Adriana. *British Women Writers and the French Revolution: Citizens of the World.* Basingstoke: Palgrave Macmillan, 2005.

Craciun, Adriana, and Kari E. Lokke, eds. *Rebellious Hearts: British Women Writers and the French Revolution.* Albany: State University of New York Press, 2001.

Gilmartin, Kevin. *Writing Against Revolution: Literary Conservatism in Britain, 1790–1832.* Cambridge: Cambridge University Press, 2007.

Grenby, M. O. *The Anti-Jacobin Novel: British Conservatism and the French Revolution.* Cambridge: Cambridge University Press, 2001.

'Politicising the Nursery: British Children's Literature and the French Revolution', *The Lion and the Unicorn* 27 (2003): 1–26.

Johnson, Nancy E. *The English Jacobin Novel on Rights, Property and the Law: Critiquing the Contract.* Basingstoke: Palgrave Macmillan, 2004.

Kelly, Gary. *The English Jacobin Novel 1780–1805.* Oxford: Clarendon Press, 1976.

Women, Writing, and Revolution, 1790–1827. Oxford: Clarendon Press, 1993.

Ty, Eleanor. *Unsex'd Revolutionaries: Five Women Novelists of the 1790s.* Toronto: University of Toronto Press, 1993.

Watson, Nicola J. *Revolution and the Form of the British Novel, 1790–1825: Intercepted Letters, Interrupted Seductions.* Oxford: Clarendon Press, 1994.

Wood, Lisa. *Modes of Discipline: Women, Conservatism and the Novel After the French Revolution.* Cranbury, NJ: Associated University Presses, 2003.

Revolutionary drama

Buckley, Matthew. '"A *Dream of Murder*": *The Fall of Robespierre* and the Tragic Imagination', *Studies in Romanticism* 44 (2005): 515–49.

Carlson, Julie. *In the Theatre of Romanticism: Coleridge, Nationalism, Women.* Cambridge: Cambridge University Press, 1993.

Green, Katherine. 'Mr Harmony and the Events of January 1793: Elizabeth Inchbald's *Every One Has His Fault*', *Theatre Journal* 56 (2004): 47–62.

Hindson, Paul, and Tim Gray. *Burke's Dramatic Theory of Politics.* Aldershot: Avebury, 1988.

Jacobus, Mary. *Romanticism, Writing and Sexual Difference: Essays on 'The Prelude'.* Oxford: Clarendon Press, 1989.

Jewett, William. *Fatal Autonomy: Romantic Drama and the Rhetoric of Agency.* Ithaca, NY: Cornell University Press, 1997.

O'Quinn, Daniel. *Staging Governance: Theatrical Imperialism in London, 1770–1800.* Baltimore: Johns Hopkins University Press, 2005.

Russell, Gillian. *The Theatres of War: Performance, Politics, and Society 1793–1815.* Oxford: Clarendon Press, 1995.

Taylor, George. *The French Revolution and the London Stage, 1789–1805.* Cambridge: Cambridge University Press, 2000.

Watkins, Daniel P. *A Materialist Critique of Romantic Drama.* Gainesville: University Press of Florida, 1993.

Politics and poetry

Abrams, M. H. 'English Romanticism: The Spirit of the Age', in *The Correspondent Breeze: Essays on English Romanticism.* New York and London: W. W. Norton and Co., 1984: 44–75.

Bainbridge, Simon. *Napoleon and English Romanticism*. Cambridge: Cambridge University Press, 1995.

British Poetry and the Revolutionary and Napoleonic Wars: Visions of Conflict. Oxford: Oxford University Press, 2003.

Barrell, John. *Imagining the King's Death: Figurative Treason, Fantasies of Regicide 1793–1796*. Oxford: Oxford University Press, 2000.

Butler, Marilyn. *Romantics, Rebels and Reactionaries: English Literature and its Background 1760–1830*. Oxford: Oxford University Press, 1981.

'Plotting the Revolution: The Political Narratives of Romantic Poetry and Criticism', in *Romantic Revolutions: Criticism and Theory*. K. Johnston *et al*. ed. Bloomington: Indiana University Press, 1990: 133–57.

Chandler, James. *Wordsworth's Second Nature: A Study of the Poetry and Politics*. Chicago: University of Chicago Press, 1984.

Clark, Timothy. *Embodying Revolution: The Figure of the Poet in Shelley*. Oxford: Clarendon Press, 1995.

Cox, Jeffrey. *Poetry and Politics in the Cockney School: Keats, Shelley, Hunt and Their Circle*. Cambridge: Cambridge University Press, 1998.

Craciun, Adriana. *British Women Writers and the French Revolution: Citizens of the World*. Basingstoke: Palgrave Macmillan, 2005.

Craciun, Adriana, and Kari E. Lokke, eds. *Rebellious Hearts: British Women Writers and the French Revolution*. Albany, New York: State University of New York Press, 2001.

Cronin, Richard. *The Politics of Romantic Poetry: In Search of a Pure Commonwealth*. Basingstoke: Macmillan, 2000.

Dart, Gregory. *Rousseau, Robespierre and English Romanticism*. Cambridge: Cambridge University Press, 1999.

Duff, David. *Romance and Revolution: Shelley and the Politics of a Genre*. Cambridge: Cambridge University Press, 1994.

Erdman, David V. *Blake: Prophet Against Empire: A Poet's Interpretation of the History of his own Time*. 3rd edn. Princeton, NJ: Princeton University Press, 1977.

Hanley, Keith. '"A Poet's History": Wordsworth and Revolutionary Discourse', in *Wordsworth in Context*. P. Fletcher and J. Murphy ed. Lewisberg, PA: Bucknell University Press, 1992: 35–65.

Hanley, Keith, and Raman Selden, eds. *Revolution and English Romanticism: Politics and Rhetoric*. Hemel Hempstead: Harvester Wheatsheaf and New York: St Martin's Press, 1990.

Heffernan, J. A. W., ed. *Representing the French Revolution: Literature, Historiography, and Art*. Hanover, NH: University Press of New England, 1992.

Johnston, Kenneth *et al*., eds. *Romantic Revolutions: Criticism and Theory*. Bloomington: Indiana University Press, 1990.

Keach, William. *Arbitrary Power: Romanticism, Language, Politics*. Princeton, NJ: Princeton University Press, 2004.

Kitson, Peter. 'Coleridge, the French Revolution, and The Ancient Mariner', *Yearbook of English Studies* 19 (1989): 177–207.

Levinson, Marjorie. *Wordsworth's Great Period Poems: Four Essays*. Cambridge: Cambridge University Press, 1986.

Liu, Alan. *Wordsworth: The Sense of History*. Stanford, CA: Stanford University Press, 1989.

Makdisi, Saree. *William Blake and the Impossible History of the 1790s*. Chicago: University of Chicago Press, 2003.

Maniquis, Robert, ed. *Studies in Romanticism*, special edn, 'English Romanticism and the French Revolution', 28 (1989).

Mee, Jon. *Dangerous Enthusiasm: William Blake and the Culture of Radicalism in the 1790s*. Oxford: Oxford University Press, 1992.

Romanticism, Enthusiasm, and Regulation: Poetics and the Policing of Culture in the Romantic Period. Oxford: Oxford University Press, 2003.

Paulson, Ronald. *Representations of Revolution (1789–1820)*. New Haven: Yale University Press, 1983.

Prickett, Stephen. *England and the French Revolution*. Basingstoke: Macmillan, 1989.

Roe, Nicholas. *Wordsworth and Coleridge: The Radical Years*. Oxford: Oxford University Press, 1988.

John Keats and the Culture of Dissent. Oxford: Clarendon Press, 1997.

The Politics of Nature: William Wordsworth and Some Contemporaries. Basingstoke: Palgrave Macmillan, 2002.

Shaw, Philip. *Romantic Wars: Studies in Culture and Conflict, 1789–1823*. Aldershot: Ashgate Publishing, 2000.

Watson, J. R. *Romanticism and War: A Study of the British Romantic Writers and the Napoleonic War*. Basingstoke: Palgrave, 2003.

Woodring, Carl R. *Politics in English Romantic Poetry*. Cambridge, MA: Harvard University Press, 1970.

INDEX

Abbé Sieyès 37
  What is the Third Estate 21–2
Abrams, M. H. 201
  'English Romanticism: The Spirit of the
    Age' 191
Acts of Parliament
  Corporation Act 8, 74
  Gagging Acts (1795) 12, 15, 127
  Married Women's Property Acts
    157
  Seditious Meetings Act (1795) 12
  Test Act 8, 74
  Treasonable Practices Act (1795) 12
adultery 148, 187
Alderson, Amelia, *see* Opie, Amelia
America 35
  constitutions 40, 82
    federal 33–4, 40
  establishment of government 80
American Revolution 24, 37–8, 192, 201
Antidote against French Politics, An 135
Anti-Jacobin 130, 142, 197
anti-Jacobin novels
  see novels, anti-Jacobin
Anti-Jacobin Review 142–3
APLP
  see Association for the Preservation of
    Liberty and Property against
    Republicans and Levellers
aristocracy, the 93, 165, 183
  breakdown of 188
  as sinister 186
  see also hereditary privilege
Ashurst, Justice William
  Charge to the Grand Jury of Middlesex
    11
assembly 19
  see also National Assembly

Association for the Preservation of Liberty
  and Property against Republicans and
  Levellers (APLP) 8, 42, 133–7, 195
  and the government 133–4
  and native advantages 134
  pamphlets and broadsheets by 134–7
  publications by 134
Astley, Philip
  Paris in an Uproar 180
Astley Circus 179
Austen, Jane 131
  Mansfield Park 148

Bage, Robert 161–2
  Hermsprong; or, Man As He Is Not
    161–2
Baillie, Joanna
  De Monfort 188
ballads 195–7
  street 197
Barbauld, Anna Laetitia 172
  *An Address to the Opposers of the Repeal
    of the Corporation and Test Acts*
    149
Barlow, Joel 49
  The Conspiracy of Kings 63
Barrell, John 118
beautiful, the 72, 75, 103
biographies 112, 156–7
  philosophical 112
  see also memoirs
Bisset, Robert
  Douglas; or, The Highlander 169
Blackstone, Sir William
  Commentaries on the Laws of England
    110
Blackwood's Edinburgh Magazine
  143

Blake, William
  The French Revolution 193, 200
  The Marriage of Heaven and Hell 63, 69
  'The Song of Liberty' 200–1
Boothby, Sir Brooke
  Observations 56
Bowles, John 142
  *Reflections on the Political and Moral
    State of Society at the Close of the
    Eighteenth Century* 140
British Critic 142
Bullock, Mrs
  Dorothea; or, A Ray of the New Light
    168
Burges, Mary Anne
  *The Progress of the Pilgrim Good-Intent,
    in Jacobinical Times* 161
Burke, Edmund 16–17
  on assembly 19
  and the British character 25
  caricatures of 50–5, 57
    on the Liverpool jug 59
  defence of liberty 27
  first reactions to news from France 23
  and Fox 14
  and the habits of a people 24
  on Marie Antoinette 147
  and Paine 32, 47–8, 49
  and radicalism 57
  Reflections on the Revolution in France
    2–3, 5, 14, 16, 17, 22, 131–2, 163
    defence of prejudice 25
    on education 59
    England addressing France 25
    epistolary form of 25, 68
    and the monarchy 177–8
    and Paine 31
    and the people 18–19, 23
    and the poor 76
    responses to, 3, 49, 56, 74: see also
      cartoons
  and the Rockingham party 17
  on Rousseau 20
  'Speech on the Army Estimates' 20, 32
  and the 'Swinish Multitude' 197
  theory of democracy 17, 28
  writing style
    and chivalry 50, 62
    demonic imagery of 63
    epistolary form of 25, 68
    metaphor in 63–5
    and Paine 69
    and theatricality 23, 176–9

writings of
  *An Appeal from the New to the Old
    Whigs* 29, 37, 56
  A Letter to a Noble Lord 63
  letter to the County Movement in
    Buckinghamshire 19
  A Letter to the Sheriffs of Bristol 19
  Letters on a Regicide Peace 6
  *A Philosophical Enquiry into the Origin
    of our Ideas of the Sublime and the
    Beautiful* 72, 75
  *Thoughts on the Cause of the Present
    Discontents* 18
Burney, Fanny 49
Butler, Marilyn
  Romantics, Rebels, and Reactionaries
    129
Byron, Frederick George 50–5
  Contrasted Opinions of Paine's Pamphlet
    55–6
  *Don Dismallo Running the Literary
    Gauntlet* 51
Byron, George Gordon, Lord 192

Canning, George 197
cartoons 50–6, 57, 63
  by Frederick George Byron 50–5
censorship 166, 179–81, 183
chapbook literature 140
chastity 147–8, 151, 161
  loss of 148, 151
  not gendered 151
Cheap Repository Tracts 10, 139–40
chivalry 27, 73, 163, 199
'Church and King' 196
Church and King clubs 8
'Citizen Lee'
  see Lee, Richard 'Citizen'
class
  aristocracy 93, 165, 183, 186, 188
  elite 176
  governing 138
  the poor 4, 76, 181, 197
  universal 21
  see also hereditary privilege
clergy, the 10, 21
Cobbett, William 132
Coleridge, Samuel Taylor 131, 192,
    197
  caricatured 198
  and chivalry 199
  on *An Enquiry concerning Political Justice*
    (Godwin) 92

Coleridge, Samuel Taylor (*cont.*)
  writings of
    'Apologetic Preface to "Fire, Famine
      and Slaughter"' 203
    'France: An Ode' 202
    'Religious Musings' 200, 202
    see also Wordsworth, William, and
      Samuel Taylor Coleridge
Coleridge, Samuel Taylor, and Robert
  Southey
  The Fall of Robespierre: An Historic
    Drama 183–5, 187
Colman the Younger, George
  The Heir at Law 182–3
commerce 41, 43, 103, 104, 182
community 109
Comparative Display of the Different
  Opinions of the Most Distinguished
  British Writers on the Subject of the
  French Revolution, A 56
conservatism 2–3, 5, 130
  evangelicals 10
  novels of
    see novels, anti-Jacobin
  propaganda by 5
  reaction against reform 8–10
  see also loyalism
constitutions 33–4, 40, 82
Convention Bills 125
  see also Acts of Parliament
Corporation Act 8, 74
counter-revolutionary culture 129
  and hereditary privilege 132
  and Romanticism 129
  and the state 130
  see also conservatism
County Movement, the 19
Covent Garden 179, 185
Crabb Robinson, Henry 98
Craik, Helen
  Adelaide de Narbonne 167

de Gouges, Olympe
  Declaration of the Rights of Woman
    146
Declaration of the Rights of Man and the
  Citizen 22, 82
democracy 17, 28, 38, 93
Dent, John
  The Triumph of Liberty: or, the Fall of the
    Bastille 180
Dialogue Between a Labourer and a
  Gentleman, A 137

Dialogue Between Mr T –, a Tradesman in
  the City, and His Porter, John W, A
  137
Dissenters 149
  Rational Dissenters 86, 149
  and the Test and Corporation Acts 74
  see also radicalism
domestic tyranny 106–11, 149
  servant and master 107–9
  and women 109
drama
  see theatre
Drury Lane 179, 185
Dunlap, William
  on *An Enquiry concerning Political Justice*
    (Godwin) 97
Dyer, Gary 130

Eaton, Daniel Isaac 122–3, 127
  Hog's Wash (journal) 122
  pamphlets 122
  tried and acquitted 122
economic growth 81
Edgeworth, Maria
  Letters for Literary Ladies 152–3
Edgeworth, Richard 152
Edinburgh Review 191
education for women 77, 147–8, 150,
  152–6
Elliot, Sir Gilbert 49
emotion 102, 113
Engels, Friedrich
  on *An Enquiry concerning Political Justice*
    (Godwin) 99
Englishman's Political Catechism 137
epic 198
equality 190–1
  gender 145–6, 148
  sexual 155
  of women 126, 149
Erskine, Thomas 12, 15
Excursion of Osman (anon.) 170

Favret, Mary 105
feminism 149, 154, 156
Fenwick, Eliza
  Secresy; or, The Ruin on the Rock 153
Fenwick, John 96
fiction
  and censorship 166
  forms of 160
  and politics 160, 170, 173
  see also novels

Fox, Charles James 13–15, 19, 74
  and Burke 14
Franklin, Andrew
  A Trip to the Nore 185
French Jacobins 5
Friends of the Liberty of the Press, the
  122
Friends of the People 7

Gagging Acts (1795) 12, 15, 127
Garrick, David 175
gender 147, 150, 164
  and equality 145–6, 148
  linked to religion and politics 149
  and morality 148–9
  and prejudice 152
general will, the
genius, notion of 131
Gerrald, Joseph 120
Gifford, William 130
Gillray, James
  The Apotheosis of Hoche 63
  The New Morality 63, 166, 198
Girondins, the 79
Godwin, William 161
  defence of sensibility 112–13
  definition of intellectual 114
  education and career 86–7
  on emotion 113
  An Enquiry concerning Political Justice 4,
    86, 88, 95–6, 163
    biblical imagery in 90
    conclusions of 95
    on democracy 93
    discredited 99
    experimental nature of 89
    further editions 88–9, 98–9
    'Mode of Effecting Revolutions' 95
    on monarchy and aristocracy 93
    and moral improvement 91–3, 95
    and the nature of government 91
    'Of the Exercise of Private Judgement'
      91
    production of 89
    and property 94
    readers of 95, 96–8
    and a society governed by reason 93–5
    style and method of 90
    success of 96
    and theory 94–6
    view of humanity in 96
    view of morality in 98
  on his intellectual deficiency 114

and Mary Wollstonecraft 101, 113
and Montesquieu 90
at Paine's trial 87
as a political journalist 87
on the public and the private 113
and Rational Dissent 92
on sympathy 112
writings of 87
  Memoirs of the Author of a Vindication
    of the Rights of Woman 102, 112
  St Leon 166
  Things As They Are; or, The Adventures
    of Caleb Williams 88, 102, 107–9,
    162, 170
  Thoughts Occasioned by the Perusal of
    Dr Parr's Spital Sermon 89
Gordon Riots (1780) 16, 168
government
  in America 39
  British 10–15, 33
    and the repression of radicals 7, 10–15,
      143
    secret service section 11
    and war operations 10
  forms of
    civil 41
    court 41
    democratic 39
    hereditary 39
    hierarchical 75
    representative 39, 43
    republican 82
  and governing classes 138
  and the home 107
  and moral improvement 91–3
  nature of 26
  and reason or ignorance 36, 39, 40
  and society 39
  vices of 91
Grey, Charles, 1
Grey's Society of the Friends of the People
  120

Hamilton, Elizabeth 155
  Letters on the Elementary Principles of
    Education 155
  Memoirs of Modern Philosophers
    169–70
Hanway, Mary Ann
  Ellinor; or, The World as It Is 152
Hardy, Thomas
  and the LCS 118, 119
  and religion 125

Hays, Mary 149
  Appeal to the Men of Great Britain in
    Behalf of Women 152
  death notice of Wollstonecraft 156
  Female Biography: or Memoirs of
    Illustrious and Celebrated Women of
    All Ages and Countries 156
  Letters and Essays, Moral and
    Miscellaneous 149–51, 155
  memoir of Macaulay 157
  Memoirs of Emma Courtney 153, 164,
    169
  'Memoirs of Mary Wollstonecraft'
    156
  on Roland 157
  Victim of Prejudice 166
Hazlitt, William
  on An Enquiry concerning Political Justice
    (Godwin) 88
  Letter to William Gifford 130
  Life of Napoleon 129, 176
  'Mr Wordsworth' 190–1, 203
hereditary privilege 34, 39, 43, 75, 78, 81,
    108, 132
  and counter-revolutionary movements
    132
hierarchy 75, 96
  social 135, 137, 140
  in the theatre 175, 178, 182–3
Hodgson, Richard 125
Holcroft, Thomas 49, 161
  Adventures of Hugh Trevor 162
  Anna St Ives 163
  Deaf and Dumb 186
  Knave or Not? 186
  A Tale of Mystery 186
Hole, Robert 140
Horne Tooke, John 118, 124
Hughes Circus 179
Hunter, Joseph 172

imagination 201–3
Imlay, Gilbert 79, 83, 102–5
  and commerce 104–5
Inchbald, Elizabeth 161
  Every One Has His Fault 180–2
  Nature and Art 162
India, reform of 19
Irish rebellion (1798) 8, 11, 168

Jacobin novels
  see novels, Jacobin
Jacobin poet, the 198

Jacobinism 142
  French 5
  see also radicalism
Jeffrey, Francis 191
Jodin, Marie Madeleine
  Vues Législatives pour les femmes
    (Legislative Views for Women) 146
'John Bull' series
  John Bull's Answer to His Brother
    Thomas's Second Letter 135
  John Bull's Second Answer to His Brother
    Thomas 137
  One Penny-worth More, or, A Second
    Letter from Thomas Bull to His
    Brother John 135–7
  by William Jones 135–7
John Horne Tooke Stripped Naked and
    Dissected, and his Political Anatomy
    Exposed (anon.) 124
Jones, William
  'John Bull' series 135–7
Jordan, J. S.
  The Brazen Trumpet (journal) 126

Kelly, Gary
  The English Jacobin Novel 161
Kemble, John Philip 188
  Henry V 185
'Kit Moris'
  The Rights of the Devil, or, The Jacobin's
    Consolation 63
Kotzebue, August von
  Pizarro 187
  The Stranger 187

Lake School of poetry 191
Land Plan 4
  see also property
Lane, William 172
Larpent, Anna 160
Larpent, John 180
law, the 175
  legislation 7, 12–13
  and property 110
  and women 109–10, 145
  see also Acts of Parliament
LCS
  see London Corresponding Society
Lee, Richard 'Citizen' 124–6, 127
  in exile 127
  King Killing 125
  and the mock playbill 60
  and religion 125

Lewis, Matthew
  The Castle Spectre 186
  The Monk 168
liberty
  civil and religious 75, 80
  and gender 147
literacy 129–30, 138
literary criticism 62, 66
literature
  as counter-revolutionary 191
  revolution in 191
  see also novels; poetry; theatre
Liverpool jug 59
London Corresponding Society (LCS) 6,
    117, 118–20, 196
  and Lee 125
  new leaders of 124
  outlawed 127
  publications by 118, 119–20
  religious matters banned 125
  and respectability 120
  and self-improvement 120
  speakers for 123, 124
loyalism
  and Burke's demonic imagery 63
  loyalist associations 8–10, 87
    actions against radicals 9–10
    militants in 10
    Paine burnt in effigy 57
    periodicals by 10
    and the war effort 9
  and the press 166
  violence of 137
  see also conservatism; novels, anti-Jacobin
Lucas, Charles
  The Infernal Quixote 168, 171

Macaulay, Catharine 147–8
  and gender equality 148
  Letters on Education 147–8
  Observations on the Reflections of the Rt.
    Honourable Edmund Burke 147
Mackintosh, James
  Vindiciae Gallicae 3, 48, 56
madhouse, the 109, 111
male oppression of women 4
marriage 163, 164, 181
  forced 162
  a form of slavery 164
  and property 110
  rejection of 172
Married Women's Property Acts 157
Mathias, T. J. 197

memoirs 109–15, 146
  and history 112
  in novel form 106, 163
Merry, Robert 120
  in exile 127
  The Laurel of Liberty 121
  Ode for the 14th of July 121
millennialism 200–1
Milton, John
  Paradise Lost 203
Minerva Press 172
Modern Gulliver's Travels (anon.) 161
monarchy, the 34, 36, 39, 81, 93
  constitutional 193
  George III 34
  Louis XVI 24
  Marie Antoinette 23, 50–1, 82, 147
  and theatre 175, 178
  treatment of 194
monogamy 164
Montesquieu, Charles-Louis de Secondat,
    baron de la Brède et de 22, 29
  mixed constitutional theory of 20
Moody, Jane 186
morality 139–40
  and spiritual concerns 140
More, Hannah 10
  and Evangelical Anglicanism 139
  on feminism 154
  on language and literacy 138
  writings of
    Cheap Repository Tracts 139–40
    Essays on Various Subjects, Principally
      Designed for Young Ladies 154
    Strictures on the Modern System of
      Female Education 154–5
    Village Politics. Addressed to All the
      Mechanics, Journeymen, and Day
      Labourers, in Great Britain
      137–9
Morton, Thomas 182
muteness in theatre 186

National Assembly, French 22, 49
national culture 132, 142
natural world, the 202–3
'new philosophy' 169
novels
  anti-Jacobin 160, 166–70, 171–3
    characteristics of 167
    as propaganda 171
    ridiculing radical ideas 168
    by women writers 169–70, 171

novels (*cont.*)
  Jacobin 160, 161–6, 171–3
    characteristics of 161, 162, 164
    and libraries 172
    as propaganda 170
    reviewers of 172
  as memoirs 106, 163
  new readers of 170, 173
  'of ideas' 170, 171, 173
  'of opinion' 160, 173
  philosophical and political 170
  satirical 168, 171
  women readers of 169

'Ode on the Restoration of Freedom to France, An' 195
Opie, Amelia (née Alderson) 193
  Adeline Mowbray 172
  The Dangers of Coquetry 151
  The Father and Daughter 151
Otway, Thomas
  Venice Preserv'd 180
ownership 107–8
  see also property

Paine, Thomas
  and Abbé Sieyès 37
  on America 35
  and Burke 31, 32, 35, 44, 47–9
  on Europe and America 42
  in France 37
  on government 38
    and society 39
  in absentia trial 67
  and Jefferson 32, 33
  and loyalism 57
  and the monarchy 34, 36, 39
  on new and old worlds 38
  and reform
    in Britain 40, 42
    in Europe 40
    in France 40
  and republicanism 37, 39
  responses to
    attacked in verse 196
    burnt in effigy 8, 57
    cartoon of 55–6
  and rights 32–3
  Rights of Man 118, 119
    and history 179
    and theatricality 177, 178

Rights of Man (1791) 3, 18, 31, 32–6
  account of events in France 34
  form of 68–9
  on hereditary privilege 34
  and radicalism 36
  responses to 49: *see also* cartoons
  and rights of generations 32
  and universal suffrage 35
Rights of Man (1792) 4, 31, 36–42
  on constitutions 40
  developments in Paine's position 43–4
  focus on the American Revolution 37–8
  French influences on 37
  and radicalism 36
  writing style
    contrasted with Burke 69
    plainness of 65–7
    use of literary allusions 67–8
    use of literary criticism and satire 66
    use of metaphor 67
  writings of
    Agrarian Justice 43
    Common Sense 33, 34, 35, 38, 39, 43, 65
    Dissertations on First Principles of Government 33, 35, 43
    a history of the French Revolution 32
    Letter Addressed to the Addressers ('Third part of *Rights of Man*') 35, 42
    Republican Manifesto 37, 42
    'To Messieurs Condorcet, Nicolas de Bonneville and Lanthenas' 38
Paley, William
  Equality, As Consistent with the British Constitution, In a Dialogue between a Master-Manufacturer and one of His Workmen 137
pamphlets 47, 68, 86, 134–7
  anthology of 56
  poems and songs in 196–7
  and poetry 191, 195
Parr, Samuel 49
patriarchy 106, 113, 164
Pedersen, Susan 139
periodical reviews 166
  and radical fiction 166
  and surveillance 142–3
personal and political 101
  see also private and public realms
philosophical history 80

philosophical novels 170
Philp, Mark 134
pig motif 59–62
Pigott, Charles 121
    The Jockey Club 121
    Political Dictionary 122
    *Strictures on the New Political Tenets of
        Edmund Burke* 121
Pitt, William 10, 134
    government of 10–15
'Pitt's Reign of Terror' 11
Pocock, J. G. A. 131
poetry 192–3, 194, 200
    anthologies of 194
    and the pamphlet war 191, 195,
        196–7
    and politics 191, 197–9, 203
    and popular tunes 195–7
    publication of 193, 194
    readership of 195
    'Romantic' 201–4
    satirical 130, 142
    versions of 195
poets
    disillusionment of 201
    of the imagination 201–3
    and political debates 194
politics 26, 47, 81, 175–6, 200
Polwhele, Reverend Richard 151
poor, the 4, 181
popular contentment, elite view of 135–7
Portland, William Bentinck, 4th Duke of
    14
Portsmouth theatre riot 180
Poullain de la Barre, François 146
Powell, James (government spy) 125
Press Act (1798) 13
Price, Richard
    A Discourse on the Love of our Country
        2, 24–6, 74
Priestley, Joseph 17, 150
print culture 117, 129–30, 176, 179, 182,
    184
private and public realms 101, 102–6, 113,
    187
propaganda 5, 170
property 4, 5, 75, 164
    children as 110
    equality of 94, 162
    illegitimate children as 110
    landed 126
    and the law 110
    and marriage 94, 110

servants as 108
women as 110, 148
prosecution of authors and distributors 11
public oratory 177

Quarterly Review 130, 143

radicalism 1–6, 77, 118–19
    and Burke 63
    elite leaders of 120–2
    and executions 146
    fiction of 166
        see also novels
    and French women 79
    in London 117–18
    popular 120
    presented as self-interest 168
    radical societies 6–10, 87
        across Britain 7
        banned by law 13
        and Burke 57
        government repression of 7, 10–15, 87,
            143
        loyalist associations against 9–10
        publications by 5
        in Scotland 7, 11, 14
    and religion 125
    and women's rights 4
reason 2, 4, 72, 80, 92
Reeves, John 133–7
    career of 134
reform 1–6, 19, 32
    in Britain 19, 35, 40
    constitutional 1–6
    in Europe 35, 40
    in France 35, 40
    gradual approach to 163
    see also radicalism
Regency Crisis 16
religion 2, 6
    hymns 196
    and radicalism 125
    see also clergy, the
republicanism 34, 37, 38, 39
reputation 145, 148–9, 163
Revolution Society, London 2, 6
rights 26, 32–3, 43
    inalienable 24
    material and social 43
    natural 3, 33, 146
    perfect and imperfect 33
    of women 146, 149
Robertson, William 73

Roland, Manon
  An Appeal to Impartial Posterity 146,
  157
Romanticism 69, 129, 191
  literary 47, 62
Roscoe, William
  *The Life, Death and Wonderful
    Atchievements of Edmund Burke* 76
Rousseau, Jean-Jacques 77
  democratic principle of 20
  Emile 152
  Julie ou la nouvelle Héloïse 111
  on sensibility 72
Rowlandson, Thomas
  The Contrast, 1792 59
royal proclamation against seditious writings
  11, 87, 119
  and Paine 31
Royalty Theatre 179

Sadler's Wells 179
St John, John
  The Island of St Marguerite 180
satire 62, 66
  in novels 168, 171
  in poetry 130, 142
Sayer, Edward
  Lindor and Adelaïde, a Moral Tale 166
Schelling, Friedrich 69
Scotland
  radical societies in 7
  trials for sedition in 11, 14
Scott, Sir Walter 131
  Marmion 62
Scottish Enlightenment writers 73
secret service 11
Seditious Meetings Act (1795) 12
seditious writings 11, 31, 87, 119
  royal proclamation against 11
sensibility 71–2, 75, 77, 80, 102, 103,
  112–13
  cult of 194
  sonnet of 193
servants 107–9
Seward, Anna 198
  'Sonnet to France on her present
    Exertions' 192–3
  on writers and poets 193
sexual freedom for women 153, 155
  see also chastity
Sheffield Society for Constitutional
  Information 5, 7
Shelley, Percy Bysshe 192

on *An Enquiry concerning Political Justice*
  (Godwin) 97, 98
'To Wordsworth' 204
Siddons, Sarah 187, 188
slavery 168, 171
  marriage as a form of 164
  rebellions in the West Indies 168
Smith, Adam 73
Smith, Charlotte 166
  The Banished Man 165, 167
  Celestina 164
  Desmond: A Novel 151, 160, 164, 165
  The Emigrants 194
  The Natural Daughter 167
  The Old Manor House 165
  The Young Philosopher 166
society 27, 93–5
  hierarchy of 135, 137, 140
    and the theatre 175, 178, 182–3
  stages of development 73
  and the condition of women 73
  see also class
Society for Constitutional Information (SCI)
  6, 117, 118
Society of the Friends of the People 14, 15
sonnets 193
Southey, Robert 131, 199
  and classical forms 198
  on *An Enquiry concerning Political Justice*
    (Godwin) 96
  Joan of Arc: An Epic Poem 198
  see also Coleridge, Samuel Taylor, and
    Robert Southey
Spence, Thomas 126–7
  The End of Oppression 126
  Land Plan of 4
  Pig's Meat (journal) 126
  The Rights of Infants 126
'Spinning Wheel, The' (anon.) 194
Spirit of Anti-Jacobinism for, 1802, The 142
sublime, the 72, 75, 103
suffrage 35, 42, 43
surveillance 142–3
sympathy 102, 112, 124

taxation 41–2, 43
  and poor relief
Test Act 8, 74
theatre 180, 181, 185, 187
  censorship and regulation of 179–81
  genres 181, 185, 187
    burlesque 177
    'German drama' 187

gothic drama 185–6
'low' forms 179–80
melodrama 185, 186–7
pantomime 177
'Romantic drama' 184
sentimental comedy 182
tragedy 177
tragi-comedy 178
'illegitimate' 180
'legitimate' 179
'minor' 179
plays for reading 183
spatial hierarchy of 175, 178, 182–3
see also drama; individual theatres
Thelwall, John 7, 57, 123–4, 127, 180
and religion 125
scientific interests 123
speaker for the LCS 123, 124
trial and imprisonment 123, 124
writings of
Daughter of Adoption 170
The Peripatetic 123
Poems written in Close Confinement 123
Third Estate, the 21–2
To the Mistaken Part of the Community, Who Assemble in Seditious Clubs for the Purpose of Obtaining a Redress of What They Suppose Grievances 135
Tom Pains Effegy or The Rights of a Sed[i]tious Poltroon 57
trade unions 13
treason trials in England (1794) 11, 40
Treasonable Practices Act (1795) 12
'Tree of Liberty, The' (shop) 124
Trial and Execution of the Grand Mufti 161
trials for sedition in Scotland 11, 15
True Briton 181
Two Acts, the 12, 15, 127
tyranny
domestic 106–9, 111, 149
political 107

violence 27, 96, 193
virginity
see chastity
Volunteers, the 9

Walker, George 161, 171
The Vagabond 168
war with France 5, 88, 103
Watson-Taylor, George
England Preserved 185

Whig party, the 13–15
coalition with Pitt 14
'Wholsome Advice to the Swinish Multitude' 197
Williams, Helen Maria
Julia, a Novel 151
Letters Written in France in the Summer of 1790 151
Williams, Raymond
Culture and Society 132
Wilson, James
pamphlet on the Federal constitution 33
Windham, William 49
Wollstonecraft, Mary 71, 78, 101, 104
and the Analytical Review 72
on commerce 104
disagreements with Burke 74
and emotion 113
and events in France 74, 75, 76, 78, 80–2, 83, 105
in France 71, 78, 105
friends of 71
and Gilbert Imlay 79, 83, 102–5
business affairs of 104–5
and intuition 114–15
on liberty 75
on Marie Antoinette 82
on the National Assembly and court 81–2
and national education 78, 79, 83
on reason 72
and the Revolution 106
on Rousseau 77, 111
on sensibility 71–2, 103, 111
and the sublime and the beautiful 103
and sympathy 104
Vindication of the Rights of Men 18, 74–7, 114, 147
Vindication of the Rights of Woman 4, 74, 77–8, 114, 148
and William Godwin 101
writings of
The Female Reader 72–3
An Historical and Moral View of the French Revolution 18, 74, 80–4, 105
Letters on the Character of the French Nation 79
Letters Written during a Short Residence in Sweden, Norway and Denmark 83, 102–6
Maria; or, the Wrongs of Woman 102, 109–11, 164, 166

Wollstonecraft, Mary (*cont.*)
  Mary: A Fiction 71–2
  review of *A Discourse on the Love of
    our Country* (Price) 74
  *Thoughts on the Education of
    Daughters* 71
'woman question', the 145
women
  education for 77, 147–8, 150,
    152–6
  equality of 126, 149
  male oppression of 4
  as property 109, 110, 148, 164
  as readers of novels 169
  rights of 4, 149
  role in the Revolution 146–7
  and sexual freedom 153, 155
  and societal development 73
    see also chastity

women writers 145, 146
  of anti-Jacobin novels 169–70, 171
  attacks on 147
  critique of gender prejudice 152
  forms used
    conversational 153
    epistolary 152–3
  and the French Revolution debate 145,
    157
Wordsworth, William 131, 192
  and conservatism 191, 204
  on *An Enquiry concerning Political Justice*
    (Godwin) 96, 97
  The Prelude 193, 194, 199, 202–3
Wordsworth, William, and Samuel Taylor
    Coleridge
  Lyrical Ballads 191

Yorke, Henry Redhead 7

Cambridge Companions to...

AUTHORS

Edward Albee edited by Stephen J. Bottoms

Margaret Atwood edited by
Coral Ann Howells

W. H. Auden edited by Stan Smith

Jane Austen edited by Edward Copeland and
Juliet McMaster (second edition)

Beckett edited by John Pilling

Bede edited by Scott DeGregorio

Aphra Behn edited by Derek Hughes and
Janet Todd

Walter Benjamin edited by David S. Ferris

William Blake edited by Morris Eaves

Brecht edited by Peter Thomson and Glendyr
Sacks (second edition)

The Brontës edited by Heather Glen

Bunyan edited by Anne Dunan-Page

Frances Burney edited by Peter Sabor

Byron edited by Drummond Bone

Albert Camus edited by Edward J. Hughes

Willa Cather edited by Marilee Lindemann

Cervantes edited by Anthony J. Cascardi

Chaucer edited by Piero Boitani and Jill Mann
(second edition)

Chekhov edited by Vera Gottlieb and
Paul Allain

Kate Chopin edited by Janet Beer

Caryl Churchill edited by Elaine Aston and
Elin Diamond

Coleridge edited by Lucy Newlyn

Wilkie Collins edited by Jenny Bourne Taylor

Joseph Conrad edited by J. H. Stape

Dante edited by Rachel Jacoff (second edition)

Daniel Defoe edited by John Richetti

Don DeLillo edited by John N. Duvall

Charles Dickens edited by John O. Jordan

Emily Dickinson edited by Wendy Martin

John Donne edited by Achsah Guibbory

Dostoevskii edited by W. J. Leatherbarrow

Theodore Dreiser edited by Leonard Cassuto
and Claire Virginia Eby

John Dryden edited by Steven N. Zwicker

W. E. B. Du Bois edited by Shamoon Zamir

George Eliot edited by George Levine

T. S. Eliot edited by A. David Moody

Ralph Ellison edited by Ross Posnock

Ralph Waldo Emerson edited by Joel Porte and
Saundra Morris

William Faulkner edited by
Philip M. Weinstein

Henry Fielding edited by Claude Rawson

F. Scott Fitzgerald edited by Ruth Prigozy

Flaubert edited by Timothy Unwin

E. M. Forster edited by David Bradshaw

Benjamin Franklin edited by Carla Mulford

Brian Friel edited by Anthony Roche

Robert Frost edited by Robert Faggen

Gabriel García Márquez edited by
Philip Swanson

Elizabeth Gaskell edited by Jill L. Matus

Goethe edited by Lesley Sharpe

Günter Grass edited by Stuart Taberner

Thomas Hardy edited by Dale Kramer

David Hare edited by Richard Boon

Nathaniel Hawthorne edited by
Richard Millington

Seamus Heaney edited by
Bernard O'Donoghue

Ernest Hemingway edited by Scott Donaldson

Homer edited by Robert Fowler

Horace edited by Stephen Harrison

Ibsen edited by James McFarlane

Henry James edited by Jonathan Freedman

Samuel Johnson edited by Greg Clingham

Ben Jonson edited by Richard Harp and
Stanley Stewart

James Joyce edited by Derek Attridge
(second edition)

Kafka edited by Julian Preece

Keats edited by Susan J. Wolfson

Lacan edited by Jean-Michel Rabaté

D. H. Lawrence edited by Anne Fernihough

Primo Levi edited by Robert Gordon

Lucretius edited by Stuart Gillespie and
Philip Hardie

Machiavelli edited by John M. Najemy

David Mamet edited by Christopher Bigsby

Thomas Mann edited by Ritchie Robertson

Christopher Marlowe edited by Patrick Cheney

Andrew Marvell edited by Derek Hirst and Steven N. Zwicker

Herman Melville edited by Robert S. Levine

Arthur Miller edited by Christopher Bigsby (second edition)

Milton edited by Dennis Danielson (second edition)

Molière edited by David Bradby and Andrew Calder

Toni Morrison edited by Justine Tally

Nabokov edited by Julian W. Connolly

Eugene O'Neill edited by Michael Manheim

George Orwell edited by John Rodden

Ovid edited by Philip Hardie

Harold Pinter edited by Peter Raby (second edition)

Sylvia Plath edited by Jo Gill

Edgar Allan Poe edited by Kevin J. Hayes

Alexander Pope edited by Pat Rogers

Ezra Pound edited by Ira B. Nadel

Proust edited by Richard Bales

Pushkin edited by Andrew Kahn

Rabelais edited by John O'Brien

Rilke edited by Karen Leeder and Robert Vilain

Philip Roth edited by Timothy Parrish

Salman Rushdie edited by Abdulrazak Gurnah

Shakespeare edited by Margareta de Grazia and Stanley Wells (second edition)

Shakespearean Comedy edited by Alexander Leggatt

Shakespeare on Film edited by Russell Jackson (second edition)

Shakespeare's History Plays edited by Michael Hattaway

Shakespeare's Last Plays edited by Catherine M. S. Alexander

Shakespeare's Poetry edited by Patrick Cheney

Shakespeare and Popular Culture edited by Robert Shaughnessy

Shakespeare on Stage edited by Stanley Wells and Sarah Stanton

Shakespearean Tragedy edited by Claire McEachern

George Bernard Shaw edited by Christopher Innes

Shelley edited by Timothy Morton

Mary Shelley edited by Esther Schor

Sam Shepard edited by Matthew C. Roudané

Spenser edited by Andrew Hadfield

Laurence Sterne edited by Thomas Keymer

Wallace Stevens edited by John N. Serio

Tom Stoppard edited by Katherine E. Kelly

Harriet Beecher Stowe edited by Cindy Weinstein

August Strindberg edited by Michael Robinson

Jonathan Swift edited by Christopher Fox

J. M. Synge edited by P. J. Mathews

Tacitus edited by A. J. Woodman

Henry David Thoreau edited by Joel Myerson

Tolstoy edited by Donna Tussing Orwin

Anthony Trollope edited by Carolyn Dever and Lisa Niles

Mark Twain edited by Forrest G. Robinson

John Updike edited by Stacey Olster

Virgil edited by Charles Martindale

Voltaire edited by Nicholas Cronk

Edith Wharton edited by Millicent Bell

Walt Whitman edited by Ezra Greenspan

Oscar Wilde edited by Peter Raby

Tennessee Williams edited by Matthew C. Roudané

August Wilson edited by Christopher Bigsby

Mary Wollstonecraft edited by Claudia L. Johnson

Virginia Woolf edited by Susan Sellers (second edition)

Wordsworth edited by Stephen Gill

W. B. Yeats edited by Marjorie Howes and John Kelly

Zola edited by Brian Nelson

TOPICS

The Actress edited by Maggie B. Gale and John Stokes

The African American Novel edited by Maryemma Graham

The African American Slave Narrative edited by Audrey A. Fisch

Allegory edited by Rita Copeland and Peter Struck

American Crime Fiction edited by Catherine Ross Nickerson

American Modernism edited by Walter Kalaidjian

American Realism and Naturalism edited by
Donald Pizer

American Travel Writing edited by
Alfred Bendixen and Judith Hamera

American Women Playwrights edited by
Brenda Murphy

Ancient Rhetoric edited by Erik Gunderson

Arthurian Legend edited by Elizabeth Archibald
and Ad Putter

Australian Literature edited by Elizabeth Webby

British Literature of the French Revolution
edited by Pamela Clemit

British Romanticism edited by Stuart Curran
(second edition)

British Romantic Poetry edited by James
Chandler and Maureen N. McLane

British Theatre, 1730–1830, edited by
Jane Moody and Daniel O'Quinn

Canadian Literature edited by
Eva-Marie Kröller

Children's Literature edited by M. O. Grenby
and Andrea Immel

The Classic Russian Novel edited by
Malcolm V. Jones and Robin Feuer Miller

Contemporary Irish Poetry edited by
Matthew Campbell

Crime Fiction edited by Martin Priestman

Early Modern Women's Writing edited by
Laura Lunger Knoppers

The Eighteenth-Century Novel edited by
John Richetti

Eighteenth-Century Poetry edited by John Sitter

English Literature, 1500–1600 edited by
Arthur F. Kinney

English Literature, 1650–1740 edited by
Steven N. Zwicker

English Literature, 1740–1830 edited by
Thomas Keymer and Jon Mee

English Literature, 1830–1914 edited by
Joanne Shattock

English Novelists edited by Adrian Poole

English Poetry, Donne to Marvell edited by
Thomas N. Corns

English Poets edited by Claude Rawson

English Renaissance Drama, edited by
A. R. Braunmuller and Michael Hattaway
(second edition)

English Renaissance Tragedy edited by
Emma Smith and Garrett A. Sullivan Jr.

English Restoration Theatre edited by
Deborah C. Payne Fisk

The Epic edited by Catherine Bates

Feminist Literary Theory edited by
Ellen Rooney

Fiction in the Romantic Period edited by
Richard Maxwell and Katie Trumpener

The Fin de Siècle edited by Gail Marshall

The French Novel: from 1800 to the Present
edited by Timothy Unwin

Gay and Lesbian Literature edited by
Hugh Stevens

German Romanticism edited by Nicholas Saul

Gothic Fiction edited by Jerrold E. Hogle

The Greek and Roman Novel edited by
Tim Whitmarsh

Greek and Roman Theatre edited by Marianne
McDonald and J. Michael Walton

Greek Lyric edited by Felix Budelmann

Greek Mythology edited by Roger D. Woodard

Greek Tragedy edited by P. E. Easterling

The Harlem Renaissance edited by
George Hutchinson

The Irish Novel edited by John Wilson Foster

The Italian Novel edited by Peter Bondanella
and Andrea Ciccarelli

Jewish American Literature edited by
Hana Wirth-Nesher and Michael P. Kramer

The Latin American Novel edited by
Efraín Kristal

The Literature of Los Angeles edited by
Kevin R. McNamara

The Literature of New York edited by
Cyrus Patell and Bryan Waterman

The Literature of the First World War edited by
Vincent Sherry

The Literature of World War II edited by
Marina MacKay

Literature on Screen edited by
Deborah Cartmell and Imelda Whelehan

Medieval English Culture edited by
Andrew Galloway

Medieval English Literature edited by
Larry Scanlon

Medieval English Mysticism edited by
Samuel Fanous and Vincent Gillespie

Medieval English Theatre edited by
Richard Beadle and Alan J. Fletcher
(second edition)

Medieval French Literature edited by
Simon Gaunt and Sarah Kay

Medieval Romance edited by
Roberta L. Krueger

Medieval Women's Writing edited by
Carolyn Dinshaw and David Wallace

Modern American Culture edited by
Christopher Bigsby

Modern British Women Playwrights edited by
Elaine Aston and Janelle Reinelt

Modern French Culture edited by
Nicholas Hewitt

Modern German Culture edited by
Eva Kolinsky and Wilfried van der Will

The Modern German Novel edited by
Graham Bartram

Modern Irish Culture edited by Joe Cleary and
Claire Connolly

Modern Italian Culture edited by
Zygmunt G. Baranski and Rebecca J. West

Modern Latin American Culture edited by
John King

Modern Russian Culture edited by
Nicholas Rzhevsky

Modern Spanish Culture edited by
David T. Gies

Modernism edited by Michael Levenson

The Modernist Novel edited by Morag Shiach

Modernist Poetry edited by Alex Davis and
Lee M. Jenkins

Modernist Women Writers edited by
Maren Tova Linett

Narrative edited by David Herman

Native American Literature edited by
Joy Porter and Kenneth M. Roemer

*Nineteenth-Century American Women's
Writing* edited by Dale M. Bauer and
Philip Gould

Old English Literature edited by
Malcolm Godden and Michael Lapidge

Performance Studies edited by Tracy C. Davis

Postcolonial Literary Studies edited by
Neil Lazarus

Postmodernism edited by Steven Connor

Renaissance Humanism edited by
Jill Kraye

The Roman Historians edited by
Andrew Feldherr

Roman Satire edited by Kirk Freudenburg

Science Fiction edited by Edward James and
Farah Mendlesohn

The Sonnet edited by A. D. Cousins and
Peter Howarth

The Spanish Novel: from 1600 to the Present
edited by Harriet Turner and
Adelaida López de Martínez

Travel Writing edited by Peter Hulme and
Tim Youngs

*Twentieth-Century British and Irish Women's
Poetry* edited by Jane Dowson

The Twentieth-Century English Novel edited by
Robert L. Caserio

Twentieth-Century English Poetry edited by
Neil Corcoran

Twentieth-Century Irish Drama edited by
Shaun Richards

Twentieth-Century Russian Literature edited by
Marina Balina and Evgeny Dobrenko

Utopian Literature edited by Gregory Claeys

Victorian and Edwardian Theatre edited by
Kerry Powell

The Victorian Novel edited by Deirdre David

Victorian Poetry edited by Joseph Bristow

War Writing edited by Kate McLoughlin

Writing of the English Revolution edited by
N. H. Keeble

For EU product safety concerns, contact us at Calle de José Abascal, 56–1°, 28003 Madrid, Spain or eugpsr@cambridge.org.

www.ingramcontent.com/pod-product-compliance
Ingram Content Group UK Ltd.
Pitfield, Milton Keynes, MK11 3LW, UK
UKHW020332140625

459647UK00018B/2116